The Oneida Indian Journey

The Oneida Indian Journey

From New York to Wisconsin, 1784–1860

Edited by

Laurence M. Hauptman
and
L. Gordon McLester III

THE UNIVERSITY OF WISCONSIN PRESS

The University of Wisconsin Press
2537 Daniels Street
Madison, Wisconsin 53718

3 Henrietta Street
London WC23 8LU, England

5   4   3   2   1

Printed in the United States of America

Published in cooperation with the Oneida History Conference Committee
composed of Gerald L. Hill, Kathy Hughes, L. Gordon McLester III,
Ernest Stevens, Jr., and the late Barbara Van Boxtel, as well as the
Oneida Tribal Business Committee, and has been assisted by a grant
from the Oneida Nation of Indians of Wisconsin.

Library of Congress Cataloging-in-Publication Data

The Oneida Indian journey : from New York to Wisconsin, 1784–1860 /
    edited by L. Gordon McLester III and Laurence M. Hauptman ; in
    cooperation with the Oneida History Conference Committee . . .
    240 pp.   cm.
        ". . . an outgrowth of a series of history conferences sponsored by
        the Oneidas"—Foreword.
    Includes bibliographical references and index.
    ISBN 0-299-16140-4 (cloth : alk. paper).
    ISBN 0-299-16144-7 (pbk. : alk. paper)
        1. Oneida Indians—History—Sources.   2. Oneida Indians—
    Relocation—Wisconsin.   3. Oneida Indians—Government policy—
    Wisconsin.   4. United States—Politics and government.   5. United
    states—Race relations.   I. McLester, L. Gordon.   II. Hauptman,
    Laurence M.   III. Oneida History Conference Committee.
    E99.045056   1999
    973'.04975—dc21   98-47296

Contents

**Part II. Oneida Community Perspectives
of Oneida Indian History**

**Part III. Doing Oneida Indian History: Needs, Approaches,
and Resources**

Illustrations

Maps and Table

Maps

Table

Foreword

This remarkable volume represents the collaboration of a Native American people, the Oneida Nation of Indians, and both Indian and non-Indian scholars. It is an outgrowth of a series of history conferences sponsored by the Oneidas, and many of the chapters are derived from papers presented at those sessions. It is appropriate that the co-editors of the volume should be an Oneida, L. Gordon McLester III, who personifies his nation's interest in its history, and a leading ethnohistorian, Laurence M. Hauptman.

In this work the Indian voice is clear, several Oneidas and one Lumbee contributing. Included also are 10 brief stories in the Oneida language, accompanied by translations. And input has been provided not only by the Oneidas of Wisconsin, but also by those of Canada and those who remained in New York.

The prime objectives of the compilers of this volume were to broaden the knowledge of Oneida history and to encourage further research. It certainly should contribute to such worthy goals.

To these ends, the editors have included several studies of the period 1784–1860, during which Oneidas were coerced into moving from New York to Wisconsin and Canada. There also is a section on the methods and sources for researching and writing Oneida history. It opens on a heartening note: "Anyone with average intelligence can dig up information after learning a few skills and tricks of working with collections of documents." In other chapters, specialists discuss manuscript collections in New York and Wisconsin and how maps have been used as social constructs.

This is a book to be read with profit not only by those interested in Oneida history but also by anyone seeking an introduction to methods and sources employed in writing about Native Americans.

Norman, Oklahoma   WILLIAM T. HAGAN

Preface

This volume is the result of the efforts of a number of Oneida people dedicated to maintaining their communal living links to the learning and experiences of their ancestors. It is an emotional tribute to the value of an identity, a tribute that says their ancestors' lives mean something *now* to the present generation, as those same lives did in the past to the people of whom these writers speak so admiringly and fondly.

The Oneidas have held four major history conferences in the past 12 years, in which they have combined the strengths of Oneida people in their direct participation in both academic and experiential aspects. Out of this, a revitalized self-respect, as seen through a previous volume, *The Oneida Indian Experience* (Syracuse University Press, 1988), and a surge of economic success have come, resulting in a vibrant, dynamic community that is reflected in this volume as well. When we examine the history of the Oneida people, the source of the discipline required for these conferences becomes more and more clear.

Federally funded cultural programs from the Work Projects Administration to the Indian Self Determination and Education Assistance Act, PL 638, helped to foster the involvement of Oneida people in language and history. Throughout these efforts the elders, native speakers, and other tribal members have given unselfishly, and it is upon their contributions and dedication that the success of these cultural programs is built and preserved for the future. The results of these programs have aided the Oneida people in making land claims and in other litigation, in curriculum development for the Oneida elementary and high schools, and in organizing the Oneida History Conferences, among other things. The work has also drawn the separate Oneida communities together in ways that politicians could only speak of. With economic success, the Oneida people have committed their own resources to these efforts and have looked at their own history with modest pride and found substance to share with others.

The Oneidas have taken a step toward the future by ensuring that the story of one Oneida community is known and understood by its own members and by using the most accomplished people it can find, both Oneida and non-Oneida, to accomplish that goal. The present volume represents a small part of the continuum that begins in time immemorial and goes to the foreseeable and the unknown future. It is this path that the Oneidas who live in Wisconsin have chosen to light for themselves and their relatives everywhere—other Oneida relatives, other Six Nations relatives, other Indians, and other human beings of any race or nationality—with this small volume. It hasn't been an easy road, however.

The Oneida Tribe of Wisconsin has been beset with problems similar to those of other tribes and communities, both internally and externally. The cultural devastation brought on by the thefts of land, broken government promises, family breakups, removals and relocations, coerced attendance and cruel regimented life at boarding schools, the undermining and belittling of tribal religion, law, leadership, and authority, and the loss of language has been terrible. Notwithstanding these sanctioned de facto depredations, some Indian communities like Oneida have hung on tenaciously. Other less fortunate Indian communities have not been able to resist this onslaught of overwhelming forces and have disappeared, leaving no present voice to bind them to their ancestors. The story of these people is left to others or, finally, lost to the world.

When a community takes responsibility for recording and interpreting its own history, however, it vibrates as a chord of identity through the generations. It is too easy just to say that the old culture maintained its history this way or that. Like other dynamic activities of a culture—language, music, and religious practices—history is alive only if it is expressed as a cultural imperative: we need to know our ancestors, what they did, thought, knew, and believed.

GERALD L. HILL

Abbreviations

CU = Columbia University, Butler Library
DHI = Francis Jennings and William N. Fenton, eds., *Iroquois Indians: A Documentary History of the Diplomacy of the Six Nations and Their League.* (Woodbridge, Conn.: Research Publications, 1985), microfilm, 50 reels
HC = Hamilton College, Clinton, New York
M = microcopy
MHS = Massachusetts Historical Society, Boston
MR = microfilm reel
MSS = manuscript collection
NA = National Archives
NYHS = New-York Historical Society, New York City
NYPL = New York Public Library, Special Collections Division, New York City
NYSA = New York State Archives, Albany
NYSL = New York State Library, Manuscript Division, Albany
OHA = Onondaga Historical Association, Syracuse
SHSW = State Historical Society of Wisconsin, Madison
SU = Syracuse University, George Arents Research Library, Bird Library
VC = Vassar College, Poughkeepsie, New York
Whipple Report = New York State Legislature, Assembly, Document no. 51, *Report of the Special Committee to Investigate the Indian Problem of the State of New York* (Albany, 1889)
WPA = Work Projects Administration

Contributors

DEBRA ANDERSON is the archivist for the State Historical Society of Wisconsin's University of Wisconsin–Green Bay Area Research Center.

EILEEN ANTONE, a member of the Oneida Band of the Thames, has written on the history of the Canadian Oneidas.

JACK CAMPISI, an anthropologist who served as the principal expert witness in the Oneida land claims cases, has worked with more than three dozen American Indian nations from Maine to Alaska on issues related to federal recognition, Indian country, and land rights. Currently he is the Director of Museum Projects for the Mashantucket Pequot Tribal Nation. He serves on the Advisory Board of the D'Arcy McNickle Center for the History of the American Indian at the Newberry Library. Campisi, who has taught at the State University of New York and Wellesley College, is the author of *Mashpee: Tribe on Trial* (1991) and co-editor of *The Oneida Indian Experience: Two Perspectives* (1988).

RICHARD CHRISJOHN, born in Ontario, raised at Onondaga, and now deceased, was the leading Oneida woodcarver-artist of the twentieth century.

AMELIA CORNELIUS, an Oneida Indian, is assistant gaming manager of the Oneida Casino. A former member of the Oneida tribal government, she now devotes much of her time to Oneida storytelling, writing, and the pursuit of Oneida genealogy and history.

JUDY CORNELIUS was the librarian at the Oneida Library for 18 years and is presently serving on the Oneida Gaming Commission. An Oneida, she has been awarded a D'Arcy McNickle Fellowship from the Newberry Library in Chicago.

JAMES D. FOLTS is senior archivist for the New York State Archives at Albany.

WILLIAM T. HAGAN is distinguished emeritus professor of history at the State University of New York at Fredonia and at the University of Oklahoma. He is the author of many books on American Indians. His most recent work is *Theodore Roosevelt and Six Friends of the Indian* (1997), published by the University of Oklahoma Press. Hagan is also a past president of the Western History Association and a founding board member of the D'Arcy McNickle Center for the History of the American Indian at the Newberry Library.

LAURENCE M. HAUPTMAN is professor of history and SUNY faculty exchange scholar at the State University of New York at New Paltz. He has served as a historical consultant to the Oneida Nation of Indians, Seneca Nation of Indians, and Mashantucket Pequot Tribal Nation. He is the author of many articles and books on Iroquois history and is the co-editor of *The Oneida Indian Experience: Two Perspectives* (1988). In 1987 and in 1998, he was awarded the Peter Doctor Indian Fellowship Award by the Iroquois in New York for his research and writings on American Indian history.

GERALD L. HILL is chief counsel for the Oneida Tribe of Indians of Wisconsin. An Oneida, he has long been active in American Indian politics nationwide. He is a former president of the American Indian Lawyers Association.

MARIA HINTON is an Oneida elder and language teacher who has worked to preserve the Oneida language over the past quarter century. A graduate of the University of Wisconsin–Green Bay at the age of 69, she translated and transcribed *A Collection of Oneida Stories* (1996), which is used today by the Oneidas in their language program.

REGINALD HORSMAN is distinguished professor of history at the University of Wisconsin–Milwaukee. Born in Great Britain, he is the author of many articles and books in American Indian and frontier histories, including *Expansion and American Indian Policy, 1783–1812* (1967), *The Frontier in the Formative Years, 1783–1815* (1970), and *Race and Manifest Destiny* (1981).

FRANCIS JENNINGS is director emeritus of the D'Arcy McNickle Center for the History of the American Indian at the Newberry Library and currently serves as a senior research fellow at that institution. The author of many books and articles on American Indians, his greatest contribution to Iroquoian studies is his editorship of the 50-volume microfilm set *Iroquois Indians: A Documentary History of the Diplomacy of the Six Nations* and three major books: *The Invasion of America* (1975), *The Ambiguous Iroquois Empire* (1984), and *Empire of Fortune* (1988).

ARLINDA LOCKLEAR, a Lumbee Indian, practices law in the Washington, D.C., area. Formerly the chief staff attorney for the Native American Rights Fund, she successfully argued two cases before the United States Supreme Court, including the Oneida Indian land claims case (1985).

Jo Margaret Mano is associate professor of geography at the State University of New York at New Paltz. She was a recipient of grants from the Newberry Library and New York State Library for research in cartographic records. At the present time, she is working at the New York State Library and New York State Archives and Records Service on an annotated index of New York's cartographic records up to 1900.

L. Gordon McLester III, an Oneida, is the coordinator of the Oneida History Conferences and founder of the Oneida Historical Society. A former tribal secretary of the Oneida Nation of Indians of Wisconsin, he is the president of Bear Claw and Associates.

Loretta Metoxen, an Oneida Indian, is former vice chairman of the Oneida Tribe of Indians of Wisconsin. She is presently working at the Oneida Cultural Heritage Department as tribal historian.

Liz Obomsawin is an Oneida from New York. Raised on the Onondaga and Oneida reservations, she is currently pursuing a Ph.D. in history at Syracuse University. A screenwriter and educator, she has developed a fifth-grade curriculum and undertaken the videotaping of 40 Oneida elders in New York State.

WPA Storytellers: Jim Antone, Abrahms Archiquette, Oscar Archiquette, Katie Cornelius, Melissa Cornelius, Guy Elm, Jonas Elm, Elizabeth Huff, Jessie Peters, Sarah Summers, and Rachel Swamp. The WPA Oneida Language and Folklore Project, administered by Dr. Floyd Lounsbury, collected hundreds of stories from Oneida elders between 1938 and 1941, which are today part of the curriculum in the Oneida schools. Unlike other WPA projects of the time, these stories are a unique portrait of an American Indian community because they were collected, translated, and transcribed by the Oneidas themselves.

The Oneida Indian Journey

Introduction

The present collection is a sequel to *The Oneida Indian Experience: Two Perspectives* published by the Syracuse University Press in 1988. This book is divided into three parts: The Way West: Tribal Dispossession and Community Rebuilding, 1784–1860; Oneida Community Perspectives of Oneida Indian History; and Doing Oneida Indian History: Needs, Approaches, and Resources. Like the earlier volume, its aims are to elucidate aspects of Oneida Indian history and to stimulate future historical research on these American Indians. It does not pretend to be the final word on the subject. Unlike the earlier volume, which spanned the entire scope of Oneida history, this book has a specific time frame, namely, the period from 1784 to 1860. During this era, the vast majority of Oneidas were dispossessed of their lands in New York State, were forced to seek new homes in Wisconsin and Ontario, and rebuilt their communities in both areas.

The Oneida Indian Journey: From New York to Wisconsin, 1784–1860 is a collection of interdisciplinary essays and community perspectives on a crucial period in this Iroquoian people's history. Two professional historians, a geographer, an anthropologist, an archivist, and an attorney join in with 18 voices of the Oneida community—local historians, folklorists, genealogists, linguists, and tribal elders—to elucidate this vital era, the treaty and removal periods of Oneida Indian history. The book grows out of a series of historical conferences sponsored by the Oneida Nation of Indians of Wisconsin over the past 11 years.

At a time when the Oneida Nation was undergoing a cultural and economic renaissance, tribal members themselves found it essential to undertake the sponsorship of these conferences to document as well as to collect the remarkable history of their nation.

Three-quarters of the book, in one form or another, was presented at the Oneida Indian History Conferences. Sixteen of the authors in part 2 of the book, and 18 in all, including one of the editors, are Oneida Indians. Of the 18, 15 are now enrolled members of the Oneida Nation of Indians of Wisconsin.

One caveat needs to be stated at the beginning. The editors are conscious of the limitations of the sources for this period of Oneida history. Because many of the journals, diaries, and official government reports and correspondence were written by males—missionaries such as Jeremy Belknap, Samuel Kirkland, and Jedidiah Morse, and policymakers such as John C. Calhoun—the voices of Oneida women are largely silenced in the primary documents. In order to get around this limitation, the editors have relied on the stories of Oneida women elders and their remembrances, as found in the WPA Oneida Language and Folklore Project in the first chapter in part 2 of the book. Half of the stories in this section are by Oneida women. Moreover, most (five out of six) of the contemporary community historians represented in the second chapter in part 2 of the book are women and bring unique insights about Oneida history.

Reginald Horsman's chapter in part 1, originally presented at one of the Oneida Indian History Conferences, was previously published in Donald Fixico's edited *Anthology of Western Great Lakes Indian History* (1987) by the American Indian Studies Program at the University of Wisconsin–Milwaukee, although much of Horsman's material was presented at Oneida, Wisconsin, in 1989. Jack Campisi's chapter is an excerpt of his 1974 Ph.D. dissertation from SUNY Albany's Department of Anthropology, "Ethnic Identity and Boundary Maintenance in Three Oneida Communities." James Folts's and Jo Margaret Mano's chapters in part 3 were specifically commissioned to fill out this volume and provide new directions for future research on the Oneidas.

The Oneida Indian Journey: From New York to Wisconsin, 1784–1860 fills a vacuum in the historical literature. Unlike the historiography of the Five Civilized Tribes, the Delawares, the Shawnees, and other prominent native peoples of the eastern woodlands, the historiography of the Iroquois has not included published studies focusing on the removal of any peoples of the Six Nations (the Mohawks, Oneidas, Onondagas, Cayugas, Senecas, and Tuscaroras, also known collectively as the Iroquois Confederacy) westward to Wisconsin or to Indian Territory. This book focuses on the process of dispossession of their New York land, but also shows the significant cultural continuity, flexibility, and adaptation that resulted from Oneida immigration to Wisconsin.

Oneida removal to Wisconsin in some ways was a unique experience, far different from our images of what befell the Five Civilized Tribes on their Trail of Tears. Although it was incredibly traumatic to be forced from their New

York homeland through a policy carefully crafted by state officials to open up central and western New York, the Oneidas were, nevertheless, not rounded up at the point of bayonets and marched westward. Moreover, unlike the Five Civilized Tribes, who found hostile southern Plains Indians upon their arrival in Indian Territory, the Oneida, Stockbridge, and Brothertown Indians were initially welcomed by culturally distinct and vastly different Algonquian and Siouan peoples, namely the Menominees and Winnebagos. Although tensions arose between the Menominees and the "New York Indians" over the size of the initial cessions, a land settlement was worked out within a decade and a half under a federal-Oneida treaty in February 1838. Indeed, in some ways, the Oneida experience in Wisconsin in its group migration from New York, its settlement, and its community building at times paralleled the same process whereby entire white communities left New England or New York via the Great Lakes route to settle in Wisconsin. Yet, unlike these white communities, the Oneidas, however long their roots became, were still subject to the whims of state and national Indian policies, which at times continued to preach removal from Wisconsin or urged the allotment of tribal lands for the "good" of the Indians.

The book begins in 1784 at a time when the Oneidas started to face pressures to cede land. Most of the Oneidas had sided with the Americans during the Revolution. They had been recruited by Lafayette, had loyally served General Philip Schuyler, and had excelled in combat, making the difference in the major American victory at the Battle of Oriskany in 1777. Although formally commended by General Washington for their service in the American Revolution, the Oneidas were forced to cede millions of acres of their land as early as 1785 at Fort Herkimer. The book clearly shows that the roots of American Indian removal policies go as far back as the end of the American Revolution and "owe" much to military men–entrepreneurs such as Philip Schuyler.

The book's end date is 1860. Two crises soon followed: the Civil War and the Dawes General Allotment Act of 1887. Both these events changed the Oneidas of Wisconsin beyond recognition and are deserving of separate book-length treatments. Out of 1,100 reservation residents, perhaps as many as 142 served in the Union army, and as many as 65 were fatalities during the Civil War. During the war, smallpox also claimed at least 15 tribal members. White communities that suffered in the war were soon replenished with immigrants, but the Wisconsin Oneida Indian community faced a 4–5 percent depopulation, which had severe and debilitating repercussions well into the future.[1]

Right after the war, policymakers on federal, state, and local levels pushed for the allotment of the 65,000-acre Oneida Indian Reservation, culminating in 1887 with the enactment of the Dawes General Allotment Act. On June 13, 1892, allotment began with the issuance of a total of 1,524 allotments and 20 trust patents to the Indians. The trust period was extended for another year in 1917. Even before the trust period was finally allowed to expire on nearly all the Oneida allotments in 1918, a federal "competency" commission began issuing fee patents to Oneidas of less than one-half Indian blood in order to quicken the pace of assimilation. After the issuance of fee patents by the federal competency commission or at the end of the trust period, Oneida lands became subject to taxation, resulting in new and impossible tax burdens, foreclosures, and subsequent tax sales of property. Moreover, land speculators, in collusion with the corrupt Indian agents, and, on occasion, Oneida leaders themselves, immediately set out separating the Indian allottee from his allotment. The Oneidas, largely uneducated rural people, were encouraged to fall into debt by borrowing money or mortgaging their homesteads to buy musical instruments, carriages, and livestock, all of which they generally did not need. Some of their homes were subsequently lost because of their inability to pay back loans. Whiskey was employed in outright swindles to dispossess them. Thus, by the time of the New Deal, the Oneidas had fewer than 90 acres of tribal lands and approximately 700 acres held in individual allotments.[2]

In spite of this misguided policy, the Oneidas have survived as an Iroquoian people in Wisconsin. Today, the over 14,000 tribal members, the largest of all the Oneida communities, take pride in their elders' perseverance and their retention of cultural traditions, some of which are set forth both in the Oneida language and in English in part 2 of this book.

Notes

1.   Laurence M. Hauptman, *The Iroquois in the Civil War* (Syracuse, N.Y.: Syracuse University Press, 1993), p. 67.
2.   Laurence M. Hauptman, *The Iroquois and the New Deal* (Syracuse, N.Y.: Syracuse University Press, 1981), p. 72.

PART I

THE WAY WEST:
TRIBAL DISPOSSESSION AND
COMMUNITY REBUILDING,
1784–1860

Introduction

The five chapters in part 1 focus on the Oneidas' dispossession of their New York homeland and their early adjustment to their Wisconsin surroundings. Laurence M. Hauptman, in chapter 1, describes Oneida society and politics in the three decades after the American Revolution and the community's many fissures that facilitated tribal land loss. In chapter 2, Hauptman shows the key role of Philip Schuyler, the former commander of Oneida soldiers during the American Revolution, in dispossessing the Indians at the New York State–Oneida "Treaty" of 1795, a blatantly fraudulent accord. Reginald Horsman then recounts, in chapter 3, the forces at work that brought the Oneidas to Wisconsin: the mysterious ministry of Eleazer Williams, the nefarious actions of the Ogden Land Company, and the calculating federal policies of Secretary of War John C. Calhoun. Horsman's chapter is followed by Jack Campisi's, which shows the cultural resilience and adaptation of the Oneidas in their early days in Wisconsin. In the final chapter in part 1, Arlinda Locklear reflects on the Buffalo Creek Treaty of 1838 and its legal implications for the Oneidas of Wisconsin. Thus, as a whole part 1 details the "time of troubles" in Oneida history, the pressures that caused their exodus from New York, and tribal efforts to rebuild their community in Wisconsin before the American Civil War.

The migrations of Oneidas west to Green Bay and its environs began in 1820; however, the pressures that led to their removal from their central New York State homeland started immediately after the American Revolution. Their homeland, whose center was the short portage between the Mohawk River and Wood Creek, the so-called Oneida Carrying Place, was strategic to the Indians and later to Euro-Americans. To the southeast are the headwaters of the Mohawk, which flows eastward until it joins the Hudson, which connects to the Atlantic Ocean at New York City. On the north is Wood Creek, which, along with Fish Creek, Oneida Lake, and the Oswego River, was a major passageway to Lake Ontario and the rest of the Great Lakes. Not surprisingly, the British constructed Fort Stanwix in 1758 at the Oneida Carrying Place, and it became one of the strongest fortifications in North America.

Because of its strategic location, entrepreneurs and state officials saw the Oneida homeland as essential to the rise of the Empire State; the founding of the region's major cities of Utica and Rome; the development of major canals—the first canal experiment, the Western Inland Lock Navigation Company, as well as the Black River, Chenango, Erie, and Oneida Lake canals; and the construction of the first state road, the Genesee Turnpike, sometimes called the Seneca Turnpike (Route 5), which originally went from New Hartford, the Oneida village of "Chicugughquate" (Kidneys), to Canandaigua, and which ran through the southern end of the principal Indian settlement of Oneida Castle. Moreover, to the west of Oneida Territory were the extensive salt mines of Salina in the environs of today's Syracuse and the vast lands of the New Military Tract, the former estate of the Onondaga and Cayuga Indians, who were allied to the British in the American Revolution. To make these lands west of Oneida attractive for sale, roads and canals had to be constructed, and, for that to happen, lands and/or rights-of-way had to be secured from the Oneida Indians.

Despite federal guarantees to protect their Oneida and Tuscarora Indian allies at Fort Stanwix in 1784, the New York State legislature, proposing to speed up white settlement, passed two laws in 1784 and 1785 to facilitate the "settlement of the waste and unappropriate lands" in the state, and set up procedures to advertise and distribute Indian lands, even before the state had bought title. Previously, state officials had pointed out to the Indians that they were going to be treated fairly and the Indians' land base would be respected. Governor George Clinton gave assurances, indicating that in order to prevent Indian-white disputes and conflict, the provision in the New York State Constitution forbidding Indian land sales to individuals without legislative permission would be enforced.

In reality, New York officials built the rising Empire State on profits from Indian land cessions. The Oneidas are a case in point. Between 1785 and 1846, these Indians lost their lands in New York State through a series of "treaties," despite being largely on the Patriot side during the American Revolution and despite provisions in the New York State and United States Constitutions, congressional acts, and federal treaty guarantees. Taking advantage of the existence of Oneida divisions, New York State officials began the process of dispossession, defrauding these Indians of over 5 million acres.

Even though the Oneidas were given guarantees of the United States' recognition of their territory at the Treaty of Fort Stanwix in 1784, New York State "acquired" the very next year at Fort Herkimer 300,000 acres of Oneida lands, the present counties of Broome and Chenango, rich, well-watered agricultural lands, for $11,500. In September 1788, at Fort Schuyler, the state "acquired" nearly 5 million acres of Oneida lands, reserving 300,000 acres in Madison and Oneida counties; in return, the state paid the Oneidas $2,000 in cash, $2,000 in clothing, and $1,000 in provisions, and provided $500 to subsidize the building of grist and saw mills. The state was also to provide an annuity of $600 to the Indians. In this 1788 agreement, the Oneidas signed an "instrument of cession" with New York State governor George Clinton, viewing the action as a lease to the state in an effort to foil the speculators' nefarious efforts. Instead, state officials soon claimed that this agreement was an Oneida cession of much of their lands. When state officials no longer could get Indians to come to the treaty table, the state granted power of attorney to a small segment of the tribe, and then signed the agreement with those Indians in the name of all Oneidas. This pattern was set in the New York State–Oneida "Treaty" of 1795, described by Laurence Hauptman in chapter 2, which became the model for all Albany's efforts at dispossession of the Oneidas for the next half century. With the death or aging of key tribal leaders at critical times, state officials tied to transportation and land interests, such as Philip Schuyler, relentlessly pursued these Indian lands, which they deemed as vital to their own ambitions as well as to the region's and the state's growth. Land "purchased" by state "treaty" from Oneida for 50¢ an acre was sold for 7–10 times its original purchasing price. Meanwhile, the state was pushing settlement of its central portion. Madison County, with fewer than 1,000 settlers in 1800, had 39,000 by 1830.

The Oneidas, already severely fractionated in their polity and religion, largely found it impossible to resist these pressures, leading a majority of the community, for its protection and survival, to migrate west to Wisconsin in the period 1820–1838 or to Ontario during 1839–1845. The incredible pressures placed upon the community as a result of this transportation revolution explain in part why the bulk of the community followed the controversial Indian missionary Eleazer Williams, a charismatic but unbalanced ecclesiastic leader of Mohawk ancestry, into the wilderness of eastern Wisconsin, where the largest contemporary Oneida community still resides.

Williams, a charismatic Episcopal missionary (lay reader and catechist), possessed a command of the Mohawk and Oneida languages, a fiery oratory style, and religious fervor, as well as significant political ability. He foresaw the establishment of an ecclesiastic empire with himself as leader, one that would include the bulk of the Six Nations, resettled in Wisconsin. In chapter 3 Reginald Horsman perceptively shows that Williams' idea fitted the times, not merely the goals of speculators such as the Ogden Land Company. Missionaries such as Jedidiah Morse had been calling for Indian isolation from the worst effects of white contact. At the time, Secretary of War John C. Calhoun (see illustration on p. 98) was promoting his idea of indirect removal, in which the Indians would decide to cede their lands in the East for resettlement in the West. By 1817, Williams won the support of the First Christian Party and subsequently converted many members of the "Pagan Party," which, by 1818, became known as the Second Christian Party.

The choosing of Wisconsin as a final Oneida destination was no accident. Discussions from 1817 onward between Williams, agents of the Ogden Land Company, missionary Jedidiah Morse, Indian subagent Jasper Parrish, Governor Lewis Cass, and Secretary of War Calhoun actually brought up a plethora of possibilities including Arkansas, Illinois, Michigan, and Missouri. Cass and Morse appeared to have influenced the decision, although several other factors also must be noted: Williams and an exploring party visited Green Bay as early as 1820; the area is the same latitude as the Oneida homeland of central New York; and the government found some Indians, the Menominees, willing to sell land to their New York Indian (Oneida, Stockbridge, Brothertown) "friends," whom they dubbed the Nottoways. In an extraordinary series of Indian-Indian negotiations in 1821 and 1822, New York Indians obtained an unbelievable estate of 4 million acres from the Menominees. The Buffalo Creek Treaty in 1838 reduced these Oneida lands to 65,425 acres, or approximately 100 acres per Oneida who resided in Wisconsin by that year.

The Oneidas who came to Wisconsin, which was part of Michigan Territory between 1818 and 1836, arrived at different times. Most of these Oneidas came by lake steamer out of the port of Buffalo. These packet boats made stops along the way at Detroit and at Mackinac Island before reaching Green Bay. Initially, exploring parties of Oneidas were led into the Wisconsin wilderness by Eleazer Williams, and most of these early arrivals were members of the First Christian Party who settled along Duck Creek. By 1825, this Williams-led group numbered about 150 Indians, and they soon were joined by more emigrants from New York. A separate migration of Oneidas had come to Wisconsin as early as 1823, led by Neddy Otsiquette, who settled at Little Chute but whose community later resettled at the Duck Creek reservation. In 1830 and after, a new wave of emigrants came from New York. This new group, the Orchard Party, first settled near the Stockbridge at Grand Kakalin on the Fox River. Three years later, the Orchard Party, by then Methodist converts, moved to the Duck Creek area, settling on the west side of the reservation at De Pere. After the disastrous Treaty of Buffalo Creek of 1838, analyzed by Arlinda Locklear in chapter 5, another wave of Oneidas migrated to Wisconsin. Those in this last migration, known as the Homeless Oneidas, were fully incorporated into the Oneida Nation of Indians, but only in the final decade of the nineteenth century.

Oneida life in New York in the 1820s and 1830s steadily worsened, effecting westward migrations. The desperate conditions were described by an

English traveler who came upon the Oneidas embarking at Buffalo for Green Bay on July 4, 1831:

... On the wharf at Buffalo we saw a number of the Oneida tribe of Indians, on their way to Greenbay, a branch of Lake Michigan. This tribe having sold their lands in the state of New York, government was conveying them to their new possessions. The poor creatures were standing in groups, dressed in their best attire, and many young and old of both sexes stupified by intoxication. I particularly remarked a grey-haired aged female, with a countenance of the deepest suffering, bearing in her arms a child of spurious origin. These descendants of the original owners of the soil have been gradually deprived of their birthright; and although Greenbay is 1000 miles from their old habitations, the white man in progress of time will envy their new possessions, and the poor Indian will retire still farther to the west, if drunkenness, and other vices acquired from the whites, do not exterminate the race. . . .[1]

Two years later, in July 1832, Maximilian, prince of Wied, traveling on the Erie Canal, visited Oneida Castle and found the bulk of the reduced community preparing for another evacuation:

At noon we were in the village of Oneida, which is irregularly built on both sides of the canal. Here we happened to meet with above 100 Oneida Indians, whose lands, assigned to them by the government, lie to the south of this place. The women wore round black felt hats; the men red woollen scarfs [*sic*] over their blue great coats. Their complexion was a yellowish-brown, not dark. They were of low stature, especially the women, as has been observed of all the remnants of the six nations, and have retained more of the national features than the men. We were informed that some of these people were to embark here and proceed to Green Bay, near which they intended to settle.[2]

The decline of the Oneida Nation not only led most of these Indians to Wisconsin, but also prompted a sizable migration of Oneidas to Ontario, in three separate groups from 1839 to 1845. Thus, by the mid-1840s, only about 200 Oneidas remained in New York State.

From the first, Oneidas attempted to rebuild their community in Wisconsin. Oneida life in Wisconsin revolved around eight clearly defined neighborhoods, described by Jack Campisi in chapter 4. The Episcopal church members settled at Oneida along Duck Creek on the west side of the reservation, and the Methodist followers, the old Orchard Party, settled along the east side near De Pere. The nuclear family was the primary unit, and reciprocal gift giving and assistance in the form of building bees were expected between kin. Marriages were arranged, and rules of clan exogamy were followed in the first decades. The Longhouse religion was not practiced, and certain Iroquois practices—such as the Little Water Society, Iroquoian funerary customs, and employment of herbal medicines—were fitted into the Christian religion.

The Oneidas brought little of their traditional political structure to Wisconsin, although they had a system of chiefs who claimed hereditary rights. The council was composed of a head chief and 12 "big men," or chiefs, appointed by the senior women of the lineages. This hereditary council could allocate lands, outlaw liquor sales, make contracts for sale of timber, enforce sentences of banishment and execution, and represent the nation in dealings with the federal government, such as in securing annuity payments. Thus, despite the great crisis caused by dispossession and removal, Oneida society had resilience enough to adapt to its new surroundings.

The Oneidas who immigrated to Wisconsin in the 1820s and 1830s faced myriad problems. The first wave of immigrants had to build temporary shelters quickly to protect themselves from the approaching Wisconsin winter. Right from the first, some of the Menominees bitterly disputed the legality of their large land cessions of 1821 and 1822, a controversy that was not fully resolved until 1838. Moreover, even as Eleazer Williams was leading Oneidas westward, a group of Oneidas were insisting that Williams was not officially sanctioned to speak for them on the removal question. Religious divisions, which were so manifest in New York, were carried by the Oneidas to Wisconsin; the Episcopalians, the First Christian Party, settled apart from the Methodists, the Orchard Party, on the Oneidas' Duck Creek reservation. Different sets of chiefs represented each group. It is little wonder that each established its own school and fielded its own lacrosse team, as Oscar Archiquette's WPA story in part 2 of the book illustrates. Missionary Williams was himself a source of factionalism; however, by the early 1830s, Williams' days of leadership were numbered largely because of charges of malfeasance against him, his erratic behavior, and his failure to get the rest of the Six Nations to join the Oneidas in the West.

Intratribal divisions went so far as to lead one group of Oneidas, claiming to represent 200 members, to petition President Martin Van Buren with an offer to exchange their lands in Wisconsin for lands farther west. Objecting to the leadership of Chief Daniel Bread of the First Christian Party, they proposed that the federal government give them 320 acres for every 100 acres they would cede in Wisconsin. They continued to press for removal until 1844. In 1845, Governor Henry Dodge of Wisconsin Territory proposed removal of the Oneidas from Wisconsin Territory, but the proposal was rejected by the vast majority of the Oneidas, including Jacob Cornelius, Bread's opponent and acknowledged leader of the Orchard Party.[3]

By the end of the first decade in Wisconsin, observers were reporting that the Oneida community was beset with problems related to alcohol abuse. In a frontier setting, a few miles from whiskey traders in and around Fort Howard, who were always willing to violate the law by selling alcohol to the Indians, the Oneidas could not isolate themselves from the problem. In one week in September 1834, nine Oneidas died as a result of hard drinking. After the arrival of a contingent of Methodist Oneidas from New York, one missionary later claimed that the group was welcomed with a celebration that was a "scene of great intoxication and degradation."[4]

Despite these wrenching problems, by 1830 the Indians at Duck Creek had cleared 237 acres of land and planted corn, potatoes, and turnips. Four years later, the Reverend Jackson Kemper noted that 400 acres were cleared and "the crops looked promising." Upon his visit, Kemper preached in English in the newly log-constructed Episcopal church, and his sermon was translated into Oneida, even though the Indians were employing Eleazer Williams' Mohawk prayerbook (see illustrations on pp. 95–96). Although it was an Episcopal service, 10 Methodists of the Orchard Party, as well as their schoolteacher, took communion, which was followed by a hearty church breakfast of pork and beans, chicken pies, squash, potatoes, peas, and rice.

Although there are few extant records of the Oneidas in the first decade in Wisconsin, two diaries written in the 1840s illustrate the rapidity of Oneida adjustment to their new surroundings. In 1840, Henry R. Colman became the Methodist missionary to the Oneidas. According to Colman, the Oneidas at the time numbered approximately one thousand persons. The largest neighborhood was around the Episcopal church. The principal road ran parallel to Duck Creek in a northeast-southwest direction. The two frame buildings in the settlement were owned by Jacob Cornelius, head chief of the Orchard Party, and Daniel Bread, head chief of the First Christian Party, who was referred to as head chief of the nation. Missionary Colman then carefully described the Episcopal church and its congregants:

On a little rise of ground stood the church, a frame building painted white, measuring about 40 × 60 feet. The pews were made of pine boards, without doors, and unsoftened by cushions. Father preached through an interpreter. This latter functionary was usually William Woodman, who received for his services from the Missionary Society, the munificent sum of $50 per annum. The hymnal used at the services was, I think, in the Mohawk tongue, which the Oneida understood. They were great lovers of harmony and sang beautifully, often employing themselves in writing music by note.

I well recall the appearance of the Sunday morning congregation. The men, who had doffed their blankets and were clad in the garb of American citizens, sat on one side. The women, still in petticoats and blankets, took the other side. The blankets were red or white, such as are now in use upon our beds, while many of the women were wrapped in large pieces of costly broadcloth. The younger women generally sat and walked the highways with their blankets over their heads, so that only one eye could by any chance be seen. The older women in church generally let the blankets fall to their shoulders. Some wore silk hats, with silver bands two inches wide; commonly one band sufficed, yet not unfrequently the hat would be nearly covered with them. These were worn throughout the service. I do not recall that the men indulged in silk hats. The women's skirts were often made of the finest cloth, bordered from one to twelve inches at the bottom with beads sewed to the cloth. The skirts never trailed in the mud, but were short and revealed pantalets of the same material and adornment.[5]

Colman added that next to the church stood a log schoolhouse that aimed to educate Oneida boys and girls on the "elements of education." They sat on "slabs with pegs for legs learning reading, writing, and spelling," and some of the "youths were quite ambitious to learn the English language." In addition to his teaching duties and his pastoral responsibilities, the missionary served almost as the "adviser-in-chief of the community," comforting, exhorting, and reproving his congregants in sermons, marriages, and funerals, as well as making "suggestions about farming."[6]

Colman also noted that the Oneidas were "an independent nation, and dispensed their own justice." Much like what Oneida Elizabeth Huff recounts in a WPA story in part 2 of this book, the Methodist missionary even witnessed a tribal council, serving as a court, finding a defendant guilty of the murder of three children. Oneida warriors, "garbed in the uniform of soldiers, with bayonetted rifles borrowed from Fort Howard, acted as guard" during the execution. Although the Oneidas themselves became rooted in Wisconsin Territory and dispensed frontier justice in the 1840s, they were not without pressures both from afar and from within. Some members of the community promoted abandoning their new home for lands in Missouri to avoid the white man who "was crowding them again."[7]

A second memoir, written in 1849 by Alfred Cope, a Quaker shipping magnate from Philadelphia, reveals even more about the Oneidas and their three decades in Wisconsin. Upon first viewing the Oneida Indian Reservation, Cope noted the "unpretending but substantial habitations of the Oneidas as far as the eye can reach," as well as the "green fields and snug buildings so prettily situated," which were the "result of their own labor and good management. . . ." After describing the umbrella-carrying Oneida women, who wore Menominee-styled head-gear, Cope commented favorably on the menfolk and their farming abilities. He was "struck with the respectability of their appearance and equipages." Comparing the Oneida forms with those of his native Pennsylvania, Cope insisted that "their horses, wagons and harness could have been creditable" to his own home state. He added that the Oneida horses "were superior in appearance and spirit" to those commonly found in Pennsylvania and that the Indians "had better teams than any other country people about the [Green] Bay."[8] Once again drawing comparisons, Cope noted:

The buildings of the Oneidas were by no means equal to those of the Brothertowns, nor were their fields in as nice condition nor their horned cattle as carefully bred as those of the Stockbridges. Yet, in all these respects they would bear pretty well to be put in comparison with most communities of whites of as recent date. In one particular—the height, material, and firmness of their fences—they excelled. No such fencing was seen elsewhere. The height seemed needless, unless for the exclusion of deer. It was asserted that these people formed the most important part of the agricultural population of this vicinity, were quite superior as farms in industry and productiveness to the farmers of French descent, and, in fact, brought to market more corn and beef than anyone else. . . .[9]

Cope observed that the Oneida houses were of unpainted wood, "well-proportioned and neatly constructed," and built along a main corridor, and that, even as early as 1849, most of the timber on the lot had been cleared, leaving no shade on these homesites. The "most conspicuous buildings" on the reservation were the Episcopal church and the home of Daniel Bread (see illustration on p. 99). The church wore "the pleasant face of a New England village meeting-house," and Chief Bread's residence was a "spacious, double house painted white and set back a considerable distance from the main road." Unlike Colman's estimate, Cope claimed that there were between 700 and 800 Oneidas, and that 500 were members of the Episcopal church and 100 were Methodists. Each church ran schools for Oneida children and, in 1848, 50 students, more than half girls, attended.[10]

The Philadelphia businessman then described the July 4, 1849, celebration at Oneida, at which time it was customary to invite the tribe to the head chief's house. Over 100 attended the feast, which included a meal of venison, fresh pork, beef, rice pudding, and coffee. Much like in other American communities, fireworks were set off. The meal was followed by a lacrosse match between teams selected from members of the Episcopal and Methodist churches, whose competition in this sport is also revealed later in a WPA story in part 2. Fully reporting the match, the pacifist Cope cringed at the combative nature of the game but delighted at the players' great agility and overall prowess. What disturbed Cope at the match was the ever-present liquor trade, a major problem in the 1820s and 1830s, which Cope now noted had been somewhat reduced. Indeed, tribal council regulation forbade "grog shops in the Nation."[11]

Cope's memoir also shows the continuing connection between Oneida communities and renewed threats to Oneida life and stability. While he was at Duck Creek, he came in contact with an Oneida delegation of Canadian deputies, "grave, sensible men" who were attempting to confer with their brethren about "the feasibility of bringing about a permanent reunion of their people. . . ." To Cope, there "was something pleasant in the thought of such a movement—the reunion of the broken fragments of a once powerful people."[12] However, there was another side to these discussions. With talk of Oneida Indian removal from Wisconsin being raised again, two Oneida communities deemed it necessary to confer about their future.

Ultimately the roots put down by the Oneidas in Wisconsin were strong enough to withstand this crisis as well as two greater ones that followed: the American Civil War and the Dawes General Allotment Act of 1887. Each of these events is worthy of a separate book in Oneida history and goes beyond the scope of this present study.

Notes

1. Clayton Mau, ed., *The Development of Central and Western New York* (Rochester: DuBois Press, 1944), p. 336.

2. *Travels in the Interior of North America,* trans. H. Evans Lloyd (London: Ackermann and Co., 1843), p. 500.

3. Reginald Horsman, "The Wisconsin Oneidas," in *The Oneida Indian Experience: Two Perspectives,* ed. Laurence M. Hauptman and Jack Campisi (Syracuse, N.Y.: Syracuse University Press, 1988), pp. 65–82.

4. Jackson Kemper, "Journal of an Episcopalian Missionary's Tour to Green Bay, 1834," *Wisconsin Historical Collections,* Vol. 14 (Madison: SHSW, 1898), pp. 431–433.

5. Henry Colman, "Recollections of Oneida Indians, 1840–1845," in *Proceedings of the State Historical Society of Wisconsin on Its Fifty-ninth Annual Meeting, October 26, 1911* (Madison: SHSW, 1912), p. 156.

6. Ibid., p. 157.

7. Ibid., pp. 158–159.

8. Alfred Cope, "Green Bay Diary [1849]," *Wisconsin Magazine of History* 50 (1967): 135–136.

9. Ibid., p. 137.

10. Ibid., pp. 137–138.

11. Ibid., pp. 139–143.

12. Ibid., pp. 143–144.

1 *Laurence M. Hauptman*

The Oneida Nation
A Composite Portrait, 1784–1816

The Oneida Indians in the post–Revolutionary War era found themselves increasingly divided, a factor that weakened them and facilitated their dispossession from their central New York State lands. Ethnohistorian Jack Campisi has identified three issues that divided Oneida society in the late eighteenth century: "control of political authority within the tribe and among its communities; the degree of acceptance or rejection of white society; and the policy concerning land sales to the State of New York." Campisi adds "These issues coalesced around two opposing groups called the 'Pagan' or Cornelius Party and the Christian or Shenandoah Party."[1] Although Campisi is quite accurate in his assessment, the splits in Oneida society were even greater than he describes. At times, these divisions were more an abyss than merely fissures. Rivalries between warriors and sachems, religious and political factionalism, social disintegration reflected in increasing alcohol abuse and internecine violence, economic dependence, class distinctions, and different strategies relating to holding onto or selling land were all apparent in the post–Revolutionary War era, but their roots began long before that period.

At the end of the American Revolution, the Oneidas, mostly Patriot-allied Indians, were a scattered people. Their villages were destroyed, their leadership was divided, and their former allies in the Iroquois Confederacy were alienated from them. The American Revolution had been a whirlwind, one which severely disrupted their universe.[2] Although prior to the war they had

19

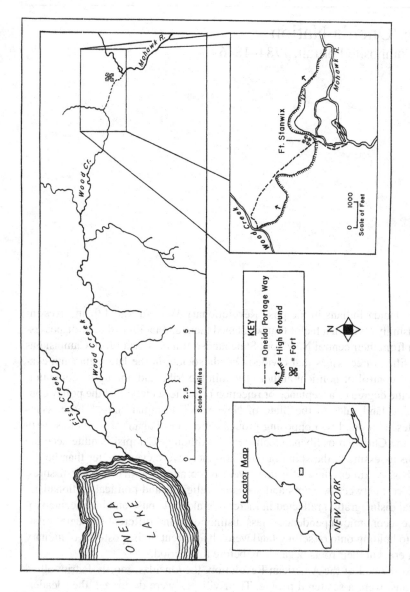

Map 1.1. The Oneida Carrying Place (Map by Ben Simpson)

been divided into factions, one led by the warriors and the other by sachems, the events of 1775–1783 exacerbated the divisions, which "never healed, and they provided the fertile ground for the exploitation of the tribe."[3]

By 1780, most Oneidas were refugees, with the majority of the American-allied seeking protection at Schenectady. A smaller pro-British faction sought refuge at Fort Niagara; this contingent either soon followed the Mohawk war chief Joseph Brant to settle at the Haldimand Patent along the Grand River in 1784 or temporarily settled in Seneca Country along the Genesee River. Even with this smaller pro-British faction included in the total, the overall Oneida population shrank by a third in the two-decade period of 1774–1794, largely as a result of Oneida battlefield deaths during the American Revolution, as well as the desperate economic situation that followed, which led to starvation and susceptibility to disease. In 1794, De Witt Clinton estimated the total Oneida population to be 1,088, with 628 Oneidas residing in the United States and 460 in British Canada.[4]

Missionary Samuel Kirkland's presence contributed to the divisions and helped shape the Oneida world long after the American Revolution ended.[5] Besides his influence in bringing most of the Oneidas to the American side during the Revolutionary War, encouraging assimilation to the white man's ways, and introducing Christianity, Kirkland (see illustration on p. 93) reinforced already existing divisions within the community, between warriors, mostly his supporters, and sachems. Thus, at the end of the American Revolution, the pro-Kirkland warriors who had been allied to the Americans and who had become converted to Christianity largely resided at Oneida Castle (Kanowaʔalohaleʔ), 12 miles south of the easternmost section of Oneida Lake; the sachems and their supporters, now organized as the Pagan Party, resided at Oriskany (Old Oriske), 8 miles west of present-day Rome, New York.[6]

Kirkland's career among the Oneidas had two stages. The first stage occurred before, during, and immediately after the American Revolution; Kirkland was seen, especially among the warrior element within the Oneidas, as their "friend" or "father." To historian James Ronda, there was more to these designations "than just Iroquois courtesy in the air. The Oneida faithful saw Kirkland as a spiritual director, a guide in the midst of troubled times." In his lengthy, unyielding, hellfire-and-brimstone sermons, which lasted hours at a time, Kirkland's rigid message emphasized the notion of a solitary believer standing naked before an all-powerful, all-knowing angry God to be judged.[7]

Despite Kirkland's demanding New Light message, some prominent Oneidas did indeed see the Presbyterian theologian as the right antidote for a growing dysfunctionalism in Oneida society. Kirkland's sermons stressed a complete reliance on farming and the abandonment of the demon rum, whose use had reached epidemic proportions among the Oneidas. The centerpiece of Kirkland's thinking was education, which he believed could prepare the Indians for the Christian white world by erasing native ways and could serve the Indians as a tool for surviving in a hostile culture. Cooperating with Skenandoah and other influential Oneidas such as Laulence and Onondiyo, he pushed his "civilization plan." Thus, to some Oneidas such as Skenandoah, a former alcohol abuser, Kirkland offered a new level of self-respect.

Kirkland's significance is easily seen in examining the lives of two prominent Indians in this period: Good Peter (see illustration on p. 91) and Skenandoah. The former, Agwelondongwas/Agwrondongwas, or "Breaking of the Twigs," was a Bear Clan chief of the Oneidas. He was born around 1715 and was converted to Christianity by the missionary Elihu Spencer in 1748 at the upper Susquehanna village of Oquaga, a village of diverse refugee Indians under the watchful eyes of the Oneidas. It was at this time that Good Peter acquired both his Christian religious faith and his ability to read and write "fairly well." A strong advocate of temperance among his people, Good Peter by 1757 was preaching at Oquaga and at neighboring villages. Soon he was being referred to as the eloquent Dominie Peter, Peter the Priest, or Petrus the Minister and was carrying out the Christian message of Spencer and Gideon Hawley, who also taught and missionized at Oquaga in the 1750s.[8]

The New Light Christianity of the Great Awakening significantly affected these Indians, especially in its call for temperance. By 1765, Good Peter visited Reverend Eleazar Wheelock's mission school at Hanover, New Hampshire, asking the missionary to send teachers to the Oneidas and other Six Nations. Later Samuel Kirkland, Wheelock's first white student at the school, was dispatched to Oneida Territory, after failing miserably as a missionary among the Senecas during a 10-month period in 1764 and 1765.[9]

Good Peter, as well as his friend and ally Skenandoah, proved to be indispensable to Kirkland's missionary efforts. Good Peter later served as one of Kirkland's deacons, becoming an active, spellbinding Indian orator, preacher, and Christian missionary throughout Iroquoia.

Although becoming somewhat disenchanted with Kirkland for the missionary's support for Indian land cessions in 1788, Good Peter still accompanied Kirkland on his official travels and remained both a Christian and the most eloquent orator-defender of Oneida land rights. At a time when the Oneidas were surrounded by swarming land sharks, Good Peter had few options open to him and his people except for reliance on self-proclaimed "friends" of the Indians. Just prior to his death, Good Peter told Pickering that Governor George Clinton, who presented himself as the protector of the Indians from the tentacles of land speculators, had tricked the Oneidas, and that they had no intention of selling any lands. He insisted that the Indians would lease "out a tier of townships, on the line of property, to any poor people of his state, who had no lands; and that we would do this on reasonable terms."[10]

Governor Clinton's strategy—flattery—was clear, as is revealed in a letter to state Indian commissioner Peter Rykman in April 1784. Clinton recognized Good Peter's high standing among the Oneidas, insisting to Rykman: "You must also pay attention to, and flatter him [Good Peter] on account of his good sense and friendship to us." When Good Peter, too late, finally realized the governor's intentions, he moaned: "After this transaction, the voice of the birds from every quarter, cried out—You have lost your country—You have lost your country!" The aged Oneida added that the alarm was made by a "white bird."[11]

With this lesson learned, the venerable Good Peter attempted to educate the United States Indian commissioner Pickering about what had transpired and sought federal protection from New York State's avaricious actions. Unfortunately for the Oneidas, Good Peter, their great advocate, died in 1792. His hope and that of Pickering—namely, that federal laws and new federal-Indian treaties (the Pickering Treaty of 1794 and the Oneida Treaty of 1794) would protect the Indians from New York State—proved to be ill founded, for the treaties were worthless guarantees, totally ignored by omnipotent Empire State politicians such as Philip Schuyler, Good Peter's wartime "friend."

A second Oneida, Skenandoah, whose name means "running deer," was the archetype of the "good Indian." Indeed, among his own people, he was known universally as "the good friend of the white man." Whether this was a derogatory designation is not altogether clear. Skenandoah, born into a Susquehanna (Andaste or Conestoga) Indian family around 1706, was later adopted by the Oneidas, rising to the role of war chief and later Pine Tree chief of the Oneida Wolf Clan. Skenandoah, described as a "tall, well-made and robust man," was known as a "brave and intrepid warrior" during his youth. He had tattoos on his chest and hands and apparently also had enormous ears. According to Oneida tradition told to William Beauchamp, the Episcopal minister at Onondaga and an anthropologist, Skenandoah, (also known as Shenandoah, Schenando, Skenandon, Skanondonagh, Skenondough, Skenandore, John Skanondo, John Skeanendon, as well as many other variations of the name) had a religious transformation after an incident in Albany in 1755. He embarrassed himself at a treaty council when he became very drunk and found himself the following morning in a naked state.[12]

Skenandoah's conversion to Christianity was complete when he met and fell under the influence of missionary Kirkland in 1765. His unbridled friendship with Kirkland, a father figure to the Indian despite the missionary's younger age, lasted until Kirkland's death in 1808. This friendship was to significantly shape Oneida history as well as Iroquois and American histories as a whole.[13] William Beauchamp writes: "In the Revolutionary War his [Skenandoah's] influence induced the Oneidas to take up arms in favor of the Americans. Among the Indians he was distinguished as the white man's friend."[14] Although he was later accused of serving the British during the war, in part because he was the former father-in-law of Joseph Brant, the famed Mohawk war chief and British ally, Skenandoah apparently was one of the keys to the Oneida-American alliance in the Revolution.[15] Two incidents during the war illustrate his commitment and unabiding loyalty to Kirkland and the Americans. About the first,

Beauchamp writes: "His vigilance once preserved from massacre the inhabitants at German Flats."[16] Second, his commitment to the Americans included his being sent by General Schuyler to Fort Niagara on a special mission, where he and his lifelong friend Good Peter were promptly imprisoned by British military authorities.[17]

After the war, nearly every prominent non-Indian visitor to the Oneida Country was taken to see the aging warrior, who by that time had become blind. To some white men in the post–Revolutionary War period, Skenandoah became the "noble savage" incarnate, a symbol of the "genius" of the Indian character.[18] By 1810, he was described inaccurately by De Witt Clinton as "first chief of the Oneidas." Clinton then compared the impressive Oneida centenarian to an English monarch or to one of Queen Anne's famous American Indian kings of a century earlier.[19]

The aged, blind warrior, who by the 1790s was described as the "second chief" of the Oneidas, was to live in his declining years through the worst upheaval in his people's history. Using an accommodationist approach to the white man's land pressures, Skenandoah apparently agreed to piecemeal land cessions in a failed attempt to keep the whites from taking all of Oneida Country, especially Oneida Castle. Faced with religious and political pressures from within the Oneida world that would spill over into internecine violence in the last three decades of his life, Skenandoah's strategy was to fail miserably. In this regard, the aged warrior used the *very same* methods that the Oneidas had used since the crisis years of the 1770s: ingratiating himself to more powerful forces supported by his "father," the white missionary Samuel Kirkland. Always drawing support from his devout Christian faith, Skenandoah appealed for harmony within the terribly divided Oneida Indian community.[20]

Despite his remarkable life, Skenandoah's insistence on cooperation with the white man, and undoubtedly his frequent accession to land sales, was to cost him his reputation among the Oneidas. According to a perceptive Polish traveler's account in 1805, Skenandoah's standing in his community had plummeted: "The King [Skenandoah] is a great friend of the white man and has thus incurred the animosity of the tribe. His power is limited to negotiations with the white man and to presiding in council; for the rest, he has not the least authority over his fellow tribesmen."[21] In other words, the great Oneida warrior had become a pathetic figure in his declining years, the archetype of "government chief," brought out to meet visiting dignitaries and needed to sign illegal state accords for Oneida land cessions. Yet, Skenandoah's cooperation goes deeper than this point. In effect, he had become psychologically as well as economically dependent on the white man, especially his surrogate father Reverend Samuel Kirkland.

Skenandoah's acceptance of the missionary's message offered him a way to free himself from the demon rum and the troubling world around him. Whatever the missionary advised him to do, Skenandoah, the faithful son, complied.

Right to Kirkland's death in 1808, Skenandoah followed his "father's" teachings. Kirkland's emphasis on hard work, self-discipline, and self-worth brought economic rewards as well. For instance, it brought presents from influential whites such as New York State governor Daniel Tompkins, who bestowed on Skenandoah an elegant silver pipe. Also, those Oneidas more closely associated with the white man had clear economic advantages and lived in better housing than their "Pagan" brothers. Skenandoah, for one, lived in a well-made house built in a Dutch style with a hearth on one side "with an open space all around and a kind of funnel above to let out the smoke." His residence, elaborate for the Oneidas, was situated on the edge of the village, commanding "an extensive and grand view all round."[22]

When Kirkland proposed his "Plan for Education of Indians," which emphasized teaching Oneidas using the English language, Western methods of agriculture, and moral reform through Christian teachings, Skenandoah, his family, and his followers in the First Christian Party faithfully endorsed it. Besides ceding land for the project, the Hamilton-Oneida Academy, the predecessor of Hamilton College, they even went as far as writing to the New York State Board of Regents and recruiting Onondaga and Seneca children from Buffalo Creek and petitioning federal authorities such as the powerful secretary of the treasury Alexander Hamilton, Philip Schuyler's son-in-law, to support Kirkland's efforts in this regard.[23] It is little wonder that at Skenandoah's death in 1816, at somewhere between 96 and 106 years of age, the Oneida was buried on the grounds of Kirkland's Hamilton College next to the grave of his white father, the missionary (see illustration of Skenandoah's tombstone on p. 92).

Despite being unable to read and write English, Skenandoah's name appears on all the Oneida Indian land cessions of the 1780s and 1790s.[24] It also appears in 1793 on the enormous 21-year lease of over 50,000 acres of land to Peter Smith, a business partner of John Jacob Astor. This lease, the New Petersburgh Tract, comprised the towns of Augusta in Oneida County and Stockbridge, Smithfield, Fenner, and northern Cazenovia in Madison County. Smith, the father of the famous abolitionist Gerrit Smith, went so far as to name his first son Peter Skenandoahah, after his alleged "friend." The 1795 state treaty with the Oneidas allowed for the purchase of Smith's leased tract. In the end, Smith later paid the state to obtain title to 22,300 acres of this "former" Oneida land.[25]

Although members of all factions advocated leasing or selling lands at one time or another, it should be noted that tribal divisions were exacerbated by debates over leasing and land sales. This concern was made clear in a council with federal commissioner Timothy Pickering on October 11, 1794, when the Oneidas were asked to explain the roots of the great dissension occurring within their community. Two Oneidas—Onondiyo or Captain John, representing the sachems, and Peter, representing the warriors—addressed Pickering. Although Peter's speech revealed little about the troubles occurring within the nation, Onondiyo's speech explained much. He insisted: "Our minds are divided on account of our land."[26] Onondiyo was basically observing that, by the decade after the American Revolution, the Oneidas had become increasingly divided upon the merits of selling tribal lands.

It is too easy to suggest that Skenandoah was a "sell-out" because he was more willing to lease or cede Oneida lands than most other Oneida leaders. Indeed, the Oneida leadership had few options open to them. Depending on the word of missionary Kirkland or Philip Schuyler, their former commanding officer, were logical strategies to be employed. Moreover, we cannot project acquisitive values onto this deeply religious man. Much of his adult life since the 1750s had been built on cooperation with the white man. A trusting man, his faith, his redemption from alcohol, his role as an intermediary between the Indian and non-Indian worlds, as well as his economic survival, were determined by that cooperation, much like so many other Oneidas who became nearly totally dependent on outsiders. Besides, to blame this aged warrior would ignore that all factions at one time or another from 1785 onward accepted state money for land. The Skenandoah, or the Christian, faction was not alone in its concessions. Although the "traditionals" in the Pagan Party, also known as the Cornelius or Doxtator Party, were initially against selling land to the state, they did accede in 1805 to the partition of the remaining Oneida reservation between themselves and the Oneidas of the Christian Party. Later, in 1809, they signed and acknowledged this partition and at the same time, leased their lands east of Oneida Creek, from Oneida Lake to Mud Creek, which flows into Oneida Creek to the south of the Genesee (Seneca) Turnpike, for an annual rent of 6 percent, based upon a value of $.56 per account and a state advance of $1,000. Moreover, later, from 1827 onward to 1846, descendants of some of the original members of the Pagan Party, by that time known as the Orchard Party, sold land to the state in a series of illegal transactions.[27]

Just before his death in 1816, Skenandoah had come to realize what had befallen the Oneidas and that his strategy of cooperation with white friends had failed. He then described himself, as well as his leadership, as a hemlock tree with its top cut off.[28] Skenandoah went on to blame in large part New York State officials and "certain white men," rather than casting aspersions on any of the Oneida leadership, himself included. He insisted that alcohol made the Oneidas "mice for white men, who are cats. Many a meal have they eaten of you. Their lips are sweet, but their heart is wicked." After stating that "there are good whites, and there are good Indians" and that he loved "all good men," Skenandoah, Kirkland's surrogate son, once again put the fate of his troubled Indian nation in terms of devotion to Christianity: ". . . Jesus, whom I love, sees all. His great day is coming, he will make straight; he will say to cheating whites and drinking Indians—'begone ye!—go! go! go!' Certainly, my children, He will drive them away." As a product of the Great Awakening, Skenandoah hoped for the Second Coming of Christ to lead the Oneidas away from troubles. Instead, one year after Skenandoah's death, Eleazer Williams, a missionary product of the Second Great Awakening, showed up at Oneida, insisting that Zion was Wisconsin, then Illinois Territory.[29]

The strategy employed by the Oneidas in the period and the aging of its leadership were only two of many reasons the Oneidas were unprepared for the foxes at the gates. In the last decades of Skenandoah's life, there occurred an important power vacuum in Oneida leadership and one not solely attributable to Indian factionalism caused by religious divisions. In the space of the brief period between 1788 and 1795, the Oneidas lost four of their most powerful voices, including the remarkable Good Peter in 1792. The Oneidas at Old Oriske were led by Colonel Hongarry until his death in 1788. He was succeeded by [Peter] Oneyanha, also known as Beechtree and Peter the Quartermaster, of the Turtle Clan. Although Beechtree was present at both of the state negotiations with the Oneidas in 1785 and 1788, which he signed, he died just prior to the key events of the 1790s. Moreover, Captain John (Onondiyo) died on September 12, 1795, three days before the sealing of the New York State–Oneida accord of that year.[30]

The death of major Indian voices and the aging of others, besides Skenandoah, created a definite crisis in the Oneida community in the 1790s. Increasingly the community was divided along religious lines. In the mid-1790s, the followers of the "Great Binding Law," who were dubbed the Pagan Party, were headed by Blacksmith (also known as Silversmith), a nephew of Good Peter and the keeper of the standing stone, the symbol of the Oneida Nation. Missionary Jeremy Belknap described Blacksmith and his beliefs:[31]

He informed us that the objects of his devotion were the rocks and mountains, which he believed were animated by some invisible Power, which had a superintendency over human affairs. To this invisible Power he addressed his devotions, and depended on it for success in hunting and in war. This had been his religion from his youth, and he had never failed of receiving answers to his prayers. He had always either killed his enemy or made him captive, and had generally good luck in hunting. Others, he said, paid the same devotion to the wind and to the thunder, believing them to be invisible powers, and put the same trust in them as he did in the rocks and mountains; and he regarded the Oneida stone as an image of the deity which he worshipped.

By the late 1790s, the aged Blacksmith—"Augweehstanis" or "Augharistonisk"—was still leader of the non-Christian Oneidas. He was "aided" by Peter II, or Pagan Peter, Good Peter's son; Peter II was the chief "Pagan" warrior, a man known for his violent behavior including his summary execution of witches within the Oneida community. From 1798 to 1805, the so-called Pagan Party was to undergo two major revivals, which resurrected ancient rituals and brought back many Christian Oneidas to their traditional roots.[32]

In the autumn of 1798, a Mohawk prophet arose along the Grand River in Ontario. In his interpretations of his visions, he claimed that the "Upholder of the Skies or Heavens" had been neglected by the Indians, and that, as a result, the Iroquois faced epidemics, famines, and unpleasant days. He urged a modified version of ceremonies that had been abandoned, such as the White Dog Sacrifice.[33] In earlier times the Iroquois had ritually strangled white dogs, usually two at a time, painted them with red spots, decorated them with ribbons and a wampum collar, and hung them upon a long pole; a few days later, they placed the dogs on a fire, recited a speech, and threw tobacco into the fire while the dogs cooked. They then took the roasted dogs off the fire, cut them into pieces, and ate part of them. The Oneidas, like the Senecas, held feasts involving dogs cooked in a soup, prior to taking off on war parties. Later, hogs and deer were substituted for white dogs.[34]

The Mohawk prophet urged the substitution of deer for white dogs and emphasized "temperance, universal love, domestic tranquillity," and respect and sympathy for each other. In his eclectic message, he also advised the Indians not to openly reject all the teachings of their missionaries and to follow the Bible's words. At least some of the Christian Oneidas were converted back to the blending of Christian and traditional religions as a result of the Mohawk prophet's message and later that of Handsome Lake, a second and more influential prophet.[35]

Blacksmith and Pagan Peter revived the ceremony in 1799, and three dogs were sacrificed in very much the traditional manner described. According to missionary Kirkland, the sacrifice was the first of its kind among the Oneidas in 30 years. The missionary indicated that the Indians refrained from alcohol for 10 days during the preparations and performance of this ceremony. The Oneidas subsequently performed a war dance, followed by a social dance that lasted all night. The ceremony ended the next day after they played the Iroquois Bowl Game, also known as the Peach Stone Game, a game of chance.[36]

The revival of this ceremony associated with war tells much about the Oneidas in the period. Good Peter and Skenandoah were not the only ones looking for answers in their acceptance of the word of Christ. Their "Pagan" counterparts were also seeking answers to deal with the crisis in Oneida society in the period, though they sought more traditional ways. Kirkland saw nefarious intentions in this revival, blaming the Quakers and Reverend John Sergeant with placating the "Pagan" elements among the Oneidas; the missionary, nevertheless, recognized the great appeal of this revival to a large number of Oneidas, the benevolence of the people involved, and the rich conversation that the ceremony engendered. Reading Kirkland's letters, one gets the overall impression that few Oneidas were unaffected by these "Pagan" doings.[37]

A second holy man, Handsome Lake, the Seneca prophet, also stirred Iroquoia in 1799 and 1800, changing it forever. Until his series of three visions, Handsome Lake was overshadowed by the political career of his younger half-brother, the Cornplanter. As a notorious drunkard before his visions, Handsome Lake had hardly played the central political role in the affairs of the

Seneca Nation, although he had been in attendance and signed the ignominious agreement with Robert Morris, the Treaty of Big Tree, in 1797.

In June of 1799, Handsome Lake lay ill, bedridden in his cabin. The Indians living at the old village on the Cornplanter grant had experienced much travail that spring, including drunken brawls, accusations of witchcraft, and even the execution of a witch who was blamed for the death of Cornplanter's and Handsome Lake's niece. Leaving his cabin on the Cornplanter grant on June 15, Handsome Lake collapsed and was aided back to bed by his nephew Governor Blacksnake. Most Senecas believed that he was about to die. After two hours in a near-catatonic state, witnessed by other Indians, Handsome Lake opened his eyes and began to recount a religious message he had just had. His vision included three well-dressed messengers who had come to him with the Creator's commands. The prophet was to choose his sister and her husband as his medicine persons and to attend the Strawberry Festival. There he was to preach the message of the *Gaiwiio,* the Good Word, one that condemned whiskey, witchcraft, love potions, and abortion. All wrongdoers had to confess and repent their wickedness or be punished.[38]

This first vision was to have a profound influence on the Iroquois, who were faced with disaster in the aftermath of the American Revolution. In part, the origins of the Handsome Lake religion stemmed from the splintering of the Iroquois Confederacy, substantial Indian land loss, constant white land pressures, social disintegration as reflected in the increased alcoholism and murder rates, and growing economic dependence on the non-Indian world.[39]

In the following months, Handsome Lake had two other visions, falling into trances and seeing many wonders and gaining insights relating to moral and social reform. In the second, he saw the punishment of wrongdoers: wife-beaters, drunkards, gamblers, witches, sinners. He traveled to the realm of the blessed, learning in this pleasant world how families among the Iroquois should live in peace in their own communities. Instructed by the sacred messenger who accompanied him on his spiritual journey, he was urged to continue to perform the Iroquois' religious ceremonial cycle.

In his third vision, which took place in 1800, he was commanded to write down the *Gaiwiio,* to preserve it for all time, and to carry the message to all the peoples of the Six Nations. Although Handsome Lake never preached among the Oneidas, the Good Word spread there. Handsome Lake combined his teaching with an emphasis on family values, condemning gossip, philandering, abortion, and alcohol, all of which were rampant at the time. The Seneca prophet also promoted men's participation in horticulture, which traditionally had been the women's domain. The Oneidas such as Good Peter, as most Iroquois Indians from time immemorial, had viewed women with high regard: "Our Ancestors considered it a transgression to reject the Council of their Women, particularly the female Governesses. Our Ancestors considered them mistresses of the Soil. Our Ancestors said who bring us forth, who cultivate our Lands, who Kindles our Fires and boil our Pots, but the Women . . . they are the Life of the Nation."[40] Yet, it should be noted, until the Age of Handsome Lake, only Skenandoah labored in the fields in the same manner as the women.[41]

Handsome Lake's message clearly contained Christian influences.[42] According to anthropologist Anthony F. C. Wallace, explicit "recognition of Christian theology is made in the code in his encounter with Jesus Christ, whom the prophet regarded as his counterpart among the whites. The images of heaven and, most particularly, hell seem clearly to have been based on a Christian model. . . ."[43] Indeed, the *Gaiwiio*'s acceptance among the Oneidas reflects this syncretization process. By 1805–1806, the so-called "Pagans" at Oneida "adopted the Christian sabbath, meeting in church from nine in the morning to four in the afternoon, when they required confession and absolution and made speeches."[44] To Oneidas faced with social disintegration and rampant alcoholism, Handsome Lake's messages proved appealing, even to Reverend Samuel Kirkland's Oneida helper, Doctor Peter, who spoke favorably of "the late revelations from the Seneka prophet, or man of God, as they stile him." Doctor Peter added: ". . . the prophet enjoined the strictest temperance and sobriety upon all Indians, and commanded them to abstain from the use of ardent spirits, which was never made for Indians; and for any Indian to drink a single glass or one swallow would be a deadly sin if not repented of."[45] He concluded by stating that the Seneca prophet exhorted his followers to live in peace with "all mankind, white people as well as Indians." Stressing family values, the holy man "spoke upon the duties of husbands and wives and the great sin of divorce."[46] Despite both "Pagan" and Christian Oneidas' advocating temperance, the ravages of alcoholism continued to plague the community, although the problem was temporarily lessened with the introduction of the message of the Seneca prophet and the leadership of Henry Cornelius (Haunnagwasuke, or "the little doctor") as head of the Pagan Party after 1800.[47] Later, in 1810 De Witt Clinton noted that the Pagan Party, which had grown considerably since 1798, had better morals "than those of the Christians," even though these Indians, according to Clinton, still practiced their "ancient superstitions" such as the White Dog Sacrifice, which had been rejected by Handsome Lake, and devoted six days to their Midwinter Ceremony.[48]

The Oneidas thus were a hopelessly divided people during this post–Revolutionary War era. To complicate matters even further, a class system had apparently developed by this time. This was reflected not only in Skenandoah's elevated economic position, but also in other areas of the community, most notably in what became known as the French Party. Francois Marbois had noted the extensive French presence among the Oneidas as early as 1784, pointing out the presence of the former captive Nicholas Jordan, who had been born along the Somme River in France. Jordan later married the widowed daughter of an Oneida sachem. He was one of several Frenchmen who married into the community and who had considerable influence in tribal affairs from 1784 to 1816.[49]

Some Oneidas, especially Kirkland's opponents, were swayed by another Frenchman, Peter Penet, a charismatic entrepreneur and merchant-trader from Nantes who had ingratiated himself to the Indians by invoking General Lafayette's hallowed name as well as that of the king of France, implying that he was in a quasi-official capacity as an envoy of Louis XVI to the Oneidas.[50] He also briefly instituted a Catholic mission among the Oneidas. Part of Penet's early success was a result of his full exposure of the nefarious plans of John Livingston, who had convinced the Oneidas to lease the bulk of their lands to his enterprise, the New York Genesee Company of Adventurers, for 999 years.[51] In return for Penet's help in foiling this chicanery, and in order to fulfill a dream that Penet allegedly had, the Oneidas granted this French schemer 10 square miles at the state-Oneida "treaty" at Fort Schuyler in 1788.[52] Penet's initial success among the Oneidas is both intriguing and significant, and it demonstrated the nature and extent of the crises facing these Indians. It was no accident that Oneidas followed grand schemers such as Penet and later Eleazer Williams, after the War of 1812, who both claimed French ancestry and promised "pie in the sky" tomorrow.

In 1789, Penet actually helped the Oneidas draft a plan of government for the establishment of a "grand council" that would map out and survey the community's lands. Article 6 of this proposal, one that drew initial support from various Oneidas including Beechtree, Blacksmith, and Skenandoah, specified emphatically: "No man, woman or child, of the said Oneida nation, shall have it in his power, to sell one foot of land that shall fall to his or her lot or share, except it to be to one of their nation. All other bargains for such land shall be void and of none effect."[53] Despite the appealing features of this proposal to a desperately divided Indian community, the Oneidas once again quickly split over Penet, his motives, and his character. His supporters, largely but not exclusively the opponents of missionary Kirkland, soon became known as the French Party. They included mostly members of the Pagan Party as well as wayward members of the Christian Party, including Atayataghronghta, also known as Lewis Cook, a Mohawk African who was adopted by Skenandoah and who had served the Americans faithfully during the Revolutionary War.[54]

Atayataghronghta may have financially benefited by the state-Oneida "treaty" of 1788, which provided for compensation to Penet and to the state's acquiring much of Oneida Country in 1788. John Tayler, the New York Indian Commission's agent, wrote Governor George Clinton: "I have further promised to Louis [Lewis] a Reward when the Treaty will be held at Fort Schuyler and have engaged him to return here [Albany] with the Messenger who is to come to Oneida from Buffalo Creek, and to render any other Assistance that will be required of him."[55]

The French influences went well beyond one Indian's disregard for scruples.

Some Oneidas had long been enamored with the French and French culture. The well-educated Peter Otsiquette, dubbed French Peter, had lived and studied in France after the American Revolution. While in Paris, he received three years of instruction in French, English, and German. He returned to Oneida, married an Oneida woman, but soon after died while on a visit to Philadelphia in 1792.[56] Otsiquette was not the only Francophile among the Oneidas either. The continuous presence of French traders—not just Jordan and Penet, who had married Oneida women—also had a direct effect on Oneida life and lands, an effect that extended beyond the Pagan Party. Angel De Ferriere, who had married an Oneida woman, one of the daughters of Lewis Denny (Dennie), and was tied to John [Jan] Lincklaen of the Holland Land Company, obtained substantial wealth and land by these ties. In 1810, De Witt Clinton described the process: After living 12 years at Oneida and fathering three children, De Ferriere, being "a man of genteel manners, sensible, and well-informed, acquired a great influence over them, and has prevailed on them to confer on him donations of valuable land—which have been sanctioned by the State."[57]

This illegal transaction, dated February 16, 1809, largely a land cession signed by the relatives of Lewis Denny, most important by John (Jonathan) Denny, transferred "1700 acres of the best land—a great deal of it on the turnpike [Genesee Road]."[58] John Denny, largely responsible for this cession, was later described by Clinton as being "addicted to intemperance," and his children were "said to be the worst tempered of any in the nation."[59]

Clinton revealed another reason for this illegal transaction besides consanguinity and alcohol. Some Oneidas themselves, such as the Denny family, saw personal gains and were willing to cut deals at the expense of the nation. In 1810, Lewis Denny told Clinton that there were "hard times with the Indians" and that deer were scarce because of the rapidly expanding white settlements.[60] Thus, securing economic advantages to his daughter's faithful husband was like money in the bank. Individual family survival, it is clear, took precedence over Oneida national and cultural integrity in desperate times.

Indeed, long before 1809, individual components of the nation took precedence over Indian national interests. Despite periodic efforts to reconcile differences, the Oneida Indians agreed to divide their remaining Indian lands in 1805, with Skenandoah's Christian Party getting ownership of the southern portion of tribal lands.[61] Thus, as De Witt Clinton noted five years later, the Oneidas "were now entirely separated in their territory, as well as in their God."[62]

Eventually the splits with the Oneida Indian community widened. In 1816 and 1817, Eleazer Williams converted some members of the Pagan Party to Christianity and encouraged the remaining members of the Christian Party to change their religious affiliation from Presbyterianism to Episcopalianism. Williams' flock became known as the Second Christian Party. In 1826, some members of the Pagan Party were converted to Methodism, assuming the name "Orchard Party." Despite this loss of membership, the Pagan Party maintained its existence by winning converts back periodically from both of the Christian parties. Under increasing pressure to migrate, by 1840, 400 of the 578 Oneidas remaining in New York decided to sell off their lands and leave the state. By 1843, the Oneidas retained two landbases in New York—approximately 190 acres at Orchard Park in Oneida County and 743 acres at Marble Hill in Madison County; however, in the same year, the New York State legislature "permitted" the allotment of Oneida lands in severalty. Within 80 years, the Oneida common landbase had shrunk to 32 acres.[63]

Notes

1. Jack Campisi, "Ethnic Identity and Boundary Maintenance in Three Oneida Communities," unpublished Ph.D. dissertation, SUNY Albany, 1974, p. 81.

2. For the Oneidas in the American Revolution, see Barbara Graymont, "The Oneidas in the American Revolution," in *The Oneida Indian Experience: Two Perspectives,* ed. Jack Campisi and Laurence M. Hauptman (Syracuse, N.Y.: Syracuse University Press, 1988), pp. 31–42. See also Barbara Graymont, *The Iroquois in the American Revolution* (Syracuse, N.Y.: Syracuse University Press, 1972), pp. 58–70, 134–143, 242. For some information about British-allied Oneidas, see Lyman C. Draper, Frontier War Papers, "Notes from Oneida Indians. . . ," Series 11U, Draper Collection, SHSW.

3. Jack Campisi, "The Oneida Treaty Period, 1783–1838," in *The Oneida Indian Experience,* p. 60.

4. Campisi, "Ethnic Identity and Boundary Maintenance," p. 35. Approximately 30 Oneidas are listed in the Timothy Pickering Census of 1792 as living in the Genesee Valley. Jasper Parrish MSS, VC.

5. James Ronda, "Reverend Samuel Kirkland and the Oneida Indians," in *The Oneida Indian Experience,* pp. 23–30; see also Christine Patrick, "Samuel Kirkland: Missionary to the Oneida Indians," unpublished Ph.D. dissertation, SUNY Buffalo, 1992.

6. Campisi, "The Oneida Treaty Period," p. 60.

7. Ronda, "Reverend Samuel Kirkland," pp. 23–24, 29.

8. Walter Pilkington, ed., *The Journals of Samuel Kirkland* (Clinton, N.Y.: Hamilton College, 1980), pp. 43–44 n 9; John [Jan] Lincklaen, *Travels in the Years 1791 and 1792* (New York: G. P. Putnam's Sons, 1897), pp. 68–69; Colin Calloway, *The American Revolution in Indian Country: Crisis and Diversity in Native American Communities* (New York: Cambridge University Press, 1995), pp. 112–113; Richard Smith, *A Tour of the Hudson, the Mohawk, the Susquehanna and the Delaware in 1769,* ed. Francis W. Halsey, paperback reprint ed. and retitled from the 1906 original, *A Tour of Four Great Rivers . . .* (Fleischmanns, New York: Purple Mountain Press, 1989), pp. 133–134. Calloway misidentified Good Peter's clan as Eel. There was no Eel Clan then among the Oneidas, nor is there one now. For more on Good Peter, see also Draper, "Notes from Oneida Indians," Draper Collection, 11U.

9. James Dow McCallum, ed., *The Letters of Eleazar Wheelock's Indians* (Han-

over, N.H.: Dartmouth College, 1932), pp. 25, 79–80; Pilkington, ed., *The Journals of Samuel Kirkland,* pp. xvii-xviii; Ronda, "Reverend Samuel Kirkland," pp. 24–25.

10.   Good Peter to Timothy Pickering, early April 1792, Timothy Pickering MSS, MR 60, MHS.

11.   Good Peter to Pickering, early April 1792, Timothy Pickering MSS, MR 60. For more on this extraordinary Oneida, see: Franklin B. Hough, ed., *Proceedings of the Commissioners of Indian Affairs Appointed by Law for the Extinguishment of Indian Titles in the State of New York* (Albany, N.Y.: Munsell, 1861), Vol. 1; Pilkington, ed., *The Journals of Samuel Kirkland,* pp. 129–130, 142–144, 159, 199–201, 215–222, 231; Barbara Graymont, "New York State Indian Policy after the American Revolution," *New York History* 57 (1976): 454–455; and J. David Lehman, "The End of the Iroquois Mystique: The Oneida Land Cession Treaties of the 1780s," *William and Mary Quarterly* 47 (Oct. 1990): 536–540.

12.   Skenandoah's obituary can be found in the *Utica Patriot and Patrol,* Mar. 19, 1816, p. 4. Hough, ed., *proceedings,* 1: 87–88; Pilkington, ed., *Journals of Samuel Kirkland,* p. 48; William W. Campbell, ed., *The Life and Writings of De Witt Clinton* (New York: Baker and Scribner, 1849), pp. 187–188; Jeremy Belknap, *Journal of a Tour from Boston to Oneida, June, 1796* (Cambridge, Mass.: John Wilson and Son, 1882), p. 20; William Beauchamp, " 'Johnko' Skeanendon [The Hemlock]," in "St. Regis Indians and Five of the Six Nations," William Beauchamp MSS, bound Vol. 3, box 15, item 184, pp. 51–53, NYSL; "Instances of Indian Genius," 1816, SHSW—reprint of an article from the *Commercial Advertiser;* William W. Campbell, *Annals of Tryon County* (Cherry Valley, N.Y.: Cherry Valley Gazette Printers, 1880), Appendix, pp. 233–236.

13.   Pilkington, ed., *Journals of Samuel Kirkland,* pp. 34, 217–218, 263–270, 289–298, 305–306, 311–315, 323–339, 344, 349, 356–357, 368, 375–386, 393–399, 407, 415–420.

14.   Beauchamp, " 'Johnko' Skeanendon [The Hemlock]," Beauchamp MSS, pp. 51–53, NYSL.

15.   Graymont, *The Iroquois in the American Revolution,* p. 53. Indeed, Brant married two of Skenandoah's daughters: Margaret and, after she died, her sister Susanna. The accusations against Skenandoah can be found in the Draper Collection, Series 11U, SHSW.

16.   Beauchamp, " 'Johnko' Skeanendon [The Hemlock]," Beauchamp MSS, pp. 51–53; NYSL.

17.   Timothy Pickering to Henry Knox, May 2, 1792, Samuel Kirkland MSS, #148b, HC; Graymont, *The Iroquois in the American Revolution,* pp. 225–235.

18.   See sources cited in n. 12.

19.   Campbell, ed., *The Life and Writings of De Witt Clinton,* pp. 187–188.

20.   Pilkington, ed., *Journals of Samuel Kirkland,* p. 264; Belknap, *Journal,* pp. 21–22. Belknap's conclusion about Skenandoah's limited power appears accurate. For a different conclusion about Skenandoah's continuing influence (as late as 1799), see Pilkington, ed., *Journals of Samuel Kirkland,* p. 315.

21.   Julian Ursyn Niemcewicz, "Journey to Niagara, 1805," ed. Metchie J. E. Budka, *New-York Historical Society Quarterly* 44 (Jan. 1960): 95.

22.   Belknap, *Journal,* pp. 21–22. See also Niemcewicz, "Journey to Niagara, 1805," p. 95. For his silver pipe, see Campbell, ed., *The Life and Writings of De Witt Clinton,* pp. 187–188.

23. Oneida Indians [Skenandoah et al.] to the Regents of the State of New York, Apr. 27, 1793, Kirkland MSS, #159b, HC; from Representatives of the Oneida Indians to Alexander Hamilton, Jan. 15, 1794, in Harold C. Syrett et al., eds., *The Papers of Alexander Hamilton* (New York: Columbia University Press, 1969), 15: 642.

24. See *Whipple Report,* pp. 234–252.

25. An original copy of this Peter Smith 1793 lease and affidavit can be found in Peter Smith MSS, SU.

26. Timothy Pickering account of Captain John's speech of Oct. 11, 1794, *DHI,* MR 43, NYSL.

27. *Whipple Report,* pp. 269–272; Hough, ed., *Proceedings,* 1: 198 n 1; Arlinda Locklear, pers. comm., June 12, 1997.

28. Hough, ed., *Proceedings,* 1: 88 n.

29. Speech of John Scanandon [Skenandoah] from article in the *Niles Register,* Oct. 12, 1816, *DHI,* MR 45, NYSL. The area that is now the state of Wisconsin was part of Indiana Territory from 1800 to 1809, becoming Illinois Territory from 1809 to 1818, Michigan Territory from 1818 to 1836, and finally Wisconsin Territory from 1836 to 1848; in 1848 it entered the Union.

30. Beauchamp, "Beech Tree—Peter Oneyana," in "St. Regis Indians and Five of the Six Nations," Beauchamp MSS, item 203, pp. 54-55, NYSL; Pilkington, ed., *Journals of Samuel Kirkland,* p. 153 nn 79–80; "Capt. John, Oneida Chief," *Charleston Gazette* (S.C.), Oct. 17, 1795, Draper Collection, 11U, SHSW.

31. Belknap, *Journal,* pp. 21, 23–24. Silversmith and Blacksmith were apparently the same Oneida. Laurence M. Hauptman, Oneida fieldnotes, June 1997.

32. Samuel Kirkland to Alexander Miller, May 24, 1800, Samuel Kirkland MSS, #211c, HC; Pilkington, ed., *Journals of Samuel Kirkland,* pp. 360–365.

33. Kirkland to Miller, May 24, 1800, Kirkland MSS, #211c, HC; Pilkington, ed., *Journals of Samuel Kirkland,* pp. 360–365; Elisabeth Tooker, "The Iroquois White Dog Sacrifice in the Later Part of the Eighteenth Century," *Ethnohistory* 12 (1965): 129–140.

34. Besides the Tooker article cited above, for more on the White Dog Sacrifice, see Anthony F. C. Wallace, *Death and Rebirth of the Seneca* (New York: Alfred A. Knopf, 1969), p. 299; Robert F. Berkhofer, Jr., *Salvation and the Savage: An Analysis of Protestant Missions and American Indian Response, 1787–1862* (Lexington: University of Kentucky Press, 1965; reprint, New York: Atheneum, 1976), pp. 131–132; Harold Blau, "The Iroquois White Dog Sacrifice: Its Evolution and Symbolism," *Ethnohistory* 11 (1964): 97–119; William N. Fenton, "Northern Iroquoian Culture Patterns," in *Handbook of North American Indians,* ed. Bruce G. Trigger, Vol. 15: *Northeast* (Washington, D.C.: Smithsonian Institution Press, 1978), p. 316; and William N. Fenton, *The Iroquois Eagle Dance: An Offshoot of the Calumet Dance* (1953; paperback reprint, Syracuse, N.Y.: Syracuse University Press, 1991), pp. 104–107.

35. Wallace, *Death and Rebirth of the Seneca,* p. 299.

36. Tooker, "The Iroquois White Dog Sacrifice," pp. 132–133; Wallace, *The Death and Rebirth of the Seneca,* pp. 299, 309.

37. Tooker, "The Iroquois White Dog Sacrifice," p. 146. Kirkland to Miller, May 24, 1800, Kirkland MSS, #211C, HC; Pilkington, ed., *Journals of Samuel Kirkland,* pp. 360–365.

38. Kirkland to Miller, May 24, 1800, Kirkland MSS, #211C, HC.

39. The literature on the origins of the Handsome Lake religion is too vast to cite

in its entirety. For a synopsis, see Anthony F. C. Wallace, "Origins of the Longhouse Religion," in *Handbook of North American Indians*, Vol. 15: *Northeast*, pp. 442–448.

40. Wallace, *The Death and Rebirth of the Seneca*, pp. 149–236.
41. Hough, ed., *Proceedings*, pp. 279–280.
42. Graymont, *The Iroquois in the American Revolution*, p. 291.
43. Wallace, "Origins of the Longhouse Religion," p. 447.
44. Quoted in Wallace, *The Death and Rebirth of the Seneca*, pp. 308–309.
45. Ibid.
46. Pilkington, ed., *Journals of Samuel Kirkland*, p. 413.
47. Ibid.
48. Pilkington, ed., *Journals of Samuel Kirkland*, p. 370 n 10; Julia K. Bloomfield, *The Oneidas*, 2d ed. (New York: Alden Bros., 1907), p. 117. Cornelius Haunnagwasuke, the little doctor, was chief at Oriske and fought at the Battle of Oriskany in the American Revolution as well as in the War of 1812, dying in 1831 at the age of 100. Abstract of Pension Application for Henry Cornelius, New York State Division of Military and Naval Affairs, Application No. 10,002, NYSA, Albany. Campbell, ed., *The Life and Writings of De Witt Clinton*, p. 187. Clinton claimed that the Christians outnumbered the non-Christians by 100 in 1810. In 1797, the Quaker missionary Joseph Clarke estimated that the Oneida population in central New York was 600 souls, and that their landbase was 12 square miles. Joseph Clarke, *Travels among the Indians, 1797* (Doylestown, Pa.: Charles Ingerman, Quixott Press, 1968), postscript.
49. Marbois, "Journey to the Oneidas," in *In the Mohawk Country*, ed. Dean Snow, William A. Starna, and Charles Gehring (Syracuse: Syracuse University Press, 1996), pp. 307–308.
50. Lafayette felt a keen responsibility to his Oneida warriors during the American Revolution, since he had helped recruit them: "Whenever the army needed Indians, or there was any business to be conducted with those tribes [Oneidas and Tuscaroras], they always had recourse to the influence of M. de Lafayette, whose necklaces and words the Indians respected." Stanley J. Idzerda et al., eds., *Lafayette in the Age of the American Revolution: Selected Letters and papers, 1776–1790* (Ithaca, N.Y.: Cornell University Press, 1977), 1: 247.
51. Franklin B. Hough, *Notices of Peter Penet of His Operations Among the Oneida Indians. . .* (Lowville, N.Y.: Albany Institute, 1866), pp. 3–24; Hough, ed., *Proceedings*, 1: 152 n; 2: 346, 352, 354.
52. *Whipple Report*, p. 239.
53. Hough, *Notices of Peter Penet*, p. 25.
54. Beauchamp, "Lewis Cook," in "St. Regis Indians and Five of the Six Nations," Beauchamp MSS, item 344, p. 62, NYSL; Hough, *Notices of Peter Penet*, p. 19 n 3; Pilkington, ed., *Journals of Samuel Kirkland*, p. 233 n 3.
55. Hough, ed., *Proceedings*, 1: 39 n 1–40, 141.
56. Beauchamp, "Peter Otsiquette," in "St. Regis Indians and Five of the Six Nations," Beauchamp MSS, item 216, p. 55, NYSL; Elkanah Watson, Journal, Sept. 1788, Elkanah Watson MSS, NYSL; Lincklaen, *Travels in the Years 1791 and 1792*, p. 69.
57. Campbell, ed., *The Life and Writings of De Witt Clinton*, pp. 190–191.
58. *Whipple Report*, pp. 266–269.
59. Campbell, ed., *The Life and Writings of De Witt Clinton*, p. 191.
60. Ibid.

61. Berkhofer, *Salvation and the Savage*, pp. 131–132; see *Whipple Report*, pp. 259–263.

62. Campbell, ed., *The Life and Writings of De Witt Clinton*, pp. 187.

63. Berkhofer, *Salvation and the Savage*, p. 132; Campisi, "The Oneida Treaty Period," pp. 60–62.

Command Performance
Philip Schuyler and the New York
State–Oneida "Treaty" of 1795

On September 15, 1795, a group of Oneidas, armed with a state-provided power of attorney, signed an accord with four New York State Indian commissioners—Philip Schuyler, David Brooks, John Cantine, and John Richardson—whereby the Indians "sold" to the state more than 100,000 acres of their choicest tribal lands in what is today Oneida and Madison counties, for a one-time payment of $2,952 and an annual payment of $2,952. Going against tribal sentiments expressed by Good Peter before his death and other Oneida sachems not to cede any more land, these Oneidas sold a portion of their land around Oneida Lake, the south and east sides, but reserved the Indians' right to lake access and fish and retained ownership rights to half-mile sections along the north shore. Although this state-Oneida accord has been written about before, the full background of this dispossession, including the major player in this high jinx, has never been disclosed.[1]

At the center of these events was Philip Schuyler, the commanding general of Oneida troops during the American Revolution. Going against restrictions about purchasing Indian lands without the presence of a federal commissioner and knowing full well that United States approval of any and all Indian land accords was required, Schuyler, through his actions and those of his cronies, violated the federal Trade and Intercourse Acts of 1790 and 1793. Realizing that the value of his lands and those of his political allies and business partners would skyrocket if transportation routes—navigable rivers, canals, and roads—made settlement attractive, Schuyler and his associates increasingly coveted Oneida Country.

Nearly every political decision and treaty negotiation involving the Oneidas between 1785 and 1798 had Philip Schuyler's personal or family stamp of approval. Indeed, few New Yorkers before or since have had the power base of this major Federalist politico. Despite his outward appearances of friendship, patronlike support of Oneidas during the American Revolution, and long-time acquaintance with several key Oneidas, Schuyler was no friend of the Indians, be they "good" Oneidas or his "savage" enemies. In the summer of 1783, Schuyler wrote that the Indians would inevitably retreat westward once faced with massive white settlement in the vicinity of their territory. He insisted that the United States had only to take the land it needed from the Indians to satisfy its immediate interests, rather than to find itself perpetually fighting bloody and costly wars. To Schuyler, the simplest, cheapest, least distressing and violent, and most advantageous national policy was self-evident: "It will be or no obstacle to our future . . . for as our settlements approach their country, they must from the scarcity of game, which that approach will induce to, retire further back, and dispose of their lands. . . ." In this late eighteenth-century version of manifest destiny, he added: ". . . they [will] dwindle comparatively to nothing, as will savages have done, who reside in the vicinity of civilized people and leave us the country without the expence, trifling as it may be of a purchase."[2] Thus, Schuyler's view of progress required rapid urbanization rather than a continued frontier setting, one that would better New York as well as America as a whole but, at the same time, would be best for his own pocketbook. In his scheme, Indian councils were better alternatives than Indian wars; however, his vision for New York had no place for Indians, be they allies or not. In fact, as late as 1796, despite his family's support for Samuel Kirkland's Hamilton-Oneida Academy, Schuyler told the missionary Jeremy Belknap that there was little or no prospect of "civilization" among the Oneidas.[3]

Schuyler's contact with the Oneidas began as early as the French and Indian War. During the American Revolution, Schuyler, who became Washington's commanding general of the Northern Department as well as federal Indian commissioner during the early years of the war, rebuilt Fort Stanwix, which was soon renamed Fort Schuyler in his honor.[4] Throughout this period, Schuyler's contacts with the Oneidas were quite extensive.

Schuyler encouraged Oneida recruitment into the Patriot army and frequently supplied these Indians during the desperate times of the American Revolution.[5] Fort Schuyler was the American outpost in the heart of Oneida Territory at Rome. When many Oneidas found themselves refugees of war during the later stages of the conflict, Schuyler appealed successfully to General Washington and financier Robert Morris for clothing and food supplies for

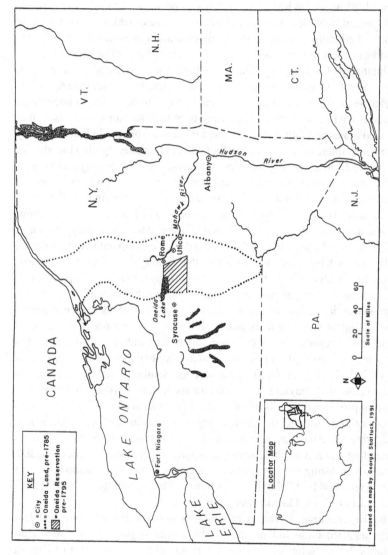

Map 2.1. Oneida Country after the American Revolution (Map by Ben Simpson [based on data created by George Shattuck, 1991])

these Indians.[6] While serving as one of the earliest United States Indian commissioners, treating with the Indians from the early days of the Revolution onward, he assured his loyal Oneida warriors that the Americans would long remember their contributions, that "sooner should a fond mother forget her only son than we shall forget you." He added that, once victory was achieved, the Oneidas would "then partake of every Blessing we enjoy and united with a free people your Liberty and prosperity will be safe."[7] Thus, Oneida leaders such as Skenandoah and Good Peter saw him as a valued ally, and Oneida officers such as Henry Cornelius, Hanyost, and Hanyere Doxtator, served Schuyler loyally throughout the war. When peace was finally achieved, Schuyler, through two Oneida intermediaries, Good Peter and Skenandoah, attempted to bring the British-allied Iroquois back into the fold and helped arrange the delivery of a peace offering, a bell, to the Continental Congress in July 1783.[8] Oneidas sought Schuyler out and saw the general as their protector and patron. Indeed, to this day, Oneidas bear Schuyler's name as both a given name and a surname.[9]

Schuyler, undoubtedly, saw himself as being above the law. He, along with his son-in-law Alexander Hamilton, the secretary of the Treasury, dominated Federalist politics of the era, well beyond the state's borders. Another of Schuyler's sons-in-law, Stephen Van Rensselaer, was perhaps the richest New Yorker in the early republic. As a United States senator throughout the postwar period, Schuyler's power was matched by few political figures in the new nation. At the end of the Revolution, his great wealth was largely in lands in Saratoga, Cortlandt Manor, and Dutchess County, as well as in banking and manufacturing in Albany and environs. Throughout his life, he took every opportunity to protect his interests and advance his great family's fortune. This New York scion, possibly taking a cue from his brother Peter, one of the New York Genesee Company of Adventurers who had attempted to defraud the Oneidas in the 1780s, himself had by the mid-1780s secured large tracts in what later became downtown Utica.

Schuyler's familiarity with Oneida Country and its vast economic potential was furthered by two other factors. First, at the end of the American Revolution, he was appointed to New York State's newly created post of surveyor general, a strategic position in which he became familiar with the vast potential of central and western New York. He later resigned from this post when he was elected United States senator from New York State in 1783. Second, as senator he was actively involved in the grand design of federal Indian policy, working with James Duane, a fellow New York Federalist, as well as other United States Indian commissioners. As early as 1783, he came to the conclusion, according to his biographer Don Gerlach, that it "would be 'advantageous' if the tribes [Oneidas and Tuscaroras] could be persuaded to exchange their lands for others 'more remote.' "[10]

Even though the Treaty of Fort Stanwix in 1784 gave the Oneidas guarantees of the United States' recognition of their territory, the very next year at Fort Herkimer, New York State "acquired" 300,000 acres of Oneida lands, the present counties of Broome and Chenango, rich, well-watered agricultural lands, for $11,500.[11]

In September 1788 at Fort Schuyler, the Oneidas under their chief Good Peter, believing they were preventing land speculators such as John Livingston, Peter Schuyler, and their New York Genesee Company of Adventurers from defrauding them, signed an "instrument of cession" with New York State governor George Clinton, viewing the action as a lease to the state in an effort to foil the speculators' nefarious efforts. State officials soon claimed that this agreement was an Oneida cession of nearly 5 million acres of their lands.[12] After this "agreement," Oneidas were increasingly reluctant to go to conference to negotiate. When state officials no longer could persuade Indians to come to the treaty table, the state "granted power of attorney to a small segment of the tribe, and then signed the agreement with those Indians in the name of all Oneidas."[13] This pattern was set in the New York State–Oneida "Treaty" of 1795, which became the model for all Albany's efforts at dispossession of the Oneidas for the next half century.[14]

At the 1788 treaty grounds, Elkanah Watson, a business partner of Schuyler, had clearly spelled out his prediction that Oneida Lake would eventually be the center of a great transportation nexus, with the salt industry as its basis. To Watson, when the "mighty canals" would be developed, a vast central New York inland empire would result. With his Federalist ally and business partner, Philip Schuyler, Watson was to put his business intuition into practice with the founding of two private "canal" companies in 1792–1793: the Western Inland Lock Navigation Company and the Northern Inland Lock Navigation Company.[15]

The aim of the Western Inland Lock Navigation Company, the more significant of the two projects and the forerunner of the Erie Canal, was to open navigable waterways from Albany west to Lake Seneca, and west-northwest to Lake Ontario. The Northern Inland Lock Navigation Company, the second project, which soon failed, was designed to improve the waters between the Hudson and Lake Champlain. Through the initiation of the former project, Watson and Schuyler hoped to open up both a channel to combine and improve the natural waterways and short canals to improve inland navigation and commerce. In that regard, they succeeded, and Durham boat traffic continued on this integrated navigation system through the War of 1812. While it may not have succeeded fully to Watson and Schuyler's grandiose expectations, it was the harbinger of "America's grand canal," the Erie, which co-opted it through purchase in 1820.

These shareholder companies were headed by Schuyler, and Watson served on the board of directors. Among the major investors were Egbert Benson, the New York State commissioner at the Treaty of Fort Schuyler in 1788, attorney general of New York State, and political ally of Schuyler and Watson; Robert

Morris, the prominent Genesee speculator who later defrauded the Senecas at the Treaty of Big Tree in 1797; Theophile Cazenove, the major representative of the Holland Land Company, which also purchased shares in the Watson-Schuyler venture; Robert Troup, a leading attorney tied to the Phelps-Gorham Purchase, one of the Pulteney Associates, and later attorney for both the Holland Land Company and the Ogden Land Company, as well as Hamilton's classmate at King's College; Stephen Bayard, leading merchant-capitalist and the largest purchaser of surveyor lots in the New Military Tract, just west of the Oneida homeland; George Scriba, who along with Peter Smith was the largest investor in lands "acquired" from the Oneidas in 1785 and 1788; and other prominent New York City businessmen such as Nicholas Low, Daniel Ludlow, Melancthon Smith, and Thomas Eddy, a leading merchant and influential member of the Society of Friends. Also represented in this enterprise were Federalists Rufus King, the soon-to-be United States senator from New York; Goldsborough Banyar, Governor John Jay's son-in-law; and Jonas Platt, one of the most important promoters of central New York lands and one of the major advocates of the later Erie Canal project.[16]

Nathan Miller, a leading economic historian of the Empire State, has written about this venture capitalist experiment, indicating that these investors saw their future profits largely in "an increase in land values." Miller insisted: "Had Schuyler carefully examined the motives of many of the directors and stockholders, and possibly his own as well, he would have discovered that a large number of them considered the matter of dividends as purely incidental to the company's plans for the improvement of transportation." Miller added that these men "were speculators to whom the broad, unsettled stretches of land in western New York seemed like an untapped gold mine whose productivity would expand in proportion to the improvements wrought in transportation and communication linking the east and the west." The economic historian then calculated that 15 of the 36 directors of the canal company "held lands which were likely to increase in value as a result of the canal company's improvements."[17] One of the directors, George Scriba, saw the canal projects as his panacea to make his undertaking pay off. A political ally of Schuyler, Scriba had purchased a vast empire in the former Oneida Territory, north of Oneida Lake and the Tug Hill Upland, bounded by Lake Ontario on the east and the Oswego River on the west, a landbase that was largely infertile and swampy in a not-so-temperate climate. He, like others, soon "took pains to advertise the fact that lands which he put up for sale were accessible to the company's system of inland communication."[18]

As early as 1793, the builders of the Western Inland Lock Navigation Company were trespassing on Oneida Indian lands, stripping the territory of its fallen timber along "Wood Creek, the stream which flows into Oneida Lake," and straightening the bounds of this water route "to the extent of shortening its length more than seven miles."[19] Thus, by the 1790s, Schuyler began to see

himself as the transportation magnate of the Empire State. With powerful connections to New York's major families, based upon politics, economics, and
consanguinity, and with "friends" among the Oneidas, Schuyler saw few im-
pediments to his grand design.

Schuyler's actions were clearly aided and abetted not only by divisions within
the Oneida polity, but also by the actions of Samuel Kirkland and his long-time
assistant among the Oneidas, James Dean. In 1788 Kirkland allegedly told his
flock that they should sell part of their lands, which led to his rejection by some
former faithful Christian Oneida followers. By his presence at six illegal state
treaties with the Cayugas, Oneidas, and Onondagas from the mid-1780s to the
mid-1790s, as well as in the negotiations for the gigantic Phelps-Gorham Purchase in 1788, the missionary gave a sense of moral legitimacy to these outright frauds and/or clear violations of federal supremacy in Indian affairs.
Moreover, as Jack Campisi has astutely observed, Kirkland encouraged the
sale of Oneida lands to whites because it could "serve to offer a model of thrift
and industry for Indians to emulate." Since he was convinced that Oneidas as a
whole "would never become farmers unless forced to by the loss of land for
hunting," the Presbyterian missionary could easily find it acceptable to serve
the Oneidas on occasions as both a minister and a government representative
dealing with the likes of John Livingston or Oliver Phelps and Nathaniel
Gorham.[20] But there were apparently other reasons for Kirkland's turnabout.

In 1790, the Oneidas and the state of New York granted Kirkland and his
sons 4,000 acres on the present site of Utica. Subsequently, after lobbying
feverishly, Kirkland obtained an additional 2,000 acres for his role in the
Phelps-Gorham Purchase negotiations.[21] The pre–American Revolution Kirkland, who sincerely saw himself as the protector of his Oneida flock, leading
them away from the fires of damnation, apparently compromised his principles
under the pressures of family and mission financial exigencies and under his
all-consuming passion to create the Hamilton-Oneida Academy. Although he
married a woman of means after the death of his first wife in 1796, Kirkland in
the early 1790s was increasingly desperate for money because of his substantial medical expenses and the extravagance of his profligate son George Whit-
field, a land speculator.[22] It appears as no coincidence that the missionary
looked the other way when the Oneidas slowly "got taken" during this period.
Increasingly dependent on outside sources for his mission, Kirkland was not
going to risk his mission sinecure by criticizing Philip Schuyler, perhaps the
most powerful New Yorker of the 1790s.

Kirkland's mindset during the period 1788–1795 was most affected by his
obsession with creating the Hamilton-Oneida Academy and promoting his specific program of Indian education. Much like some modern college presidents,
although he never officially served in that capacity, Kirkland apparently never
questioned the sources of his funding or the aims of the donors. He traded fa-
vors for donations and appointed "moneybags" to the board of trustees of his

institution. Although he gave 3000 acres of land he had obtained from the Oneidas as well as most of his remaining money, not drained away by his profligate son, to build the school, Kirkland clearly made "compromises" in the period after 1788 that alienated many of his flock.

In the late 1780s and 1790s, Kirkland's relationship with Oliver Phelps, the major land speculator, raised eyebrows. From 1788 onward, Kirkland attended land negotiations with the Senecas, adding his moral suasion, whereby Phelps furthered the building of his vast landholdings. Soon Phelps was writing Kirkland about the laying out of roads in the Phelps-Gorham lands. By November 1790, Iroquois Indians, including Cornplanter, accused Phelps, Kirkland, and the Mohawk war chief Joseph Brant of altering deeds in favor of Phelps. Indeed, when the Hamilton-Oneida Academy was chartered in 1793 by the regents of the state of New York, Oliver Phelps was the largest financial contributor to the project.[23]

The school and its founding illustrate much about Kirkland and his motives. In the same month the Hamilton-Oneida Academy was chartered, the nefarious Peter Smith asked Kirkland to do him a favor. Smith requested that Kirkland mention to Israel Chapin, the federal superintendent to the Six Nations, that "if any of the Indians should inquire that you think they ought to be satisfied with the rents which I gave them as I should wish the Indians all to be satisfied. . . ."[24] It is little wonder that Smith, in the same month, matched Phelps's financial contribution to Kirkland's Hamilton-Oneida Academy. Indeed, the list of donors and trustees of the school in the early years illustrates much. Other donors included Jonas Platt and Moses De Witt, with Platt also serving as an original trustee of the school.[25]

Even more revealing were Kirkland's notes of 1792, in which he discussed his "Plan of Indian Education." Kirkland optimistically saw a bright future for the institution because of the support of the state's scion, Philip Schuyler: "The Honorable Philip Schuyler, Esq. of Albany, much approves of the plan, and says he will most cheerfully contribute his influence for carrying it into effect."[26] Hence, it was no mere coincidence that Kirkland named the school Hamilton, in honor of Schuyler's illustrious son-in-law. Less than three years later, when the school faced disaster because it needed to complete its only building, Kirkland "hit" Schuyler's other prominent son-in-law, Stephen Van Rensselaer, for the then exorbitant sum of $1,000–1,200, mortgaging him "three hundred acres of lands, including the Academy plot or lot of ground on which the Academy is erected." Insisting it was a sound investment, Kirkland, in the manner of later college hucksters, added that his institution was "better situated to be a means of diffusing useful knowledge, and enlarging the bounds of human happiness, and aiding the reign of virtue."[27]

By the time of the signing of the federal treaty with the Six Nations on November 11, 1794, which was negotiated by Timothy Pickering and guaranteed the federal government's protection of the Indians against actions of the state, the Oneida homeland had shrunk from between 5 million and 6 million acres of land to 250,000 acres within Oneida and Madison counties, with its central focus being Oneida Lake and Oneida Castle, approximately 12 miles south of the eastern end of the lake. Three weeks later, representatives from the United States and the Oneidas signed a second treaty of friendship, again with Pickering, whereby Washington recognized the important service of these Indians as well as that of his Stockbridge and Tuscarora allies in the American Revolution, awarded them compensation for "their individual losses and services," and provided moneys for mills and millers as well as for the construction of a church to replace "the one which was there burnt by the enemy, in the late war."[28]

Within 10 months, state actions, undertaken largely by Philip Schuyler, were consciously and systematically to undo the actions of Pickering, the Indians' benefactor, and set in motion a series of transactions that nearly rid the state of its entire Oneida Indian population. Despite Schuyler's being a federal official, namely a United States senator from New York, he would further his own interests and, at the same time, flout congressional laws, consciously violating the United States Constitution and the federal Trade and Intercourse Acts, which, as stated above, required the presence of a United States commissioner and/or prior federal approval for any and all land purchases from the Indians. Indeed, Pickering knew about the state's intentions and warned Albany officials, including the newly installed governor John Jay, about the illegality of negotiating with the Iroquois without federal approval. Pickering also secured an opinion from the attorney general of the United States, William Bradford, who maintained that Indian lands could be purchased only at a treaty held under the authority of the United States.[29]

In 1793, state officials led by Simeon De Witt and John Cantine had earlier approached the Oneidas about new negotiations over land.[30] State plans for the construction of the Genesee Turnpike necessitated these deliberations with the Oneidas. In March 1793, De Witt noted in a report that the Oneidas expressed clear contempt over these deliberations and their bitterness over past land dealings with the state. Acknowledging the cooperation of Kirkland and James Dean in trying to obtain "the object of the state," De Witt was, nevertheless, frustrated in his efforts to secure any more Indian lands. Beechtree (Captain Peter), one of the Oneida chiefs, forthrightly responded to De Witt's request: "You have been told that it is our determination not to sell or lease our lands." In the end, De Witt, blaming "evil-minded people" for giving the Oneidas bad advice, went back to Albany and reported his failed mission to Governor George Clinton.[31] It was to take an "old friend" of the Oneidas, two years later, to accomplish what De Witt and Cantine had failed to secure in 1793.

On February 27, 1795, a group of Oneidas recommended that the New York State legislature appoint commissioners to treat with the Indians who were desirous of "making fresh disposal of some part of our land." The petitioners recommended the appointment of Schuyler and Dean as state commissioners, since "from our long acquaintance" they believed "them to be friends to us."[32] Instead, the legislature confirmed Schuyler, John Cantine, and David Brooks as state commissioners. Two weeks later, Israel Chapin indicated that "some white people in their vicinity have been making them [the Oneidas] offers for their land and a part of their chiefs wish to sell but the best part of them I believe are not desirous to do it hastily."[33]

Schuyler and his partners needed to gain title to lands they were already clearing between Oneida Lake and Wood Creek and lands for development around the lake. The New York State–Oneida "Treaty" of 1795 provided both the means and opportunity to secure this goal. Important to this was Schuyler's strategic placement as one of the state commissioners to negotiate this land cession. His longtime acquaintance with the Oneidas was to serve him well through his dealings in 1795.

Schuyler's presence in the negotiations was a conscious one. Both Indians and non-Indians knew that few outsiders had his standing among the Oneidas and Tuscaroras or his knowledge about or overall experience with American Indians. For nearly 40 years, he had known Skenandoah and other prominent Oneidas of the day. On June 9, 1795, he wrote to Governor John Jay about his state assignment, which included treating with the Cayugas, Onondagas, and Oneidas, as well as a wide variety of other Indian issues. In the letter, he dismissed the "very extensive" claims of Mohawks to lands west of Lake Champlain and the River Sorel and south of the St. Lawrence River, which he termed "suspect" and ill-founded. Then he elaborated on his planned negotiations with the Onondagas, Cayugas, and Oneidas, asking for provisions for the conference and requesting the governor's attendance to aid Schuyler himself, David Brooks, John Cantine, and John Richardson in securing Indian approval. Lastly, Schuyler mentioned one caveat to Jay, namely his poor health. While on a visit to one of his daughters, the Albany politico had been thrown out of his carriage when his horses bolted, damaging his ribs, causing him "not [to be] able to stir out of my room since." Despite his painful injury, Schuyler assured Jay that he would probably be able to travel to Onondaga by July 15.[34]

The state-Oneida "treaty" of 1795 was one of three that Schuyler negotiated with the Iroquois in that year and can be understood only in conjunction with the other two earlier agreements. On July 27, 1795, the Federalist secured Cayuga lands around Cayuga Lake. Schuyler obtained part of this valuable lakefront property, which he needed for his transportation scheme, the Western Inland Lock Navigation Company, but only after threats to seize all the remaining Cayuga lands in New York State. The next day after the signing of the Cayuga-state agreement, Schuyler negotiated a "treaty" with the Onondagas for all the land around Onondaga Lake, thus securing full access to the immense salt deposits of the region.[35]

On August 6, 1795, Philip Schuyler met with the sachems and warriors of the Oneida Nation. After moralizing about the evil effects of liquor among the Indians and advocating sobriety, Schuyler announced that his goal was to obtain land on the south side of Wood Creek to the area opposite Canada Creek to the eastern bounds of the Oneida Indian Reservation. Knowing full well that his negotiations required the presence of a federal commissioner to protect Indian interests as required under the federal Trade and Intercourse Acts and having been warned repeatedly by Chapin and Pickering about this requirement, Schuyler, nevertheless, proceeded with his negotiations.[36]

Captain John, or Onondiyo, the Oneida chief, immediately responded to the presence of his old friend and patron. Addressing him as Brother Schuyler, Captain John asserted that his people had "always had reason to believe you have our welfare at heart." Recalling the Revolutionary War, the Oneida chief insisted that Schuyler in the past "had gave [sic] us good council and advised us to persevere to the end." The chief then stated that the Oneidas had become poor and weak—"we are nothing but a wreck of Bones! Our lands are almost all gone from us, for almost nothing"—and that the nation was slowly becoming ashes. Captain John appealed to his former white patron, Schuyler: "It is true your doors have always been open to us and when we called upon you, you always gave us good advice." The Oneida chief then informed Schuyler that he had been warned by both Chapin and Pickering to be careful in state land negotiations, and then noted that he was disappointed that Schuyler had not brought with him "an agent from the United States." Yet the chief, nevertheless, maintained that the Oneidas were willing to sell lands if they received just value, were protected by their white patron Schuyler in the future, and were guaranteed that the Indians' grievances would be dealt with by the state. Undoubtedly the presence of his wartime commander had brought Captain John to this conclusion. The Oneida grievances included being denied equal access to fishing in and around Fish Creek. They also insisted that in order to protect their fishery, the north side of Oneida Lake, North East Bay, should be reserved for the Indians.[37]

The Oneidas' requests did not interfere with Schuyler's own strategy. He was more concerned with securing concessions over the east side of Oneida Lake, the Fish Creek–Wood Creek region, which he needed to further his canal interests. He was also intent on securing lands through the southern end of Oneida Castle, which the state needed for the Genesee Turnpike and which land speculators lusted after as well. Finally, an accord was reached on September 15, 1795, less than two months after the conclusion of state treaties with both the Cayugas and Onondagas.[38]

Besides filing a detailed expense account for the Oneida as well as for the other two treaties, Schuyler sent a revealing report about these negotiations to the New York State legislature. In it, he explained the Oneidas' motivation for ceding land, which also included confirming grants to his Federalist allies, namely Dean, Van Eps, and Wemple. Schuyler claimed that the Oneidas had been "indebted" to Van Eps "in a considerable sum of monies," and the Wemples had "afforded them [the Oneidas] very considerable pecuniary aid." Consequently, financial obligation to surrounding whites apparently led some Oneidas to cede lands.[39]

Schuyler continued by citing two other reasons for Oneida land cessions. According to the New York scion, the Oneidas were once again attempting to be good, trusting Indians. They wanted to show their loyalty, adding that they made their cessions "in consideration of the many advantages derived" from their past relationships with the state, starting from the state's succor while the Oneidas were refugees at Schenectady during the American Revolution. Schuyler concluded that the Oneidas also came to the treaty table in 1795 in order "to prevent embarrassment in future negotiations," an ambiguous reference, which possibly meant that the state as well as the Oneidas had to clear up outstanding unresolved issues, most specifically the state's assumption that it still had the right, despite the contentions of Pickering and the United States attorney general, to negotiate with the Oneidas *after* the federal Trade and Intercourse Acts, the federal Treaty with the Six Nations at Canandaigua in 1794, and the federal Oneida Treaty of 1794.[40]

In open defiance of federal law, Schuyler's position was consistent from 1783 to 1795, namely that Albany, not Washington, was supreme in all matters dealing with New York Indians and their lands. Drawing upon certain Indians' trust based on Schuyler's wartime experiences with them, the former general was to undo this reciprocal obligation, dispossess the Indians, and, in the process, become the first great transportation "pioneer" of the state. His vision was to make New York the Empire State, but at a cost to his faithful allies, the Oneidas. Indeed, it was a command performance, one that was repeated many times after 1795 by public officials and private speculators claiming to be the Indians' friends while undoing the Oneidas and their landbase in New York State.

Notes

1. For the text of the 1795 accord, see *Whipple Report,* pp. 242–249. See also Jack Campisi, "New York-Oneida Treaty of 1795: A Finding of Fact," *American Indian Law Review* 4 (Summer 1976): 71–82.

2. Philip Schuyler, "Thoughts Respecting Peace in the Indian Country," July 29, 1783, Philip Schuyler MSS, MR 7, NYPL. Throughout 1783 Schuyler, Washington, and Duane corresponded about the "Indian question." See John C. Fitzpatrick, ed., *The Writings of George Washington* (Washington, D.C.: Government Printing Office, 1938), 27: 133–137.

3. Jeremy Belknap, *Journal of a Tour from Boston to Oneida, June, 1796* (Cambridge, Mass.: John Wilson and Son, 1992), p. 5. For Belknap's final report, see *The Re-*

port of a Committee of the Board of Correspondents of the Scottish Society for Propagating Christian Knowledge Who Visited Oneida and Mohekunuh Indians in 1796, MHS Collections, Vol. 5, 1st series (Boston: Samuel Hall, 1798), pp. 12–32.

4. John F. Luzader et al., *Fort Stanwix* (Washington, D.C.: National Park Service, 1976), pp. 3–26; Lee Hanson and Dick Ping Hsu, *Casemates and Cannonballs: Archaeological Investigations at Fort Stanwix* (Washington, D.C.: National Park Service, 1975), pp. 6–13.

5. Don R. Gerlach, *Proud Patriot: Philip Schuyler and the War of Independence, 1775–1783* (Syracuse, N.Y.: Syracuse University Press, 1987), pp. 212, 303, 336–338, 347, 350, 418–420, 429, 441, 463, 478, 504, 506; Barbara Graymont, *The Iroquois in the American Revolution* (Syracuse, N.Y.: Syracuse University Press, 1972), pp. 242–243.

6. Fitzpatrick, ed., *The Writings of George Washington,* 11: 284–285, 364, 384–385; E. James Ferguson, ed., *The Papers of Robert Morris* (Pittsburgh: University of Pittsburgh Press, 1975–1977), 2: 169–171, 256–257, 273–274; 3: 188–191, 194–197. John Thornton Kirkland Notes, Feb. 1795, Draper Collection, 11U, SHSW.

7. Quoted in Colin Calloway, *The American Revolution in Indian Country: Crisis and Diversity in Native American Communities* (New York: Cambridge University Press, 1995), p. 286.

8. Graymont, "The Oneidas in the American Revolution," in *The Oneida Indian Experience: Two Perspectives,* ed. Jack Campisi and Laurence M. Hauptman (Syracuse, N.Y.: Syracuse University Press, 1988), pp. 31–42. Skenandoah and Good Peter delivered a bell on behalf of the British Indians, July 1783, Philip Schuyler MSS, MR 7, NYPL.

9. Laurence M. Hauptman, Oneida fieldnotes, 1977–1996.

10. Gerlach, *Proud Patriot,* p. 514. See also Gaillard Hunt, ed., *Journals of the Continental Congress* (Washington, D.C.: Government Printing Office, 1922), 24: 501 n 1; 25: 680–695.

11. For the federal Treaty of Fort Stanwix of 1784, see Charles J. Kappler, *Indian Treaties, 1778–1883* (New York: Interland, 1972), pp. 5–6 (reprinted from the original, *Indian Affairs: Laws and Treaties,* Vol. 2 of 5 [Washington, D.C., 1903–1941]); for the state accords of 1785 and 1788, see *Whipple Report,* pp. 234–243.

12. Franklin B. Hough, ed., *Proceedings of the Commissioners of Indian Affairs Appointed by Law for the Extinguishment of Indian Titles in the State of New York* (Albany, N.Y.: Munsell, 1861), 1: 45–47.

13. Jack Campisi, "The Oneida Treaty Period, 1783–1838," in *The Oneida Indian Experience,* ed. Campisi and Hauptman, p. 54.

14. *Whipple Report,* pp. 243–249; Jack Campisi, "New York–Oneida Treaty of 1795," pp. 71–82.

15. Elkanah Watson, Journal, Sept. 1788, Elkanah Watson MSS, NYSL; Noble Whitford, *History of the Canal System in the State of New York* (Albany, 1905), 1: 25–47; Nathan Miller, "Private Enterprise in Inland Navigation: The Mohawk Route Prior to the Erie Canal," *New York History* 31 (Oct. 1950): 398–413; Ronald Shaw, *Erie Water West* (Lexington: University Press of Kentucky, 1966), pp. 15–20, 31–32, 51, 56.

16. Miller, "Private Enterprise in Inland Navigation," pp. 398–413. See also Dixon Ryan Fox, *The Decline of Aristocracy in the Politics of New York, 1801–1840,* ed. Robert V. Remini (New York: Columbia University Press, 1919; reprint, New York: Harper Torchbook edition, 1965), pp. 151–157.

17. Miller, "Private Enterprise in Inland Navigation," p. 403. See Nathan Miller's

The Enterprise of a Free People (Ithaca, N.Y.: Cornell University Press, 1962), pp. 18–29, 43–44, 72.

18. Miller, "Private Enterprise in Inland Navigation," p. 403, 411 n 24.

19. Noble E. Whitford, *History of the Canal System of the State of New York* (Albany: Brandon Printing, 1905), 1: 37.

20. Hough, ed., *Proceedings,* 1: 141. Jack Campisi, "Ethnic Identity and Boundary Maintenance in Three Oneida Communities," unpublished Ph.D. dissertation SUNY Albany, 1974, pp. 80–81.

21. Samuel Kirkland to Governor of New York State and Commissioners of Indian Affairs of New York State, Dec. 18, 1788, Kirkland MSS, #111b, HC; Campisi, "Ethnic Identity and Boundary Maintenance," pp. 80–81; cf. James Ronda, "Reverend Samuel Kirkland and the Oneida Indians," in *The Oneida Indian Experience,* ed. Campisi and Hauptman, pp. 23–30.

22. For Kirkland's lands and financial exigencies, see Samuel Kirkland to John Thornton Kirkland, Sept. 30, 1795, Kirkland MSS, #189–193, #279–280; Campisi, "Ethnic Identity and Boundary Maintenance," pp. 93–94; Walter Pilkington, ed., *Journals of Samuel Kirkland* (Clinton, N.Y.: Hamilton College, 1980), pp. 122, 189–193, 279–280.

23. Petition of Gorham and Phelps, Feb. 7, 1789, Kirkland MSS, #113a; Oliver Phelps to Samuel Kirkland, Nov. 14, 1790, Kirkland MSS, #130c; List of Donors to Hamilton-Oneida Academy, Apr. 1793, Kirkland MSS, #159e, HC.

24. Peter Smith to Samuel Kirkland, Apr. 29, 1793, Kirkland MSS, #159d, HC.

25. List of Donors to Hamilton-Oneida Academy, Apr. 1793, Kirkland MSS, #159e; Trustees of Hamilton-Oneida Academy to New York State Board of Regents, Nov. 12, 1792, Kirkland MSS, #154a, HC.

26. Samuel Kirkland notes discussing his "Plan of Indian Education," 1792, Kirkland MSS, #143b, HC.

27. Samuel Kirkland to Stephen Van Rensselaer, Feb. 24, 1795, Kirkland MSS, #176c, HC.

28. The two federal treaties can be found in Kappler, *Indian Treaties,* pp. 34–35.

29. Timothy Pickering to Israel Chapin, Aug. 26, 1795, and William Bradford to Pickering, June 16, 1795, both in *DHI,* MR 43, NYSL; Pickering to John Jay, July 16, Sept. 1, 1795, John Jay MSS, CU.

30. Simeon De Witt Report on Council with Onondaga, Oneida, and Cayuga Indians, Mar. 11, 1793. New York State Land Records, 2d series, A 4016, Book 21: 120, NYSA; John Cantine and Simeon De Witt Report on Proceedings with Onondaga, Oneida, and Cayuga Indians, 1793, *DHI,* MR 42, NYSL.

31. De Witt Report, Mar. 11, 1793.

32. Speech of Oneida Indians to New York State Assembly and Senate, Feb. 27, 1795, *DHI,* MR 43, NYSL.

33. Israel Chapin letter to ?, Mar. 10, 1795, *DHI,* MR 43, NYSL.

34. Philip Schuyler to John Jay, June 9, 1795, John Jay MSS, CU.

35. *Whipple Report,* pp. 199–203, 224–228.

36. Timothy Pickering to Israel Chapin, Jr., Apr. 6, May 22, June 29, July 3, 1795; and Chapin to Pickering, May 6, May 22, June 13, Oct. 9, 1795, all in Henry O'Reilly MSS, box 11, Western Mementoes Papers, NYHS; Fitzpatrick, ed., *The Writings of George Washington,* 34: 250–251.

37.   Philip Schuyler et al. to Brothers, Sachems, and Warriors of the Oneida Nation, Aug. 6, 1795, Philip Schuyler MSS, MR 7; Notes of Aug. 6, 1795, Council with Oneidas, Aug. 8, 1795, Philip Schuyler MSS, MR 7; John Schenando [Skenandoah] et al. to New York State Commissioners, Aug. 16, 1795, Philip Schuyler MSS, MR 7; Draft of Oneida Treaty Council negotiations, Sept. 12, 1795, Philip Schuyler MSS, MR 7a, NYPL.

38.   *Whipple Report,* pp. 242–249.

39.   For Schuyler's expenses, see Philip Schuyler MSS, box 2, folders 23–25, Financial Documents, NYSL. The commissioners received £5000 to cover their expenses. For Schuyler, Cantine, and Brooks's report, see Report of Agents Appointed to Negotiate a Purchase of Lands, July 6–Sept. 15, 1795, *DHI,* MR 43, NYSL. Schuyler did provide cash payments to prominent Oneidas, including Skenandoah, who received $15. The largest one of the nine payments was to "White Hongarry," who received $30. These were hardly "bribes," unlike the large payments made by Robert Morris to the Seneca chiefs at the Treaty of Big Tree (1797), which were more than 25 times as large and were indeed payoffs. List of Payments/Presents to the Oneidas made by M. General Schuyler and G. W. Edwards, Sept. 1795, Philip Schuyler MSS, MR 7a, NYPL.

40.   Report of Agents Appointed to Negotiate a Purchase of Lands, July 6–Sept. 15, 1795, *DHI,* MR 43, NYSL.

3 *Reginald Horsman*

The Origins of Oneida Removal to Wisconsin, 1815–1822

The individual who was of greatest importance in the removal of the Oneidas to Wisconsin was Eleazer Williams, but the Oneida move was also shaped by a variety of public pressures and individual desires: by the efforts of New York land speculators, New York population growth, the policies of the United States government, the hopes of missionaries, and the wishes of individual Oneidas. In the decade after the War of 1812, the state of New York and the United States government were optimistic that they would be able to arrange for the removal of all the remaining peoples of the Six Nations either to what is now Wisconsin or to the region of the Arkansas River. To explain why most of the Six Nations remained while many of the Oneidas emigrated to the West, it is necessary to examine the impact of Eleazer Williams on the beliefs and thinking of the Oneidas as well as his interaction with those white officials and missionaries who supported removal.[1]

Like the rest of the Six Nations, the Oneidas had suffered greatly in the years since the American Revolution. In that conflict many of the Oneidas had sided with the Americans rather than the British, but that had not prevented the state of New York from wresting huge cessions of land from the tribe in the 1780s. The tribe had also been beset with internal divisions. Early in the nineteenth

Reprinted with permission from Donald Fixico, ed., *An Anthology of Western Great Lakes Indian History* (Milwaukee, Wis.: American Indian Studies Program, 1987).

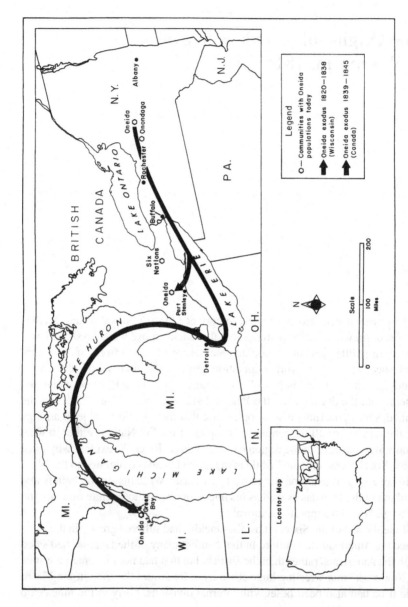

Map 3.1. Oneida removal to Wisconsin and Ontario, 1820–1845 (Map by Ben Simpson)

century, the remaining tribal land, on the reservation around Oneida Lake, was divided between "Pagan" and "Christian" groups within the tribe. The total tribal population at that time was not much more than 600, although it was to grow in the following years. White influence had been strong within the tribe since the coming of Presbyterian missionary Samuel Kirkland in the 1760s, but the Christian impact temporarily declined after the death of Kirkland in 1808.[2]

In the years after the Revolution, Oneida men had been reluctant to take up agriculture, but a visitor to the reservation in 1810 reported that he saw "indian boys trying to kill birds, others driving cattle over plains. Some Indians plowing with oxen, and at the same time their heads ornamented with white feathers; some driving a wagon, and the women milking and churning,—all the indications of incipient civilization." The Christian and Pagan parties still lived on different parts of the reservation, and there were Quaker missionaries on the reservation teaching agriculture. The visitor also commented that because the Oneidas had been pressed by famine during the previous winter, they now intended to plant wheat, a crop to which they had previously been opposed. They had large crops of corn and seemed well-provided with cattle and hogs. A more ominous sign was the presence of numerous white settlers in the vicinity of the reservation.[3] Oneidas, who lost most of their tribal land since the Revolution, might well be ready to listen to suggestions of broader acres farther to the west.

The population of the state of New York increased dramatically in the early years of the nineteenth century, from 589,051 in 1800 to 1,372,812 in 1820.[4] As the population increased, the desire to obtain all the Indian lands within the state intensified. The situation in regard to Indian lands was complicated because the state had granted the right of preemption to private land companies, whose owners, managers, and shareholders were anxious to see the Indians leave the state. Particularly active in the years after 1815 was the Ogden Land Company, which in 1810 had gained preemptive rights to Indian land in western New York from the Holland Land Company. This company was now particularly anxious to open the lands of the Seneca reservations to settlement, and used all its influence to try to secure federal support for the removal of the Six Nations from New York.

One contemporary writer who considered the plight of the New York Indians wrote that an important factor in the effort to persuade the Indians to leave New York was the interest of the companies in enhancing the value of their stock, "the value of which in the market depends entirely upon the nearer or more remote prospects of the removal of the Indians—in other words in their ejectment." He argued that it was in the interest of the land companies to use all possible means to get the Indians to leave. He also commented that, although it was always said that the removal of the Indians was voluntary, the companies had used all possible means to shape an Indian decision: ". . . from the cupidity of these preemption companies, no pains have been spared to multiply the causes and hasten the occasions of their removal."[5]

The officials of the land companies were, of course, of sufficient standing to be able to exert pressure on both the state and the federal governments, and this special pressure, added to the general New York desire to see the Indians leave, meant that in these years the officials of the federal government were constantly urged to use what influence they had to secure the removal of the Indians from New York.

In the years after 1815 the federal government was slowly reaching the conclusion that the Indians in the path of the white advance should be removed to the West. The general arguments justifying this decision were clear, but the motivations were complex. The "civilization" of the Indians was still the stated objective of the government, and most public arguments justifying the removal of the Indians were cast in terms of removing them from pernicious white pressures and providing a setting in which assimilation measures could be given time to work. Yet, for the next 20 years there were also politicians and missionaries who argued that to move those Indians who were in the process of civilization and assimilation on their present lands was a betrayal of the promises made in the 1790s and under the presidency of Thomas Jefferson.[6]

In the decade after the War of 1812 the federal government was also under great pressure from those who wanted to remove the Indians because they desired their lands. The most influential and fervent arguments in this regard came from the southern states. Tennessee and Georgia took the lead in demanding the removal of the Indians, and they received strong support from Mississippi and Alabama. Although, at times, lip service was paid to the well-being of the Indians, here the basic motive was land hunger. The southern states desired the removal of the Indians from potentially rich cotton lands. Tennessee and Georgia were just as eager to remove those Indians who were successfully adapting to white ways as they were to remove those who might be suffering from white contact. From 1816 the federal government was under constant and determined pressure from southern politicians who wished to see the Indians driven beyond the Mississippi.[7]

In New York, as in the South, self-interest was dominant in the pressures for the removal of the Indians, but those who desired the lands of the Indian reservations also received support from missionaries and government officials who believed that the Indians would have a better chance to survive, and that civilization efforts would have more effect, if the Indians were farther away from white settlements.

Immediately after the War of 1812 Governor Daniel D. Tompkins of New York urged the federal government to move the Six Nations, or part of them, to lands on the western frontier. The initial response of the federal government was cautious. Acting Secretary of War Alexander J. Dallas told Governor Tompkins in August 1815 that if the Senecas were moved to the West a critical question was whether they were to move onto Indian lands or onto lands to which the title had been extinguished. If to the latter, then the move would be of major concern to settlers in adjacent areas. State officials also tried to persuade the Six Nations that it would be in their interest to move to the West. Those of the Six Nations that seemed willing to move suggested that they should settle in or west of the state of Ohio, but the precise location for a possible move still presented problems. Secretary of War William H. Crawford stated in January 1816 that the president was willing to hold a treaty, but that in view of the possibility of a future war with Great Britain it was absolutely necessary to connect Ohio and the settlements in Michigan Territory, and it was also important to extend American settlements to the southern part of Lake Michigan. An additional problem, argued Crawford, was how much land the Six Nations wanted. Because the Six Nations were "more civilized" than some Indian groups, they would charge more when they sold the land.[8] Clearly, even after any possible move, it was not envisioned that any future home was likely to be permanent.

As the pressures for general Indian removal from New York increased, the Oneidas were experiencing changes that were to make them more susceptible than the other tribes of the Six Nations to removal pressures. In 1816 Christianity among the Oneidas was given a major boost by the coming of Eleazer Williams to the reservation. Williams was a St. Regis Indian. He numbered among his ancestors Eunice Williams, who had been captured by the Indians in 1704. She was the daughter of the Reverend John Williams of Deerfield. As a boy Williams had been taken to New England and had received a white education. After helping the American forces on the Lake Champlain front in the War of 1812, Williams became an Episcopalian. In 1816 he was appointed as lay reader, catechist, and schoolmaster among the Oneidas. Williams was a fine orator, and his preaching in his native Mohawk could be readily understood by the Oneidas. He had dramatic success in rekindling an enthusiasm for Christianity.[9] Williams also had the advantage that, with his New England education and excellent English, he was able to deal skillfully with white missionaries and government officials. He was able to obtain considerable influence by interpreting the intentions of the government to the Oneidas and the intentions of the Oneidas to the government.

First working among the Oneidas who had remained Christian, Williams soon created the strong First Christian Party. He then began to preach to the old Pagan Party, and quickly achieved additional success. In early 1817 the chiefs of the old Pagan Party publicly professed their Christianity and became the Second Christian Party. This group, at the instigation of Williams, ceded a part of their section of the reservation to build an Episcopal church. At the urging of Williams most of the Oneidas became professing Christians, although in the following years his influence was much stronger among the First Christian Party than among the rest of the Oneidas.[10]

In these years from 1816 to 1818, as Williams won great success among the Oneidas, a more determined drive was developing to try to remove the whole of the Six Nations from New York. The main leadership in this effort was taken by the Ogden Land Company, particularly by David A. Ogden, who was elected to the U.S. House of Representatives as a member of the Fifteenth Congress. Ogden took up his seat in Congress in January 1818, and during the following year used what influence he had to convince the War Department that it should do all that it could to encourage the emigration of the Six Nations to the West. Secretary of War John C. Calhoun did what he could to accommodate Ogden, but he also made it clear that ultimately any decision for removal would have to be made by the Indians themselves. During the following years, as the New York speculators did all they could to use the influence of the federal government to secure the Indian lands in New York, Calhoun consistently argued against the use of force. He was willing to tell the Indians that it was in their interest to move and was prepared to give moderate aid in their plans to secure lands from other Indians in the West, but he insisted both to the Indians and to the representatives of New York that the ultimate decision would have to rest with the Six Nations.

The initial concern of the War Department remained what it had been since the end of the War of 1812: where to settle the Six Nations if they moved to the West. The problem was complicated by Calhoun's limited knowledge of the geography of the Great Lakes region. In May 1818 Calhoun commented in a letter to Ogden that he saw almost insuperable difficulties in putting the Six Nations in the region between the Ohio, the Great Lakes, and the Mississippi, because there would be strong objections from the states of Ohio and Indiana and the territory of Illinois, and he did not see that there was a possible location in that region beyond the bounds of those entities. Calhoun argued that the Arkansas region would be the best area for the relocation and that he would try to encourage such a move.[11]

On the same day that Calhoun tried to cooperate with Ogden's wishes, he wrote to Jasper Parrish, the subagent for the Six Nations, stating that, although he did not wish threats or force to be used, he would like to see the Six Nations move for their own happiness. "Experience proves," he wrote, "that when surrounded by the whites, they always dwindle and become miserable. This is now the case with the Indians of the State of New York." He also corrected a rumor that the Six Nations would have to exchange their existing lands for new lands in the West. If they could get another tribe to accept them, this would simply be an arrangement between the Indians themselves.[12]

Throughout 1818 the Ogden interests, assisted by the federal agents, tried to influence the Six Nations in favor of a decision to move to the West. By August 1818 David Ogden was able to report to Calhoun that while the Six Nations were probably unalterably opposed to immigration to the Arkansas River region, they might be willing to move to the Fox River region west of Lake

Michigan. Calhoun quickly responded to this suggestion from Ogden and wrote to Lewis Cass, the governor and superintendent of Indian Affairs in Michigan Territory, asking him to find out if the Indians in the Fox River area, or any of the tribes north of Indiana and Illinois Territory, might be willing to grant land to the Six Nations. If this was the case, Cass was told that he would be instructed to help in arranging the removal of the Six Nations.[13]

Once again there was some confusion, for when Calhoun learned that the Fox River area was within the territory of Illinois, he quickly wrote to both Ogden and Cass to tell them that the Six Nations could not move there, because the government was anxious to extinguish all the Indian title in Illinois Territory. In December 1818, however, Illinois became a state with boundaries far to the south of the Fox River, and presumably it was explained to Calhoun that settlers seemed unlikely to press on up the western shores of Lake Michigan for some time to come, so the Fox River area was quickly resurrected as a possible home for the Six Nations.[14]

As the pressures on the Six Nations increased, sharper divisions began to develop between the various tribes. Some of the strongest support for removal came from the small group of Stockbridge Indians, who were composed of survivors of the Mahicans and other New England Indians. In the mid-1780s the Stockbridge had moved from Massachusetts to live on land allotted to them by the Oneidas. A little earlier, a small group of Indians from southern New England had accepted Oneida hospitality, and settled at Brotherton, New York. Both the Stockbridge and the Brothertons [Brothertowns] had been more assimilated to white society than most Indian groups. The Reverend John Sergeant, who had long been a missionary to the Stockbridge Indians, and Solomon U. Hendricks, a Stockbridge chief, became strong advocates of the benefits of a move to the West.[15]

In advocating removal, Hendricks and Sergeant were joined by Eleazer Williams. Williams took up the idea of removal with great enthusiasm, and he soon had success in convincing many of the First Christian Party of Oneidas of the desirability of emigration. The Second Christian Party and those who had joined neither group were far more reluctant and expressed hostility to any move westward. From this time Williams became a controversial figure within the Oneida tribe, but he was able to maintain the firm allegiance of many of the First Christian Party until the early 1830s. Others within the tribe consistently attacked his advocacy of a western move. In the fall of 1818 a group of 33 Oneidas petitioned President James Monroe to the effect that they were gaining in civilization on their present reservation, and they feared that a quick move would be a threat to their progress. They asked the president to block any steps for their immediate removal.[16]

Throughout 1819 the efforts to get the Six Nations to leave New York continued. Not only was Williams trying to get the Oneidas to agree to this plan, but also he was anxious to broaden the effort to include the rest of the Six

Nations as well as the St. Regis Indians. The promoter of the move at the national and state levels, however, continued to be David A. Ogden, and at the end of the year he was given influential Church support. The Reverend Jedidiah Morse of Boston became convinced after visiting the Six Nations in New York that it would be best for them to move to the West and be consolidated into one group. He met with David Ogden, and there was now to be an alliance of land speculators and missionaries in an effort to persuade the Six Nations that it would be in their best interest to move westward.[17]

In the winter of 1819–1820 proposals for removal west began to come to a head. The Reverend Mr. Morse proposed to the War Department that he should visit the Indian tribes to report on their condition and to help devise suitable plans to advance their civilization. During this tour he could visit the area west of Lake Michigan and examine its suitability for the emigration of the Six Nations. In February, Secretary of War Calhoun told Morse that he was to be allowed $500 toward his expenses and that he was to report the result of his visit to the War Department. Morse was also acting on behalf of the Society in Scotland for Propagating Christian Knowledge and the Northern Missionary Society in New York.[18]

Eleazer Williams became more decisively involved in plans for removal when he visited the War Department in Washington, carrying a letter of introduction from the Reverend John Henry Hobart, the Episcopal bishop of New York. In his letter Hobart commented that Williams was the son of an Indian chief, had received a very good education, and possessed more influence with his countrymen than any other person. Williams wanted financial support from Calhoun to further his plans for the removal of the Six Nations to the West. Williams intended to visit the Green Bay area to examine the region and to try to make arrangements with the tribes there for the future emigration of the Six Nations.[19]

Calhoun, of course, was happy to further, at a very small cost, his own desire for the Six Nations' removal and agreed that Williams and a deputation of Six Nations and St. Regis would receive government rations, rifle powder, and lead for their visit to the West in the summer of 1820. They would also receive $300 in general expenses, and there would be $150 in personal expenses for Eleazer Williams. Officials in the Old Northwest were ordered to help the deputation to achieve its objectives. In regard to the St. Regis Indians, Calhoun specified that there could be deputies only for those of the St. Regis within the United States, not for those in Canada.[20] Williams was now one of the most influential proponents of removal among those who could claim to have a direct influence on the Indians, and he worked consistently, against considerable opposition, to try to persuade the Six Nations to move to the area west of Lake Michigan. The proponents of removal were well aware that there was bitter Six Nation opposition to the idea, and in May, Morse told Calhoun that the question of Six Nations removal was a "delicate subject," with a diversity of opinions among both the whites and the Indians.[21]

This first trip of Williams and his deputation to the West proved a failure. After reaching Detroit they discovered that John Bowyer, the Indian agent at Green Bay, had just concluded a treaty with the Menominees, obtaining land for the government in the vicinity of Green Bay. Williams and his deputation had several meetings with the Reverend Jedidiah Morse, but, assuming that Bowyer's treaty had forestalled their plans, they returned to New York without visiting the Green Bay area. Morse told Calhoun that the Williams party had been very hurt by Bowyer's action, and, following his conversations with Williams, he recommended to Calhoun that it would be desirable for the Northwest Territory to be set aside exclusively for the Indians. There they could create a state that could in time be admitted to the union.[22] It appears that Williams imagined himself playing a vital role within a great Indian state west of Lake Michigan.

In the summer of 1820, on his return from the West, Morse visited the Oneida reservation, and using Williams as his interpreter, he spoke strongly in favor of a removal to the area west of Lake Michigan. It was later claimed by Albert Ellis, who worked with Williams at Oneida and later turned against him, that Williams had misinterpreted the Second Christian Party's answer to Morse. Morse had left the meeting with the impression that the Second Christian Party was not amenable to a move, and was surprised in the following year to discover that this group of the Oneidas was still strongly opposed.[23]

Although the government was in no way ready to accept Morse's suggestion that it should permanently set aside a huge area of the country for a possible future Indian state, Calhoun was still anxious to respond to New York pressures by moving the Six Nations to the region west of Lake Michigan. He also still argued that he believed this to be in the best interests of the Indians themselves. In April 1821 he informed Lewis Cass that the president had decided not to submit Indian agent John Bowyer's treaty to the Senate, and that the Menominees should be informed that land possession now remained the same as before the treaty was made. Plans were already being made for another visit of a New York delegation to the region west of Lake Michigan.[24]

Albert Ellis later stated that in the spring of 1821 he accompanied Williams on a trip to New York City and Philadelphia, and that in New York they had a long consultation with Thomas L. Ogden of the Ogden Land Company. From this time on, Ellis wrote, Williams received money from the Ogden Land Company. In Philadelphia, Williams met with the officials of the Episcopal Domestic and Foreign Missionary Society in order to try to get support from them for a Green Bay mission. They were to give him some support in the following years.[25]

In the spring and summer of 1821 Eleazer Williams made plans for another visit to the West. Again his main support came from the First Christian Party of the Oneidas. Calhoun was asked to give support. He agreed, asserting that the treaty signed the previous year with the Menominees had been unauthorized and had not been submitted to the Senate for ratification. The Six Nations, he stated, were free to obtain lands directly from the Menominees. Calhoun was helpful, but he was not generous. He said that, as before, rations would be supplied, but that he was unable to give any money for the trip. He also later told Williams that his party could not receive more than 14 rations a day.[26]

In June 1821, when Williams' delegation set out from New York for the West, it was clear that there were deep divisions both within the Oneida tribe and within the Six Nations. The First Christian Party of the Oneidas and the Stockbridge Indians were well represented, but there was no proper representation from the rest of the Six Nations. Ellis stated that there were single, unofficial delegates from the Onondagas, the Tuscaroras, and the Senecas, and that Williams was the sole representative from the St. Regis Indians. The First Christian Party of the Oneidas and the Stockbridge Indians were the only groups looking favorably on removal to the West.[27]

While Williams and his party were on their western trip, Oneida and Onondaga Indians at Oneida Castle protested to Monroe that Eleazer Williams had no authority to try to persuade the New York Indians to remove to the West, and that a delegation would visit Washington to lay their complaints before the government. Their visit came to naught. In September 1821 Calhoun wrote to state that the deputation of Oneidas and Onondagas had been obliged to leave Washington without effecting the object of their visit, because both he and the president had been absent. He recommended in the future that all visits should be planned through the agent. He repeated, however, that though he believed it would be in the interest of the Indians to move beyond the white settlements, it was never intended that anyone be compelled to emigrate. While the Oneida opponents of Williams were happy that the president had shown an interest in their desire to remain where they were, they still wanted their missionary to be replaced.[28]

As in the previous summer, Williams and his delegation traveled west through Detroit. Cass, who had been ordered by Calhoun to cooperate fully in the efforts to have the Six Nations move to the region west of Lake Michigan, appointed his own representative, Charles C. Trowbridge, to accompany the delegation to the Fox River. In August at Green Bay the Menominees and Winnebagos were called into council. At first they refused to cede any land, but under pressure they agreed on August 18, 1821, to cede a small strip of land on the Fox River in return for a payment of $1,500. It was not a satisfactory result of the plan to obtain a large area west of Lake Michigan for the New York Indians, but it was the opening wedge.[29]

When the delegation returned to New York, Williams and the rest of the delegation were bitterly criticized by those Oneidas who opposed the move. The center of opposition was among the Second Christian Party, but there were even divisions among the First Christian group. Williams, however, pressed ahead to get further government backing for the arrangement. He wrote to Calhoun late in November, stating that the chiefs of the First Christian Party had particularly requested him to secure permission for them to visit Washington during the winter to procure a confirmation of the grant that had been obtained from the western Indians. Calhoun quickly replied to say that because the agreement had already received the approval of the president, there was no need for a whole delegation to visit Washington. The government was, of course, anxious to avoid the expense and trouble of welcoming a whole delegation to the capital. Calhoun, however, appeased Williams by stating that one deputy could be sent to Washington if it was thought such a visit was important.[30]

In the winter of 1821–1822 the Six Nations were sharply divided on the issue of removal, and their chiefs and warriors were unable to agree on any single stance in regard to the treaty with the Menominees and Winnebagos. There was strong opposition both to removal and to the general white civilization policy among the Pagan Party of the Senecas, and Red Jacket, the great Seneca orator and spokesman of the Pagan Party, was to take an increasingly strong role in resisting any effort to move to the West. Jedidiah Morse admitted that the greater part of the Six Nations wanted to remain on their reservations in New York, and that some religious associations and individuals agreed with that position, believing that the Indians could better be civilized in their present location. Morse was hopeful, however, that if some removed west others would follow.[31]

Although the Oneidas were the tribe of the Six Nations most favorable to removal, they continued to be bitterly divided on the issue. Oneida opposition to Williams and his followers had been strong throughout the fall, and the disaffected petitioned their Episcopal bishop, John Hobart, asking that Williams be removed as their missionary. They told President James Monroe that they had dismissed Williams from his post, but Williams was to work for other Oneidas for more than a decade after his rejection by this group. It was becoming quite clear, however, that only the First Christian Party of the Oneidas, though not all of them, and the Stockbridge Indians seemed prepared to migrate westward.[32]

Although the majority of the Six Nations, including a considerable number of Oneidas, wanted to remain in New York, Williams' party of Oneidas now pressed forward with more ambitious plans for the area west of Lake Michigan. Those Oneidas who supported Williams asked Calhoun for the authority to try to enlarge the area that had been secured from the Menominees and Winnebagos in the previous summer. There was dissatisfaction with both the size and the location of the cession, which was farther away from the bay than was desirable.[33] Among the tribal leaders in New York, the main supporters of removal were Cornelius Baird of the Oneidas and Solomon Hendricks of the Stockbridge Indians. Baird worked closely with Eleazer Williams, and Hendricks had the support of the Reverend John Sergeant. Williams continued to play a key role because he had considerable credibility and support among those whites who were urging Indian removal and also had strong support among a portion of the Oneidas.

In writing to the First Christian Party, Calhoun made it clear that he had not changed his long-held position that though he thought it was in the interest of the Six Nations to leave New York, they would not be compelled to move west. He also reiterated this to the New York politicians who were so anxious to see the Six Nations leave the state. In April 1822 he told Representative William B. Rochester from New York that "the Government has endeavoured to impress upon the Indians the advantages of changing their present residence for one further West, and will continue to do so upon every suitable occasion; but no steps for their removal can be taken without their consent."[34]

Again in the summer of 1822 the federal government encouraged Eleazer Williams and his supporters to visit the West. Calhoun was happy to support an attempt to enlarge the purchase that had been made the previous year. Because the land involved was still all Indian and distant from any sizable white settlements, he could cooperate with the New York politicians and land speculators without raising any other political problems. Also, he again saved money by insisting that the delegation should be small.[35]

Williams and his party arrived at Green Bay at the beginning of September 1822, and the Menominees and Winnebagos gathered in great numbers for the treaty. The two tribes were given goods to the value of $1,500, which had been promised the year before, and a request for a larger cession was made. At first both tribes refused, and the Winnebagos left the council. After further discussion, some of the Menominees were persuaded to sign an agreement that gave the New York Indians a right in common to all their country—several million acres. The price for this princely domain was less than $4,000 in goods. In the following years, the Menominees bitterly disputed the validity of both this treaty and the agreement signed in the previous year, arguing that their chiefs had not agreed to it.[36]

In the winter of 1822–1823 Williams and his delegates stayed west of Lake Michigan, and at the end of 1822 Williams told Calhoun that he had taken his "final abode" there. In the following March he married the young daughter of a French Canadian and a Menominee woman. In the summer of 1823 other Oneidas of the First Christian Party immigrated to the region west of Lake Michigan, at first settling at the Little Kakalin on the Fox River. By 1825 there were some 150 Oneidas there. That summer a large party of Oneidas arrived from New York, and with the immigrants who were already there made a settlement at Duck Creek. This was to become the permanent Oneida reservation in Wisconsin.[37]

In the 1820s and 1830s a bitter dispute arose when the Menominees challenged the validity of the cessions. They argued that the whole arrangement should be annulled by the federal government. The dispute dragged on for years, but by 1838 the dreams of a huge Iroquois landholding west of Lake Michigan had been reduced to the 65,000-acre Oneida reservation at Duck

Creek. There were also small Stockbridge and Brotherton [Brothertown] reservations east of Lake Winnebago.[38]

The news of the supposed grant of a huge acreage west of Lake Michigan did not persuade the majority of the Six Nations to move. In the winter of 1822–1823, Red Jacket continued to lead resistance not only to removal but also to the general white civilization policy among the Indians. He visited Washington, and he and his party were told by Calhoun that it would be in their interest to remove to the West but that they would not be forced to go. The Ogden Land Company was still hoping that all the Six Nations would leave and had been urging the government to allow its surveyors onto the Seneca reservation, but in March 1823 Calhoun told Thomas L. Ogden that Red Jacket appeared inveterately opposed to removal, "and declared it his intention to live and die on the lands he now occupies."[39]

In the 1820s the Oneida immigrants to the Wisconsin area were almost exclusively of the First Christian Party, were professed Episcopalians, and were strongly under the influence of Eleazer Williams. This situation began to change after 1829, for in that year a successful Methodist mission was established on the Oneida reservation in New York and began to win converts among the Second Christian Party, creating the Orchard Party. In 1830 these Methodist converts of the Second Christian Party began to move to Wisconsin. They first settled near the Grand Kakalin on the Fox River, but from 1833 they lived on the Duck Creek on the reservation. By the fall of 1838 there were some 654 Oneidas on the Duck Creek reservation, and over the next 50 years Oneidas continued to move to this area both from New York and from Canada. Williams did not die until 1858, after achieving notoriety by claiming to be the lost dauphin of France. His influence over the Oneidas had come to an end long before, in the early 1830s.[40]

The original impetus for the removal of the Six Nations from New York had been provided by the state of New York and by the land speculators who acquired the preemption rights to the Indian reservations in the state. Strong support was provided by some of the missionaries, particularly by Jedidiah Morse on a national level and among the Oneidas and the Stockbridge Indians, and by the Reverend John Sergeant among the Stockbridge. For the Oneidas Eleazer Williams played a decisive role. As a native Mohawk speaker and fine orator, he was able to bring particular conviction to his efforts as an Episcopalian missionary. He was willing to listen to the persuasions of the Reverend Jedidiah Morse, the Ogden Land Company, and government officials, for he saw himself playing a major role in a new Six Nation homeland beyond Lake Michigan. Gaining the support of several Oneida chiefs, particularly Cornelius Baird, Williams was able to use his own eloquence and the chiefs' influence to convince many Oneidas that they would have a better life in a new land in the West. Even without the coming of Eleazer Williams to the tribe in 1816, it seems likely that some of the Oneidas would have joined their Stockbridge neighbors in removing to the West, but it was the coming of Eleazer Williams that provided the major impetus for the emigration to Wisconsin of a large part of the Oneida tribe.

Notes

1. The most detailed and best researched account of the circumstances leading to the removal of the Oneida is in Philip Otto Geier, "A Peculiar Status: A History of Oneida Indian Treaties and Claims: Jurisdictional Conflict within the American Government, 1775–1920," Ph.D. dissertation, Syracuse University, 1980.

2. See Jack Campisi, "Oneida," in *Handbook of North American Indians,* ed. Bruce G. Trigger, Vol. 15: *Northeast* (Washington, D.C.: Smithsonian Institution Press, 1978), pp. 482–485. There is also information on these years in Jack Campisi, "Ethnic Identity and Boundary Maintenance in Three Oneida Communities," Ph.D. dissertation, SUNY Albany, 1974; and in Geier, "Peculiar Status."

3. William W. Campbell, ed., *The Life and Writings of De Witt Clinton* (New York: Baker and Scribner, 1849), pp. 186–190.

4. *Historical Statistics of the United States. Colonial Times to 1957* (Washington, D.C.: U.S. Bureau of the Census, 1960), p. 13.

5. Calvin Colton, *A Tour of the American Lakes and among the Indians of the Northwest Territory in 1830,* 2 vols. (1833; reprint, Port Washington, N.Y.: Kennikut Press, 1972), 1: 99–101, 124–125.

6. William H. Crawford, who was secretary of war in the years immediately after the War of 1812, believed that the Indians should be assimilated into American society, and was opposed to forced cessions. See Reginald Horsman, *The Origins of Indian Removal, 1815–1824,* Clarence M. Burton Memorial Lecture (East Lansing: Michigan State University Press, 1970), pp. 5–6.

7. Ibid., pp. 5–16.

8. See Alexander Dallas to Governor Daniel Tompkins, Aug. 5, 1815, and William H. Crawford to Tompkins, Jan. 22, 1816, War Department, Secretary's Office, Letters Sent, Indian Affairs, C: 271–272, 294–295, NA; also Geier, "Peculiar Status," pp. 147–149.

9. For Williams see William Wight, "Eleazer Williams," in Parkman Club *Papers* (Milwaukee, 1896), 1: 133–203. Also see Colton, *Tour of the American Lakes,* 1: 157–166; Albert G. Ellis, "Advent of the New York Indians into Wisconsin," *Wisconsin Historical Collections* (Madison: SHSW, 1856), 2: 418–420; Albert G. Ellis, "Recollections of Rev. Eleazer Williams," *Wisconsin Historical Collections* (Madison: SHSW, 1879), 8: 329–330; Lyman C. Draper, "Additional Notes on Eleazer Williams," *Wisconsin Historical Collections* (Madison: SHSW, 1879), 8: 353–369; John N. Davidson, "The Coming of the New York Indians to Wisconsin," *Proceedings of the Wisconsin State Historical Society* (Madison, SHSW, 1900), pp. 176–177; Jedidiah Morse, *A Report to the Secretary of War of the United States of Indian Affairs* (New Haven, 1822), Appendix, pp. 79–80; George Graham to John Taylor, Aug. 16, 1817, War Department, Secretary's Office, Letters Sent, Indian Affairs, D: 80, NA.

10. Ellis, "Advent of the New York Indians," pp. 418–420; Geier, "Peculiar Status," pp. 152–153, 170; Campisi, "Ethnic Identity," pp. 104–105.

11. Calhoun to David Ogden, May 14, 1818, War Department, Secretary's Office, Letters Sent, Indian Affairs, D: 164–165, NA; also see Clyde N. Wilson, W. Edwin Hemphill, and Robert L. Meriwether, eds., *The Papers of John C. Calhoun* (Columbia, S.C.: University of South Carolina Press, 1959–1984), 2: 144–145.

12. Calhoun to Jasper Parrish, May 14, 1818, War Department, Secretary's Office, Letters Sent, Indian Affairs, D: 165–166.

13. See Wilson, Hemphill and Merriwether, eds., *Papers of Calhoun,* 2: 368, 3: 10–11; Calhoun to Lewis Cass, Aug. 19, 1818, to David Ogden, Aug. 19, 1818, War Department, Secretary's Office, Letters Sent, Indian Affairs, D: 204–206, NA.

14. Calhoun to David Ogden, Aug. 28, 1818, in Wilson, Hemphill, and Meriwether, eds., *Papers of Calhoun,* 3: 78; Calhoun to Lewis Cass, Sept. 2, 1818, War Department, Secretary's Office, Letters Sent, Indian Affairs, D: 208, NA.

15. For the Stockbridge see T. J. Brasser, "Mahican," in *Handbook of North American Indians,* Vol. 15: *Northeast,* pp. 207–209; Joseph Schafer, *The Winnebago–Horicon Basin: A Type Study in Western History* (Madison, Wis., 1937), pp. 35–42. For the Brothertowns see Laura E. Conkey et al., "Indians of Southern New England and Long Island: Late Period," in *Handbook of North American Indians,* Vol. 15: *Northeast,* pp. 181–182; Schafer, *Winnebago–Horicon Basin,* p. 39; also Ellis, "Advent of the New York Indians," pp. 415–417.

16. Ellis, "Advent of the New York Indians," pp. 420–422; Chiefs and Warriors of the Oneidas to James Monroe, Nov. 11, 1818, Letters Received, Secretary of War, Registered Series M221, MR 82, NA; Wilson, Hemphill, and Merriwether, eds., *Papers of Calhoun,* 2: 262–263.

17. See David Ogden to Calhoun, Dec. 10, 1819, Wilson, Hemphill, and Merriwether, eds., *Papers of Calhoun,* 4: 475.

18. Calhoun to Jedidiah Morse, Feb. 7, 1820, War Department, Secretary's Office, Letters Sent, Indian Affairs, D: 362–364, NA; Morse, *Report to the Secretary of War,* pp. 11–12.

19. John Henry Hobart to Calhoun, Jan. 25, 1820, Wilson, Hemphill, and Merriwether, eds., *Papers of Calhoun,* 4: 603–604; Ellis, "Recollections of Williams," pp. 333–336.

20. Calhoun to Eleazer Williams, Feb. 9 and May 9, 1820, to Lewis Cass, Feb. 9, 1820, to Morris Miller, May 9, 1820, War Department, Secretary's Office, Letters Sent, Indian Affairs, D: 364–367, 421, 422, NA.

21. Jedidiah Morse to Calhoun, May 31, 1820, in Wilson, Hemphill, and Merriwether, eds., *Papers of Calhoun,* 5: 160–161.

22. Jedidiah Morse to Calhoun, Aug. 15, Oct. 3, 1820, ibid., 5: 331–333, 371–372.

23. Ellis, "Recollections of Williams" pp. 326–328; Jedidiah Morse to Calhoun, Aug. 15, 1820, Wilson, Hemphill, and Merriwether, eds., *Papers of Calhoun,* 5: 331–332.

24. Calhoun to Lewis Cass, Apr. 4, 1821, War Department, Secretary's Office, Letters Sent, Indian Affairs, E: 81, NA.

25. Ellis, "Recollections of Williams," pp. 333–334.

26. See Wilson, Hemphill, and Merriwether, eds., *Papers of Calhoun,* 6: 30; Calhoun to Cornelius Baird et al., Apr. 14, 1821, and Calhoun to Eleazer Williams, June 4, 1821, both in War Department, Secretary's office, Letters Sent, Indian Affairs, E: 91, 108, NA.

27. Ellis, "Recollections of Williams," pp. 334–335.

28.   Chiefs of the Oneidas and Onondagas to James Monroe, Aug. 8, 1821, Letters
Received, Secretary of War, Registered Series, M221, MR 93, NA; Wilson, Hemphill,
and Merriwether, eds., *Papers of Calhoun,* 6: 326, 438; Calhoun to the Reverend Oba-
diah Brown, Sept. 27, 1821, War Department, Secretary's Office, Letters Sent, Indian
Affairs, E: 154–155, NA.

29.   Ellis, "Recollections of Williams," pp. 335–336; Patricia K. Ourada, *The
Menominee Indians: A History* (Norman, Okla.: University of Oklahoma Press, 1979),
p. 76; Calhoun to Lewis Cass, June 21, 1821, War Department, Secretary's Office, Letters Sent, Indian Affairs, E: 120, NA.

30.   Ellis, "Advent of New York Indians," pp. 426–427; Ellis, "Recollections of
Williams," p. 336; Eleazer Williams to Calhoun, Nov. 29, 1821, Wilson, Hemphill, and
Merriwether, eds., *Papers of Calhoun,* 6: 543; Calhoun to Lewis Cass, Nov. 22, 1821;
and Calhoun to Eleazer Williams, Dec. 11, 1821 (wrongly written as "1822" in the original); both in War Department, Secretary's Office, Letters Sent, Indian Affairs, E: 194,
204, NA.

31.   See Jasper Parrish to Calhoun, Jan. 11, 1822; David Ogden to Christopher Van-
deventer, Mar. 2, 1822; and David Ogden to Calhoun, May 9, 1822; all in Letters Received, Secretary of War, Registered Series, M221, MR 93 and 94, NA; Wilson,
Hemphill, and Merriwether, eds., *Papers of Calhoun,* 6: 615–616, 723; 7: 103–104;
Morse, *Report to the Secretary of War,* pp. 24–26; Calhoun to Jasper Parrish, Aug. 27
and Sept. 6, 1822, War Department, Secretary's Office, Letters Sent, Indian Affairs, E:
317, 323–324, NA.

32.   Ellis, "Recollections of Williams," pp. 336–337; Peter Sumner et al. to James
Monroe, Jan. 22, 1822, Letters Received, Secretary of War, Registered Series, M221,
MR 93, NA; Wilson, Hemphill, and Merriwether, eds., *Papers of Calhoun,* 6: 632.

33.   Cornelius Baird to Calhoun, Jan. 25, 1822, Letters Received, Secretary of War,
Registered Series, M221, MR 92, NA; Wilson, Hemphill, and Merriwether, eds., *Papers
of Calhoun,* 6: 633; Calhoun to Solomon Hendricks, Feb. 13, 1822, War Department,
Secretary's Office, Letters Sent, Indian Affairs, E: 215–216, NA.

34.   Calhoun to the Chiefs of the First Christian Party of the Oneidas, Apr. 15,
1822; and Calhoun to Jasper Parrish, Apr. 15, 1822; both in War Department, Secretary's Office, Letters Sent, Indian Affairs, E: 234–235, NA; Calhoun to William Beatty
Rochester, Apr. 15, 1822, in Wilson, Hemphill, and Merriwether, eds., *Papers of Calhoun,* 7: 44–45.

35.   Calhoun to Eleazer Williams, May 8, 1822; Calhoun to Lewis Cass, May 8,
1822; and Calhoun to Solomon Hendricks, June 22, 1822; all in War Department, Secretary's Office, Letters Sent, Indian Affairs, E: 253, 254, 287, NA.

36.   Albert G. Ellis, "General Ellis' Recollections," *Wisconsin Historical Collections,* Vol. 7 (Madison: SHSW, 1873–1876), pp. 223–225; Ourada, *Menominee Indians,*
pp. 76–77; Ellis, "Recollections of Williams," pp. 337–338.

37.   Eleazer Williams to Calhoun, Dec. 27, 1822, in Wilson, Hemphill, and Meriwether, eds., *Papers of Calhoun,* 7: 394–395; Ellis, "Recollections of Williams," p. 338;
Davidson, "Coming of the New York Indians," pp. 176–177; Geier, "Peculiar Status,"
p. 159; Julia K. Bloomfield, *The Oneidas,* 2d ed. (New York, 1907), pp. 180–181.

38.   See Ourada, *Menominee Indians,* pp. 77–94; Colton, *Tour of the American Lakes,*
1: 145–152, 2: 163–185; Ellis, "Recollections of Williams," pp. 341–343; Charles J.

Kappler, *Indian Affairs: Laws and Treaties,* 5 vols. (Washington, D.C., 1903–1941), 2: 517–518.

39. See Jasper Parrish to Calhoun, Oct. 21, 1822, Wilson, Hemphill, and Meriwether, eds., *Papers of Calhoun,* 7: 311–312; Calhoun to Thomas L. Ogden, Feb. 14 and Mar. 15, 1823; Calhoun to Jasper Parrish, Feb. 14, and Mar. 14, 1823; Calhoun to Red Jacket et al., Mar. 14, 1823; all in War Department, Secretary's Office, Letters Sent, Indian Affairs, E: 386–387, 403–407, NA.

40. Wade C. Barclay, *History of Methodist Missions,* 2 vols., Vol. 1: *Early American Methodism, 1769–1844* (New York, 1949–1957), pp. 146–147; Elizabeth Wilson, *Methodism in Eastern Wisconsin: Section One, 1832–1850* (Milwaukee, 1938), pp. 13–15; Philo S. Bennett and James Lawson, *History of Methodism in Wisconsin* (Cincinnati, 1890), pp. 13–16; John Porter Bloom, ed., *The Territorial Papers of the United States,* Vol. 27: *The Territory of Wisconsin* (Washington, D.C.: National Archives, 1969), p. 117 n; Campisi, "Ethnic Identity," pp. 133–134; Bloomfield, *Oneidas,* p. 213.

4 *Jack Campisi*

The Wisconsin Oneidas between Disasters

By the time the Oneidas had settled their boundaries in Wisconsin with the United States, they had endured some 200 years of European and American intrusion in their affairs. First came the Dutch to trade for furs, then the French priests to save their souls, followed by a legion of English missionaries, traders, colonial officials, land speculators, and settlers seeking dominion over the same souls and the land they occupied. The Oneidas spent two centuries embroiled in the imperial wars of first the French and the English, and later the English and their rebellious colonies, always serving on the side of the victor and always paying in people and land for the privilege.

Despite their loyalty, the new republic treated the Oneidas no better than had the crown. At the same time that the Oneidas were receiving guarantees to their lands by treaty and act, the state of New York was busy acquiring their territory and paying a pittance in return. A succession of Protestant ministers came seeking converts and splitting the tribe from its past and its members into disputing factions. Wisconsin seemed a refuge, but no sooner had the Oneidas left New York and negotiated a land base than the federal government reduced their

Revised and reprinted with permission from Jack Campisi, "Ethnic Identity and Boundary Maintenance in Three Oneida Communities," unpublished Ph.D. dissertation, State University of New York at Albany, 1974.

territory and pressed once again for their removal. By 1838 the Oneidas in Wisconsin had less than a fifth of the land they had purchased and were already being impinged upon by white settlers. The tribe was divided into first two and then three Oneida tribes, located in Wisconsin, New York, and Ontario. The divisions crossed family, clan, and religious lines. It is against this background that the next fifty years of Wisconsin Oneida tribal history is to be understood.

The area of Wisconsin where the Oneidas settled was similar to the region from which they had emigrated. The land was heavily forested and interspersed with lakes and streams. Game, furs, and fish were plentiful, as were wild plants used for medicine and food. These, together with berries, laboriously collected, provided a staple base for tribal members, and the surpluses could be sold at the local trading places in Green Bay. In the spring, families could move to a sugarbush to make maple syrup.[1]

In 1838 the Wisconsin Oneida population totaled 654. Within 30 years their number had nearly doubled, to 1,218. From then on the population increased by about 25 a year, so that by 1887, the time of the passage of the Dawes General Allotment Act, there were 1,732 people on the tribal rolls.[2] While there was sufficient land available, this growth was to have profound effects on social organization in the years to come.

The agricultural pursuits of the Oneidas were largely of a subsistence nature and included the raising of cattle, horses, pigs, and sheep. Wheat, oats, and hay were grown, but apparently there was insufficient production of hay in the early days of the settlement for winter feed. To make up the deficit, the Oneidas adopted the expediency of tying down the branches of trees so the animals could feed on the buds.[3] While farming had become primarily a male occupation, there was one important exception. Corn, planted in fields cleared in the traditional Iroquois manner, provided the mainstay of the diet. Men and women shared equally in the labor of this crop.

There was one task, however, that wives and mothers would not give up; they always worked in the corn fields with the men, planting, hoeing, and harvesting the maize. This they considered their privilege of birthright, a holiday task bequeathed to them by their knonshioni mothers of bygone days.[4]

The sale of surplus animals, berries, braided cornhusk mats, and maple syrup provided cash. As the fur trade upon which the city of Green Bay depended declined, there was a shift to lumbering. By the 1870s the Oneidas had been drawn into a cash economy, which led to the increased exploitation of their forest reserves. Men spent the winter working in the pine forests, returning home in the spring, often with little of their earnings left after the enticements of lumber towns. These adjustments were built upon and made possible by the maintenance of small, self-sufficient farm units that provided the staples for the households.[5]

In the nineteenth century the Wisconsin Oneida tribe was organized around three foci of solidarity: kinship, religion, and neighborhoods. Although each of these tended to be related to the other two, kinship was the most significant. The Wisconsin Oneida kinship system continued the tendency to place the emphasis on the importance of the extended family as a unit of solidarity, but with a narrowing of its application. In this regard there were changes in the use of the kinship terms. The use of sibling terms was restricted to the nuclear family, and the term for cousin was applied to the children of one's parents' siblings. In addition, parents limited the use of terms for son and daughter to their own children and referred to their siblings' children as nephew and niece. Similar limitations in terminological usage occurred in other relationships.

Along with the narrowing of the extended family came an increasing emphasis on the nuclear family, which, in turn, brought about a change in the relationship between husband and wife. Girls married young, generally by the age of 14 or 15.[6] Marriage was arranged by parents who gave due consideration to the rules of exogamy, as well as the social prestige and economic condition of the families concerned. Ellen Goodnough, the Episcopal minister's wife, described the procedure:

After baptism this morning there was a marriage. The bride but 15 and looked modest and childlike. As a rule the young people have not had a word to say in regard to their own marriages. The mother of the young man picks out a wife for him and makes the bargain with the girl's mother. Then the young man sends the girl a present of cloth, etc., through his mother, in value according to his circumstances. In case the girl breaks off the match she must send back the presents, but if the young man breaks off the match the presents are kept by the girl.[7]

Once a family's choice was made known, there was little likelihood of the individual refusing. The seriousness of defying the wishes of one's family is reflected in an entry in Joseph Powless' diary of 1862: "Skywiped or Clear Sky, cut his throat, he was to be married but he did not like the action of his intended wife's father, is the reason why he killed himself."[8] Ellen Goodnough noted that until her husband became a minister, couples were still being forced into marriages and that he put a stop to this by refusing church service unless they consented.[9]

Married couples were expected to stay together for life. Divorce or infidelity was considered a serious offense against the church and could lead to expulsion and social ostracism. Wives were subordinate to their husbands, who made the major economic decisions. Generally women kept control of the funds they earned from selling berries, vegetables, and baskets. Husbands allocated funds to operate the households, and women were expected to make do. Normally, men did not consult their wives regarding business transactions, and women were expected to accept their husbands' decisions without question. As Harry Basehart has noted: "The burden of adjustment rested upon the woman, who was expected to become accustomed to such male foibles as occasional drinking sprees. A woman who rebelled was unlikely to receive the support of relatives except where actual ill-treatment or definite failure to provide was involved."[10] One elderly woman told me that the first time her mother became aware that their allotment had been sold by her father was when the sheriff came to evict the family.

Husbands and wives acted with reserved decorum toward each other when in public and avoided situations where they would be in close contact with others of the opposite sex. The separation of the sexes and the women's circumspect behavior were reflected in their public appearance:

I well recall the appearance of the Sunday morning congregation. The men, who had doffed their blankets and were clad in the garb of American citizens, sat on one side. The women still in petticoats and blankets, took the other side. The blankets were red or white, such as are now in use upon our beds, while many of the women were wrapped in large pieces of costly broadcloth. The younger women generally sat and walked the highways with their blankets over their heads, so that only one eye could by any chance be seen. The older women in the church generally let their blankets fall to their shoulders.[11]

Brothers and sisters maintained close relationships throughout life, mediated in later years by the obligations they had to their children. Older brothers and sisters had authority over the younger siblings. Brothers were expected to protect and show respect to their sisters; sisters followed the wishes of their brothers, sometimes in opposition to those of their husbands. For example, the sister of one tribal leader married a man who became very prominent in the community. On one occasion the commissioner of Indian affairs directed the Indian agent to give a United States flag to the most prominent and respected Oneida man. The agent, unable to decide between the woman's brother and her husband relied on public opinion, which, after extended debate, designated her husband. However, the issue was not settled, and relations between the two men became increasingly strained until the sister-wife was forced to choose between them. She supported her brother, whereupon her husband sold his property, gave the flag to the brother, and left the community for good. The resulting estrangement between the families lasted for nearly a century.

The situation described above is unusual because the Oneida kinship system tended to minimize such disputes. The bilateral descent system tied two families together; the emphasis on children and their relation to their grandparents supported that cohesion. The arrangement of marriages implied a compatibility between the families concerned, while the religious prohibition against divorce encouraged efforts by both families to prevent or at least settle disputes amicably. Families with a number of married siblings developed a complex network of affinal and consanguineal ties, which resulted in individuals occupying a number of different kinship positions, depending upon the point of reference used.

Of the various kinship ties, that between grandparent and grandchild was the strongest and most valued. Grandparents were to be shown respect; they were considered good companions who helped ameliorate the more rigid discipline of the parents. In times of crisis grandparents were the first ones looked to for support. They occasionally raised their grandchildren, and extended visits by grandchildren were a common occurrence. Next came aunts and uncles on both sides of the family. These kin found themselves affected by two opposing trends. On the one hand, the emphasis on the nuclear family diminished their influence over their siblings' offspring while, on the other hand, their close ties to their brothers and sisters led to the assumption of obligation, particularly during periods of stress. Basehart has characterized their role in kinship solidarity as being next to grandparents and describes the limits of their obligations: "Gifts may be expected from these relatives at such life crises as marriage; their support may be counted upon at a 'bee' for house building, planting, harvesting and so on; hospitality, in the form of a meal and a place to sleep, was always available."[12] Most Oneidas could trace their kinship lines to each other, the common denominator being that individuals were cousins. First cousins were viewed as "close relatives" and treated as members of the nuclear family.

The ties of parents and children, siblings, aunts and uncles, nephews, and first cousins made up the extended family by the midnineteenth century among the Wisconsin Oneidas. Radiating from this core were a number of social relationships varying in degree of importance and forming a larger social unit, the kindred. The kindred was also a bilateral unit and included all relatives through third cousins. Second and third cousins were considered too close for marriage.[13] The group's primary importance was that it served as an emotional focus. According to Basehart,

It was distinguished as a kinship membership unit primarily by attitude and sentiment— the feeling of closer and more binding ties within the unit. When the norms of behavior were violated by a member of the kindred, these errors of omission or commission were felt more keenly and the offender would be reproached for failure to behave "like a relative."[14]

One elderly Oneida lady elaborated on these attitudes toward the kindred. She described to me how, as a child, she was admonished about the proper ways to behave in specific situations, with the frequent reminder that others would judge the kindred by her acts. She reported:

Some families we didn't associate with because they couldn't be trusted or else they drank a lot. When I got old enough to marry, my mother watched me all the time—even made sure my brothers kept an eye on me—to see I didn't fall in with some families. If I married the wrong person our whole family would be criticized, and maybe some people wouldn't want to marry my sisters or cousins. I think it was a good way because it kept you in line.

In this context the role of the parents in choosing spouses for their children took on added importance. Marriage bound kindreds together through the children, since spouses remained tied to the bilateral units of their parents. Onei-das were largely endogamous in the nineteenth century, and this placed great importance on the acceptability of the family of the prospective spouse. Social position could shift with changes in a family's fortune and prestige. The kindred, therefore, became an important index to social position as well as a mechanism of social control.

Except for their function in curing illnesses, clans declined in importance and exerted little influence on the daily life at Oneida. Basehart found that "Oneida elders believe that the clan (*oᵓda·hLa*) had greatly decreased in im-portance prior to emigration from New York and hold, in effect, that clans did not function as effective kinship membership units in Wisconsin."[15] Three clans were recognized: Turtle, Wolf, and Bear. Basehart found that older informants associated the existence of chiefs with specific families as well as with the presence of "condolence mothers," that is, clan matrons.[16] These positions had been eviscerated of any previous political content. What importance clan affil-iation retained was related to the supernatural, and in particular to witchcraft, which was believed to descend through the mother's line. Clans were believed to possess curative rites for certain nervous disorders referred to by some as the "vities."

The Oneida community of the midnineteenth century reflected the divisions resulting from the factional politics of the emigration period. Thus the differ-ences between the First Christian Party and the Orchard Party became a reli-gious division of north and south ends of the reservation, Episcopal and Metho-dist. The first emigrants had been Episcopalians, followed in the 1830s by a smaller contingent of Methodists. A quid pro quo soon developed between the groups; each managed the affairs of its sector, and each was represented in tribal councils in rough proportion to its membership. The Episcopalians generally controlled two-thirds of the political positions. In spite of the specific religious differences, the leadership of each religious group consisted of the more suc-cessful and prosperous farmers with similar views toward a work ethic and Christian morality.

Marriage between the two groups was frowned upon, and social contacts were few. Each had a number of voluntary associations, such as the altar, singing, and mutual aid societies. The leaders of each group were concerned that their members act "properly," lest the church be subject to ridicule from the other group. The political position of church leaders enabled them to bring pressure to bear on the community to maintain religious values. This tie between church and governance is epitomized by the career of Cornelius Hill, who was the last head chief of the Oneidas and an ordained priest of the Episcopal church.

In addition to the division along religious lines, the Wisconsin Oneida tribe was divided into a number of neighborhoods. Basehart identified eight:

1. *latinatakuha·ka*—the "village people." People of the South end, centering on the Methodist Church.

2. *kʌtsyaⁿohaleha·ka*—"fish–out up people." A settlement in the southwest of the Reservation. The name is said to refer to a wooden fish nailed to a pole.
3. *tatsmʌha·ka*—"Dutchman's people." People near the south boundary of the Reservation.
4. *tiksʌha·ka*—"Dixon's people." People living in the part of the Reservation near the town of West De Pere. The name is derived from the surname of the white proprietor of a favorite trading store.
5. *taluⁿkowanha·ka*—"Duck Creek people." The settlement centering around the Protestant Episcopal Church.
6. *latihulahelaⁿa·ka*—"Their guns are set up people." People of the north-central part of the Reservation. The name is said to refer to a trap for deer which made use of a trigger device for discharging a gun.
7. *tekahsokʌha·ka*—"people between its lips." A group in the northeast corner of the Reservation. The name is said to be based on analogy with Green Bay and its peninsula, conceived as lips.
8. *simoha·ka*—"Seymour people." People residing near the town of Seymour.[17]

Much of the social and economic life of the community revolved around these neighborhoods. Neighbors helped each other in clearing fields, planting, harvesting, constructing and repairing buildings, and constructing and maintaining roads. Social gatherings and Sunday visits were neighborhood activities, and each neighborhood tended to view itself as superior to the others.

Generally speaking, the neighborhoods were residential manifestations of the previously discussed foci of integration—kinship and religion. They consisted of individual farms strung along the main roads, and it was common for sons to establish homesteads near those of their fathers. The neighborhoods were integrated at one additional level: one was either a Southender or a Northender. This coincided with the religious separation. Sharp rivalries existed between the two, and these found expression in games such as lacrosse and its attendant gambling. Alfred Cope, a Quaker businessman visiting the reservation in 1849, noted that

good temper [was] maintained throughout a very severe contest in which opposing parties frequently prostrated each other with great force and hard, though accidental, blows were given and received in the melee. . . . There were two companies to contend for the palm, selected severally from the western and eastern sides of Duck Creek.[18]

In addition to this competition, there were stereotypical insults, with the Northenders being considered "talkers" rather than workers, and the Southenders looked upon as hard-working but "stingy."[19] One elderly Northender said to me that "They [Southend Methodists] were never as progressive as us. When I was a little girl we used to say they were backward—they even spoke Indian backwards. Some believed in old Pagan things. No wonder they didn't amount to anything." By contrast, a Southend resident suggested that Northenders "tried to act like whites too much" and "forgot they're Indians like the rest of us."

It is difficult to determine the degree to which the traditional Iroquois belief system permeated the culture of the Wisconsin Oneidas or was incorporated into their Christian religious attitudes. It seems certain that the Oneidas of Wisconsin performed none of the calendrical ceremonies, nor were any followers of Handsome Lake. It is equally clear that the great epics of Creation and the Peacemaker, which validated the traditional sociopolitical system, were no longer recited, nor was the condolence of sachems performed. However, the ceremonial giving of names appears to have been continued, although it took place during Fourth of July celebrations.[20] As previously described, clan and moiety arrangements atrophied when the emphasis shifted to religious and neighborhood affiliations and to nuclear family and bilateral kindred membership.

A few Iroquois beliefs were integrated into Christianity, losing much of their original meaning. Thus the good twin in the Iroquois Creation, Thaluhyawa·ku (He Who Holds Up the Sky), became synonymous with Jesus Christ. In another example, the Oneidas collected water before sunrise on Easter morning. This water, called *kanekka·nol* (holy water), was thought to have therapeutic powers.

The Oneidas brought with them to Wisconsin the complex of beliefs associated with individual health, societal well-being, and balance and equilibrium in the universe, and these continued to exert influences throughout the nineteenth century. In addition, the medicine societies continued curative practices well into the twentieth century. An informant described to anthropologist Robert Ritzenthaler a curing ceremony he had witnessed around 1880:

The medicine men are eligible to act as medicine men only after they have been sick and cured. None of the clan can attend unless they have been sick before and cured. The dancers wear masks (false faces) and something on their back. . . . the medicine men had the sickness and have gotten over it so they have supernatural power. The sick person would be placed near the fire and the dancers would come in and act fearful and make weird noises, shake rattles, and pound on the walls with clubs to scare the evil spirits. One of the medicine men would dip his hands into hot coals of the fire and drop some over the head of the sick person. Neither the medicine man nor the sick person would be burned, although the coals fell into his clothes and over his hands.[21]

In addition, Oneida herbalists administered to the sick. Dreamers were called upon to diagnose the specific cause of ailments and recommend an appropriate curing agent. Medicines were prepared to ward off witches, guarantee success in love, and assure victory in games such as lacrosse. In one case where the medicine failed, the irate losers caught the medicine man and poured the concoction down his throat. According to Ellen Goodnough's diary, he died within an hour.[22]

The Oneidas' complex funerary practices reflect another manifestation of the belief in witchcraft. These practices included runners' announcements of a death, a wake accompanied by songs and eulogies in Oneida and lasting three days and nights, and the burial followed by a Tenth-Day Feast during which the possessions of the deceased were distributed to kin and friends. These activities centered around the church and neighborhood instead of the clans, as in former times.

The Oneidas brought with them from New York a political system, which was an adumbrated version of its eighteenth-century form. Factionalism, which can be traced back at least as far as the mideighteenth century, led to confusion in leadership roles with a plethora of chiefs representing a number of factions vying for power. The movement to Wisconsin did not eliminate factional dispute, but it did remove one of its more serious causes—the issue of emigration. As representatives of the three factions arrived in Wisconsin—the First and Second Christian parties and the Orchard Party—their leaders took a place in the political structure, basing their legitimacy on chiefly prerogatives attained in New York. The result was a political system consisting of 12 hereditary chiefs and a variable number of Pinetree chiefs. In traditional Oneida political structure, the position of Pinetree chief was held by an individual who had achieved that status on the basis of his leadership and oratorical abilities.

In the early days of the settlement, recognition of an individual's ability as a political leader brought prestige. Most of the early leaders, such as Elijah Skenandoah (see illustration on p. 101), Daniel Bread, and Jacob Cornelius, had no claims to hereditary rights. They were leaders of political groups and considered Pinetree chiefs. Along with this, it was necessary that an individual be a "good Christian" and a church leader. He was expected to be temperate and generous in his behavior, giving to the needy as the occasion demanded.

By the 1860s, a number of changes had occurred. First, the prestige garnered by giving surplus to support the needy was replaced by the "development of attitudes favoring accumulation and of an organization oriented to the production of a surplus for market exchange."[23] Second, some families were recognized as having "hereditary" claims to chieftaincy that assured access to political power. These families enjoyed high status in the community, and because of their positions as religious and civil leaders, they could determine social values and enforce them. They placed a strong emphasis on education, hard work, sobriety, and family responsibility. Without the presence of wide wealth differentials, these factors became the criteria for determining social position.

The council, as it developed prior to 1871, had two classes of chiefs, a head chief and the "big men." Decisions required the concurrence of the big men, and although unanimity was not required, in practice action was assured only if the agreement represented the consensus of all councillors. The system brought from New York was modified in Wisconsin by the merging of hereditary chiefs and Pinetree chiefs, who became the big men. The chiefs were appointed by clan mothers, whose position descended along the male line from father to eldest daughter, but the title was more honorific than politically effective. For a while the system served to maintain clan affiliations, since the claims to chiefly rights were supposedly traceable to the pre-emigration period. When the elected council was instituted in the 1870s, this function of clan identity disappeared, as previously described, and clanship became important mainly in terms of curing, or medicine, societies.

The hereditary council exercised considerable power over affairs on the reservation. They acted as a court, trying cases and meting out punishment. In one case, "Peter G. was hanged in 1842. He murdered three of his children with a two foot blade or knife on February 2. He was asked why he killed his children, he said their mother is never home and they have suffered much, by killing them they would go to heaven and suffer no more. He was tried by Indian Court by chiefs and convicted to be hanged on February 18. . . ."[24] In other cases punishment involved banishment:

Daniel P. was killed, he was stabbed several times by Thomas D. It took place at night December 22, 1846. He had a trial before the Oneida, Chiefs of Oneida Nation of Green Bay. He found guilty. He was ordered to leave the Oneida Reservation and never come back, to Duck Creek, Green Bay. He lost his rights to land and everything, he left at night for Canada West. This is what happened to T. D.[25]

The criminal jurisdiction of the hereditary council was limited to the reservation. In one case, an Oneida killed another Oneida near Green Bay and was tried, convicted, and sentenced to prison by the territorial court.[26]

Oneida lands were held in common, which necessitated rules regarding their use. The hereditary council granted permits to cut wood, settled boundary disputes, and determined the citizenship of individuals. The last was a particularly vexing problem because of an influx of Oneidas, called the Woodman Party, from New York and Canada, who were considered homeless. Citizenship at this time depended upon being a member of one of the three major groups that had arrived prior to the 1838 land settlement.[27] A long and sometimes acrimonious debate ensued over the status of this group: whether they could live on the reservation farmland or even cut wood.[28] Finally, in 1887, this issue was resolved by the adoption of the 200 "homeless" Oneidas into the tribe.[29]

The tribe was also troubled by dissatisfied members who sought to sell their rights to reside on the reservation and to leave for lands further west. In 1838, shortly after the completion of the Treaty of Buffalo Creek, a group of Wisconsin Oneidas, calling themselves the Missouri Emigrating Party, claimed that the Oneida signatories did not represent the tribe, that the moneys allocated in the agreement were applied to the wrong parties, and that they wished to exchange their allocation of 100 acres per person in Wisconsin for 320 acres per person west of the Missouri. They gave as their reason that they wished to be "out of the reach of the White Settlement; and those malign influences which overcome and overreach the half civilized Indian relative to their property and Moral habits."[30] A total of 196 persons signed the petition. In response, Commissioner of Indian Affairs Crawford authorized the negotiation of a treaty permitting individuals to surrender 100 acres of their land deemed to be communal by the tribal government. This treaty was not ratified by the Senate, nor did any of the group emigrate. However, the case does illustrate the continued friction within the Oneida community as well as the willingness of the federal government to negotiate with any party offering to move. As the federal land agent noted in his report, the government stood to gain because "about thirty thousand acres of good land will be disencumbered of its Indian title and may be brought into market."[31]

Underlying the Missouri party's efforts was the important issue of representation on the tribal council. As described, early councils reflected the relative power and size of groups. The deaths of the early leaders, the erosion of power of subsequent hereditary chiefs, and the increased pressure from younger men for participation in the political process, led to the introduction in 1871 of an elective system modeled after local town governments. It is not clear whether this first attempt succeeded, but in 1880 a new elective system consisting of one sachem and six councillors was established.[32] This structure continued until the reservation was converted into townships by the second decade of the twentieth century.

Besides managing the affairs of the reservation, the council carried on negotiations with the federal government involving a wide range of activities. One critical problem was the failure of the federal government to pay the Oneidas the annuity due them under the Treaty of Canandaigua (1794). The council was able to recover a sum of $4,260 and get the annuity restored.[33] To suppress the illegal liquor trade, the council negotiated with the federal and local governments, getting a number of laws passed, although their enforcement was often less than vigorous. Milo Quaife gives the following example of the local public's attitude toward the efforts of the Oneidas:

The proximity of the Oneidas to De Pere and Green Bay and the hostile attitude of the local courts made it impossible to prevent the debauching of these Indians by crooked liquor dealers. As illustrative of the attitude of the courts, Judge Miller pointedly complained that cases against illicit liquor dealers were brought before him, and lamented the expense and inconvenience caused the accused thereby. In one case the district attorney had presented his proofs in such a convincing fashion that it seemed the jury could not avoid a verdict of guilty, when Judge Miller, in his charge, observed that the prosecution had not proved the defendants knew the men they sold to were Indians, and another verdict of acquittal was returned.[34]

In the management of their political affairs, the Oneidas took cognizance of two important external positions: the missionaries and the Indian agent. The relationship of the churches to the Oneida society is difficult to assess. Clearly ministers exerted influence in secular matters, but it is equally certain that the tribal leaders had an immense impact on religious affairs. Eleazer Williams, Episcopal minister during the migration to Wisconsin, goes so far as to say:

The Oneidas living as they do under the Patriarchal government, the civil and Ecclesiastical affairs of the tribe being entirely under the control of the chiefs and this is one of the greatest hindrances to the peace of the church and the progress of the pure religion in the tribe. The affairs of the church have often been made by the chiefs an engine for political purposes, to serve their own ends. The choice and the disposition of missionaries stationed among them, as in the hands of a small number.[35]

Since Williams had been removed as minister at the behest of these same chiefs, it is difficult to argue that he overstates his case.

The ministers, for their part, brought pressure to bear upon institutions such as marriage, which resulted in the further weakening of the clan system. The medicine societies were discouraged, while education and adjustment to white values were encouraged. The churches took over the formal teaching of Oneida children, operating the reservation schools throughout most of the century. After the establishment of a government school, the churches continued to exert influence through the Indian agent.[36] Their interest in education was spawned by the need to communicate church doctrine, which was sorely inhibited by the tribal members' continued use of the Oneida language. One Episcopal priest, Burleson, described the problems that arose for him as a result of his language problem:

Only two-thirds of the people can understand and speak the English language. As I cannot speak the Oneida tongue, I am cut off from one-third, except as I call an interpreter to my aid. . . . As one-third of the people cannot speak English, they must be held for the church through their own tongue. On Sundays, and at all services, an interpreter stands beside me. The lessons, epistles, and gospel and sermon are sung. The interpreting consumes much time. A sermon which would require twenty minutes in English, will require forty minutes more for interpreting.[37]

The church emphasis on the use of English and the federal system of boarding schools that punished children who spoke Oneida gave parents strong reasons for not teaching Oneida to their children. They were convinced by church and government that it was somehow inferior as a vehicle of expression, and they had learned from hard experience that it would result in children receiving the harsh treatment that some adults had endured. The policies and attitudes of church and federal government resulted in a decline of Oneida language skills among children.

The role of the missionary extended beyond the boundaries of the reservation. He was the Oneidas' representative to the church and their contact with the larger sector of white society through the functioning of various missionary societies. The missionary regularly appealed for help, submitted progress reports, and acknowledged the gifts he received. The following is typical of this role. Father E. A. Goodnough, the Episcopal minister, in acknowledging the receipt of $37 worth of seed, said: "This gift is a great blessing to the Indians at this time, because they are so hard pressed for means owing to the fact that they have been so long out of employment."[38] Oneidas regulated their own internal religious affairs, which were intertwined with civil matters. Ministers advised the tribal council and, in turn, accepted direction and advice from it.

The relationship of the agent to the tribe was of a different order. While the council exercised considerable authority over internal matters, the influence of the agent was increasingly felt, particularly after 1871, when an elected council replaced the hereditary one. Joseph Powless' diary of 1867, referring to a dispute over a payment for logs, illustrates the growing importance of the agent: "He was given two weeks starting February 15, 1867 to March 1867 to settle for the logs, if not the Indian Agent will settle the log question."[39]

During this period there were frequent changes in agents, complicating the relationship between the Oneidas and the federal government. In general, the agents were critical of the tribal system of holding the land in common and the maintenance of hereditary chiefs, attributing to these practices a lack of agricultural development and, worse, a breakdown of governmental control. In 1858 the agent reported: "There seems to be little or no parental or preventative authority in the chiefs. They have lost their influences of domestic government. . . . Cattle are stolen, driven off, and sold to the whites; and crimes of various kinds, and even murders, are committed."[40] Although the policies of the agents were strenuously opposed by a majority of the tribe, they were nonetheless put into effect, resulting in major changes in traditional Oneida social organization. Agents commonly portrayed the tribal government as impotent, despite the evidence to the contrary.

Indian agents were agents for the United States and not for the tribe, and consequently there existed an adversarial system, with the council negotiating with the federal government through the agent, often over rules promulgated by the agent in the name of the government. On various occasions the Oneida chiefs applied to the agent for assistance or to rectify wrongs. For example, during the 1830s the Oneidas appealed to Agent George Boyd for food supplies for the tribe and their missionary in order to survive the winter and on at least one occasion requested assistance in suppressing the sale of liquor on the reservation.[41]

Despite the efforts of the federal Indian agents to denigrate tribal government in the half century between the Treaty of Buffalo Creek (1838) and the Dawes General Allotment Act (1887), the Wisconsin Oneidas steadfastly maintained their independence and control over their affairs. To be sure, adjustments in their social and political organization occurred (as they did in non-Indian society), but the essential elements of tribal life and sovereignty remained uncompromised. By 1880 the tribe had altered some of its institutions in order to preserve its autonomy, without doing violence to its sense of itself as a sovereign people. There was occurring a shift to market agriculture, although most of the tribal land was still untouched by the plow. As late as 1887, the Oneidas had under cultivation approximately 2,700 acres out of 65,000, and this with a population of 1,732.[42] The kinship system was in transition, with the nuclear family growing in importance, but with the extended family remaining the important kin unit. Protestant churches flourished but were dominated by tribal members and subtly influenced by Iroquois traditions. The Oneida language and values remained an important part of the culture, despite the efforts of Indian agents and ministers to eliminate them. The shift to an elected council was more apparent than real because there was no change in the underlying dynamics of the society. The divisions along religious and kin lines and by neighborhoods resulted in little change in the distribution of power.

By the third quarter of the century the state of Wisconsin had undergone enormous changes. Much of the forest had been clear-cut and replaced with expanses of fields, made possible by the technological revolution in agricuture and transportation following the Civil War. Surrounded on all sides by towns and farms filled with people who had little knowledge and less appreciation of the Oneidas, the reservation was an inviting target for exploitation. The Oneidas over the century had been forced to adjust to myriad changes and had done so with relative success. But in 1887 they faced a societal disaster of others' making. The Oneida tribe in Wisconsin, along with all tribes west of the Mississippi River were to see their insularity destroyed by a combination of the well-meaning and the greedy. In that year Congress passed and President Cleveland signed the Dawes General Allotment Act, and within two decades most of the tribe's land was gone. The Oneidas faced yet another succession of adjustments.

Notes

1.   Henry Coleman, "Recollections of Oneida Indians, 1840–1845." In *Proceedings of the State Historical Society of Wisconsin at Its Fifty-Ninth Annual Meeting* (Madison: SHSW, 1912), pp. 152–159.

2.   United States Department of the Interior, *Annual Report of the Commissioner of Indian Affairs for 1887* (Washington, D.C., 1887), appendices.

3.   Colman, "Recollections of Oneida Indians."

4.   Julia Keen Bloomfield, *The Oneidas,* 2d ed. (New York: Alden Bros., 1907), p. 242.

5.   Harry Basehart, "Historical Changes in the Kinship System of the Oneida Indians," unpublished Ph.D. dissertation, Harvard University, 1952, p. 130.

6.   Bloomfield, *The Oneidas,* p. 265.

7.   Ibid., p. 273.

8.   Joseph Powless Diary (1862), SHSW, Madison.

9.   Bloomfield, *The Oneidas,* p. 273.

10.   Basehart, "Historical Changes," p. 145.

11.   Colman, "Recollections of Oneida Indians," p. 156.

12.   Basehart, "Historical Changes," p. 150.

13.   Ibid., p. 151.

14.   Ibid., p. 157.

15.   Ibid., p. 152.

16.   Ibid.

17.   Ibid., pp. 159–160.

18.   Alfred Cope, "Green Bay Diary [1849]," *Wisconsin Magazine of History* 50 (1967): 141–142.

19. Basehart, "Historical Changes," p. 158.
20. Cope, "Green Bay Diary [1849]," p. 142.
21. Robert Ritzenthaler Fieldnotes [1939?], Milwaukee Public Museum.
22. Bloomfield, *The Oneidas,* p. 271.
23. Basehart, "Historical Changes," p. 192.
24. Joseph Powless Diary (1866), p. 8, SHSW.
25. Ibid. (1862–1864), p. 12.
26. Ibid., p. 26.
27. *Green Bay Advocate,* July 20, 1871, p. 3.
28. John Archiquette Diary (1870–1874), trans. Oscar Archiquette, SHSW.
29. *Annual Report of the Commissioner of Indian Affairs for 1887,* p. 228.
30. Petition to the President by the Oneida Indians, Oct. 23, 1838, in John P. Bloom, ed., *Territorial Papers of the United States: Wisconsin Territory* (Washington, D.C.: National Archives, 1969), 27: 1078–1087.
31. Ransom Gillet to Commissioner Crawford, Jan. 14, 1839, ibid., 27: 1146–1147.
32. Minutes of the Oneida Board of Sachems and Councillors, 1892, Records of the Oneida Nation of Indians of Wisconsin, Oneida, Wisconsin.
33. U.S. Congress, House, Doc. 18, 31st Congress, 2d sess., Jan. 29, 1851.
34. Milo M. Quaife, "The Panic of 1862 in Wisconsin," *Wisconsin Magazine of History* 4 (1920–1921): 170.
35. Eleazer Williams Journal (1832), Neville Museum, Green Bay, Wis.
36. Talbot Rogers, ed., *The Works of the Rt. Rev. Charles E. Grafton . . .* (New York: Longmans, Green and Co., 1914), p. 163.
37. J. N. Davidson, *The Diocese of Fond du Lac* (Fond du Lac, Wis.: Episcopal Church, 1891), p. 2.
38. Episcopal Church, *Wisconsin Calendar* [Diocese of Fond du Lac] (1880), p. 2.
39. Joseph Powless Diary (1867), SHSW.
40. *Annual Report of the Commissioner of Indian Affairs for 1858,* p. 382.
41. George Boyd Journal [1830–1840], SHSW.
42. *Annual Report of the Commissioner of Indian Affairs for 1887,* pp. 362, 378.

5 *Arlinda Locklear*

The Buffalo Creek Treaty of 1838 and Its Legal Implications for Oneida Indian Land Claims

The Oneida Nation of Indians of Wisconsin is one of three modern-day Oneida governments that are asserting a claim to title for their aboriginal homeland in Madison and Oneida counties in central New York State. The Oneida Nation plaintiffs claim title to approximately 250,000 acres. In these lawsuits the Oneidas assert that (1) they occupied that landbase since time immemorial; (2) their title to this territory was confirmed to them in a series of three federal treaties—the Treaty of Fort Stanwix (1784), the Treaty of Canandaigua (1794), and the separate Oneida Treaty of 1794; and (3) they were deprived of that territory by illegal acts of the state of New York.[1] Basically the state concluded approximately 25 separate actions (see Laurence Hauptman, chapter 2, in part 1, and James Folts, chapter 9, in part 3) between 1795 and 1846, whereby the state now claims it legally acquired possession of the Oneida territory. The Oneidas assert in these lawsuits that those transactions were not legal, that they did not have the consent or approval of the federal government, and as such they are void by virtue of the federal Indian Trade and Intercourse Acts and federal common law principles with regard to protection of tribal lands. The first of these suits was filed in 1970, the second in 1974, and they have already involved much litigation.[2] The general issue at the heart of this case—whether or not a tribe such as the Oneida can be dispossessed of its land by a state without the consent of the federal government—has now been considered by the United States Supreme Court twice. In both cases, the Court held that the basic principles relied on by the Oneidas are sound federal law principles that do apply, and those principles indicate that the Oneida *still* have title to that territory.

The folks who are now in possession of these Indian lands raised a number of defenses in an effort to try to negate the Oneida claim. One defense is that the Treaty of Buffalo Creek of 1838 precluded the Oneidas from legal redress. Besides the loss of the Senecas' Buffalo Creek Reservation, the center of Iroquois traditional life after the American Revolution, this treaty led to the removal of many Indians, including Oneidas, from the state. Under this fraudulent treaty, consummated with alcohol and bribery and never properly ratified by the United States Senate, the Indians "accepted" a 1,824,000-acre Kansas reservation that had been set aside for all of the Six Nations as well as for the Stockbridge-Munsees, which they had to occupy within five years or forfeit title. For a total of 102,069 acres that the Senecas were to cede in New York, the Indians were to receive $202,000, $100,000 of which was to be invested in safe stocks by the president of the United States; the income earned was to be returned to the Indians. The United States was also to provide a modest sum to facilitate removal, establish schools, and purchase farm equipment and livestock for the Indians' use. Under Article 1 of the Treaty of Buffalo Creek, the "New York Indians" also agreed to "cede and relinquish to the United States all their right, title and interest to the lands secured to them at Green Bay by the Menominee Treaty of 1831, excepting the following tract, on which a part of the New York Indians now reside." Article 13 of the Treaty of Buffalo Creek dealt with the Oneidas, specifically the First Christian and Orchard parties:[3]

The United States will pay the sum of four thousand dollars, to be paid to Baptista [*sic*] Powlis, and the chiefs of the first Christian party residing at Oneida, and the sum of two thousand dollars shall be paid to William Day, and the chiefs of the Orchard party residing there, for expenses incurred and services rendered in securing the Green Bay country, and the settlement of a portion thereof; and they hereby agree to remove to their new homes in the Indian territory, as soon as they can make satisfactory arrangements with the Governor of the State of New York for the purchase of their lands at Oneida.

Less than three weeks later, the Oneidas of the First Christian and Orchard parties signed a separate amended treaty with the federal government in Washington, D.C. In it, the federal government received from the Oneidas "all their title and interest in the land set apart for them in the 1st article of the treaty with the Menominees of February 8th, 1831, and the second article of the treaty with the same tribe of October 27, 1832." Article 2 of the amended treaty of 1838 "reserved to the said [Oneida] Indians to be held as other Indian lands are held a tract of land containing one hundred acres, for each individual, and the lines of which shall be so run as to include all their settlements and improvements in the vicinity of Green Bay."[4]

Treaties are not merely quaint documents of historic interest.[5] Indian treaties, just like all treaties, are contracts between governments, and, as such, they represent a bargain between those two governments on matters of importance to them. As in every contract the two parties exchange commitments or obligations with each other on matters that concern them. Those commitments and obligations reflected in the terms of the contract are legally enforceable. Just like foreign treaties, Indian treaties are legally enforceable documents between the two contracting parties. The United States and Indian tribes contracted with each other on a number of subjects of importance to them: war and peace, commercial relations, extradition, fixing of boundaries, land claims, and so on. Under the law Indian treaties have really the same force and effect that treaties with foreign nations do. Just like foreign treaties, Indian treaties were negotiated under the Constitution by the authority of the president of the United States. Just like foreign treaties, Indian treaties were ratified by two-thirds of the Senate. Just like foreign treaties, Indian treaties fall within the provisions of the Supremacy Clause of the Constitution, which has the effect of making Indian treaties paramount to and superior to any conflicting state laws. Just like foreign treaties, Indian treaties can be abrogated or voided by the Congress. Congress does have the same authority with respect to Indian treaties that it has with foreign treaties: the authority to change the terms unilaterally or to decide not to abide by commitments made in treaties.

Because of the so-called trust responsibility between the United States and Indian tribes, the Supreme Court has formulated a number of special rules that apply to the provisions of Indian treaties. The United States Supreme Court has indicated that where the terms of an Indian treaty are ambiguous, that is, subject to one or more interpretations, the treaty will be interpreted in a way that is most favorable to the Indian tribe involved, which is most likely to reflect that Indian tribe's understanding of its bargain. This is particularly important for this discussion. Even though Congress has the power to abrogate or void an Indian treaty, a federal court will find that the Congress has done so only if the Congress has expressed its intention to do so in plain and unambiguous language. In other words, Congress cannot indirectly or by implication void the terms of an Indian treaty.

In 1871 the Congress decided to end treaty-making between the United States and Indian tribes. Up to that time, as the Constitution provides, the treaties were negotiated and signed by the president or his representative and ratified by a two-thirds vote of the Senate. This had the effect of cutting the House of Representatives out of the formulation of federal Indian policy. Until 1871, Indian treaties were the major tool for the formulation of Indian policy, and the Constitution's specification of the Senate's role in the ratification of treaties meant that, as a practical matter, that the House of Representatives played virtually no role in the formulation of federal Indian policy prior to this time. In the 1871 statute, Congress provided that it would no longer conduct business with Indian tribes through the form of federal treaties. The United States Supreme Court has construed this statute to mean that Congress did not intend to change its basic relationship with Indian tribes; it meant only to change the method by which it handled its relations with Indian tribes so that, from then onward, the House of Representatives would have as much influence in the formulation of Indian policy as the United States Senate had. The statute expressly provided that none of the Indian treaties negotiated and ratified up to that point was to be construed as voided or modified by the statute. In other words, even though treaty-making ended in 1871, treaties concluded and ratified up to that point continued to have the same effect in law that they had before that time. This means that unless a treaty negotiated before 1871 was expressly modified by a later act of Congress or voided by the Congress, it is still a legally enforceable document. Because Indian treaties are legally enforceable and because they are a primary source of federal Indian law, the nearly 400 Indian treaties are often the focus of disputes between tribes, with the United States, and sometimes with third parties.[6]

The Treaty of Buffalo Creek of 1838 provided for an exchange of land involving Wisconsin Territory and Kansas Territory. With the exception of some special provisions made for Seneca reservations in New York, there is no express language in the Treaty of Buffalo Creek that involved Oneida Territory in New York State. Nonetheless, some of the defendants in the Oneida land claims cases have asserted that the Treaty of Buffalo Creek was a defense. Some have argued that this treaty represented a commitment by the signing tribes, including the Oneidas, to abandon or relinquish all the claims to their New York territory in exchange for the territory promised in Kansas. It also has been argued that the United States Senate ratification of the 1838 Treaty of Buffalo Creek, albeit without two-thirds approval, gave it the legal standing necessary under the federal Trade and Intercourse Acts and confirmed earlier New York State transactions with the Oneidas.

Even though the Treaty of Buffalo Creek is a legally enforceable document, since most of its provisions were formally ratified by the so-called "Compromise" Treaty of Buffalo Creak in 1842, I disagree with those who argue that it has the particular effect of limiting Oneida Indian land claims. I have a number of reasons for disagreeing: First, there is nothing in the language of the treaty itself that refers explicitly to an exchange of claims in New York State for lands in Kansas. In the absence of an explicit extinguishment of the Oneida claim in New York State, the treaty cannot have that legal effect. The United States Supreme Court has ruled in other cases that if a tribe's claim is going to be extinguished because of the federal trust responsibility between the United States and tribes, it can be done only by an explicit act of Congress. In the Treaty of Buffalo Creek, we do not have an explicit statement by Congress extinguishing the Oneida claim in New York State.

Second, the Treaty of Buffalo Creek was negotiated by the president under an 1830 statute, the Indian Removal Act, which set down limitations that must apply to the interpretation of the treaty. The 1830 statute authorized the president to exchange existing territory of an Indian tribe for territory located farther west. The statute expressly provided, however, that it was not to be construed as abrogating or voiding the terms of any Indian treaty.[7]

Third is the existence of the Treaty of Canandaigua of 1794. The Treaty of Buffalo Creek of 1838 does not explicitly refer to or abrogate the Treaty of Canandaigua, by which the United States confirmed title to the Oneida Territory in New York. The Treaty of Canandaigua gives the Oneida claim added protection, since the United States Supreme Court has held that Indian treaties cannot be abrogated or voided without an express act of Congress. Thus, the Treaty of Buffalo Creek cannot be read as extinguishing Oneida claims.

What this shows us is that Indian treaties are not merely dry documents of historic interest. They are documents—legal documents—that represent and contain rights and obligations of the parties involved.

Notes

1. For the Treaty of Canandaigua (1794) and the Oneida Treaty of 1794, see Charles J. Kappler, *Indian Treaties, 1778–1883* (New York: Interland, 1972), pp. 34–37, 37–39. For the history of the Oneida Indian land claims, see Laurence M. Hauptman, *The Iroquois Struggle for Survival: World War II to Red Power* (Syracuse, N.Y.: Syracuse University Press, 1986), chapter 10; George C. Shattuck, *The Oneida Indian Land Claims: A Legal History* (Syracuse, N.Y.: Syracuse University Press, 1991); and Arlinda Locklear, "The Oneida Land Claims: A Legal Overview," in Christopher Vecsey and William A. Starna, eds., *Iroquois Land Claims* (Syracuse, N.Y.: Syracuse University Press, 1988), pp. 141–154.

2. The two Oneida cases are: 414 U.S. 661 (1974), and 470 U.S. 226 (1985).

3. Kappler, *Indian Treaties,* pp. 502–512. For the frauds under the Treaty of Buffalo Creek (1838), see Laurence M. Hauptman, "Four Eastern New Yorkers and Seneca Lands: A Study in Treaty-Making," *Hudson Valley Regional Review* 13 (Mar. 1996): 1–19; Laurence Hauptman, *Tribes and Tribulations: Misconceptions about American Indians and Their Histories* (Albuquerque, N.M.: University of New Mexico Press, 1995), chapter 4; and Henry S. Manley, "Buying Buffalo from the Indians," *New York History* 28 (July 1947): 313–329.

4. Kappler, *Indian Treaties,* pp. 517–518.

5. For a different perspective on American Indian treaties, see Francis Paul Prucha, *American Indian Treaties: The History of a Political Anomaly* (Berkeley: University of California Press, 1994), especially his treatment of the Treaty of Buffalo Creek, pp. 202–207.

6. *U.S. Statutes at Large* (May 28, 1830), 4: 411–412.

7. Ibid. (Mar. 3, 1871), 16: 566.

Receipt from twenty-two Oneida warriors for blankets and Indian clothing distributed by the state of New York for their services rendered on the Patriot side during the American Revolution. Fort Schuyler, June 8, 1792. (Courtesy of the New York State Library)

Good Peter—Chief of the Oneida Indians, by John Trumbull (Courtesy of the Yale University Art Gallery, Trumbull Collection)

Skenandoah's tombstone at Hamilton College, Clinton, New York (Courtesy of Hamilton College)

Samuel Kirkland (Courtesy of Hamilton College)

Philip Schuyler (Courtesy of the New York State Library)

Eleazer Williams as a young man, by George Catlin (Courtesy of the State Historical Society of Wisconsin, WHi (X28)1078)

Eleazer Williams (Courtesy of the Neville Public Museum of Brown County, Green Bay, Wisconsin)

Eleazer Williams' Mohawk prayerbook (Courtesy of the Neville Public Museum of Brown County, Green Bay, Wisconsin)

John C. Calhoun (Courtesy of the Library of Congress)

Daniel Bread, by Samuel M. Brookes (Courtesy of the State Historical Society of Wisconsin, WHi (X3)43526)

Letter from Daniel Bread, Henry Powlis, and John Antony to Silas Wright, New York State comptroller, August 16, 1830, Green Bay, Wisconsin (Courtesy of the New York State Library)

Elijah Skenandoah, from Thomas H. Ryan, editor-in-chief, *History of Outagamie County, Wisconsin, being a general survey . . . including a history of the cities, towns and villages. . . .* (Chicago: Goodspeed Historical Association, 1911) (Courtesy of the State Historical Society of Wisconsin, WHi (X3)20956)

PART II
ONEIDA COMMUNITY PERSPECTIVES OF ONEIDA INDIAN HISTORY

Introduction

Part 2 of the book focuses on Oneida community members' perspectives of their history. It is divided into two chapters. The first, chapter 6, is composed of stories of Oneida life and customs collected by Oneida Indians employed by the Work Projects Administration (WPA) from 1938 to 1941. Ten of these WPA stories are included. Today, the Oneida Nation of Indians employs these many stories to teach children in their own school system the Oneida language and the rich traditions of their people. In chapter 7, contemporary Oneidas write their own view of their history, starting with the Oneida time of troubles after the American Revolution and ending with Oneida existence in midnineteenth-century Wisconsin, Ontario, and New York.

The Oneida Language and Folklore Project, 1938–1941, which was conceived of by Morris Swadesh, administered by Floyd G. Lounsbury, and funded by the WPA as the Federal Writers' Project, was a unique undertaking. The project resulted in three major contributions. Most important, there is the legacy of several thousand pages of text, written in Oneida with English translations. Beyond their obvious value as folklore, the collected stories provide an insight into Oneida values, adjustments, and feelings regarding the 100 years of trauma since their emigration from New York. The project's storybooks, virtually untapped by ethnohistorians, are one of the better all-Indian archival repositories in the United States describing Indian life of the nineteenth and early twentieth centuries.

The subjects range from lists of place names to aspects of Oneida culture, including Iroquois animal symbolism, herbalism, games, proper names, and recipes; ghost and trickster stories; Indian school experiences; major turning points in Oneida history such as the American Revolution and the Oneida removal and resettlement in Wisconsin and the Kansas claim; and reactions to contemporary events including the New Deal. Taken together, they are a chronicle of an Indian nation's history and the failure of successive United States government Indian policies. Elders recalled special recipes for many different varieties of Iroquois corn soup, cracked dried corn, pumpkins, and Indian hominy. Others told of Indian salves that are good for sore throats, rheumatism, and sprains. Many of the stories are devoted to moral lessons discouraging Indian laziness, blind obedience, and greed, and promoting family responsibilities to the elderly. This Oneida project was also quite different from others of the WPA Federal Writers' Project. Grant Foreman's WPA Indian-Pioneer History of Oklahoma had whites interviewing Indians; another project involved whites interviewing African Americans in the accumulation of the famous WPA ex-slave narratives. At Oneida, Wisconsin, Indians listened to other Oneidas while learning to write their language.

A second result of this project, one of a more functional nature from the standpoint of the community, is the compilation of an Oneida hymnal. Ever since the mideighteenth century, the Oneidas had been writing and singing Christian hymns, sometimes translating English verse into Oneida, other times writing new verse for English melodies, and occasionally writing both words and music. Over time, they had developed a distinctive style of singing and had organized a number of choirs. The project brought together more than a hundred of these hymns. This revised hymnal, which is still used by the famous Oneida Singers today, is viewed by the Oneidas themselves as a major accomplishment of the project.

Third, the project also influenced the direction of Iroquois scholarship. A vast body of linguistic data on an Iroquoian language was accumulated for the first time. Although Lounsbury was later to change the orthography, his research and teaching virtually founded the contemporary interest in Iroquoian linguistics. The published hymnal and morphology are in themselves worthy monuments to the project, but beyond this, Lounsbury's example and approach dramatically changed the direction of Iroquois studies.

In assessing the significance of the Oneida Language and Folklore Project, it is important to note that the experiment was not designed to produce an overnight turnaround in the language at Oneida, Wisconsin. Even by 1939, a large percentage of Oneidas had already lost their language. With the coming of war and in the postwar climate that followed, teaching Indians their own language became out of step with American society's increasing emphasis on assimilation. Soon what had been accomplished, as was true in other WPA experiments, became a hazy memory. Even to the Oneidas, the preservation of language became less important than economic survival in the white man's world. The enthusiasm had to be recaptured, and the country had to be reawakened to the old social consciousness of the 1930s. This new awareness was to be rekindled and was to result in another attempt at language restoration at Oneida in the 1970s.[1]

Special thanks for the reprinting of these WPA stories should be given to Maria Hinton. Hinton, an Oneida elder and language teacher for more than 30 years, and many other Oneida first-language speakers including her brother, Amos Christjohn, and sister, Anna John, have been steadfastly devoted to perpetuating the use of the Oneida language and to the preservation of records, stories, and customs of Oneida ancestors. Hinton was awarded her B.A., cum laude, from the University of Wisconsin–Green Bay in 1979 at the age of 69. She was also awarded an honorary degree from Mt. Senario College. She has coauthored, with her brother, Amos, an Oneida-English dictionary, published in 1997. Hinton has also been granted lifetime certification as a native Oneida language teacher from the Wisconsin Language and Culture Board, one of three native-language speakers in Wisconsin to be so honored. She is a faith-keeper of the Turtle Clan in the Oneida Longhouse.

These WPA stories are a small part but a representative sample of her 1996 publication, *A Collection of Oneida Stories,* which are entirely her own translation and are here with her kind permission reproduced exactly as they appear in her edition. These stories are a moving tribute to the history of the Oneida people.

The vast body of stories collected can be categorized into 16 varieties: animal; animal-man; early history; ghost; holiday; how-to; joke; legend; lesson; marriage; medicine; names; personal history; recent history; religious; and witchcraft stories. Included below are five types: one animal-man; two early history; one how-to; one marriage; and five personal histories. The first five selections in chapter 6 clearly show the Oneidas' cultural continuity with their original New York homeland. Melissa Cornelius tells of the traditional use of wampum and its importance to the Oneidas, to Indian law, and to the dispensing of justice. Jim Antone then describes the importance of the seasonal ceremonial cycle to the Oneidas as well as the evolution of the White Dog Sacrifice while they lived at Oneida Castle. Antone's selection is followed by Jonas Elm's "Corn Is Planted in the Spring," which is a how-to story, describing the Oneida traditional way of making Indian corn soup, a delicacy first noted by seventeenth-century Europeans visiting the Iroquois. Guy Elm and Oscar Archiquette, reminiscent of Alfred Cope's observations, then recount the importance of lacrosse, a game brought to Wisconsin in the early years of the Oneida settlement; how the Episcopal church team vied with its Methodist church rivals; and how a medicine man "inflicted" a body slam on an opposing team player, thus ending the contest. A story by Katie Cornelius follows, describing the traditional custom of arranged marriages that was practiced in New York and in the early days in Wisconsin.

The next series of five stories focuses on Oneida life and adaptation to the Wisconsin surroundings. According to Sarah Summers, her family left Oneida Castle for Wisconsin because they "didn't want to change their ways to a white man's way of living and his laws." After arriving by ship, her grandfather (Broken Spine) had to wade through forests and swamps and endure mosquitoes as well as crop failures before finally succeeding as a hunter, fisherman, farmer, and in the maritime trades on ships out of Green Bay. In "Crime Story," Elizabeth Huff describes an Oneida murder trial that resulted in a public hanging, an event similar to one that Alfred Cope wrote about in the 1840s. Of importance, Huff notes that the Oneida chiefs themselves, not Wisconsin or the federal government, tried and convicted the Oneida for murder, because "Oneida still had their own laws so the white people weren't able to punish him." In the next selection, Rachel Swamp shows how the Oneidas undertook all kinds of work once they arrived in Green Bay. They cut and sold wood, trapped and sold hides, and shelled corn brought to the port on Great Lakes ships. In "Driving Logs," Abrahms Archiquette recalls the days Oneidas worked as loggers on the river for the great Oshkosh lumber companies. In "Fish Story," Jessie Peters nostalgically reflects on olden times, before environmental pollution and damming, when the Oneidas would spend their entire evening in a family event, catching the plentiful trout at their Duck Creek reservation and cooking "sucker head soup" in open fires.

Chapter 7, the second section of part 2, begins with two essays by Amelia Cornelius, Oneida storyteller, genealogist, and former member of the Oneida tribal government. Cornelius tells the story of two famous Oneida brothers, Peter and Neddy Otsiquette and, with it, the origins of the family name "Archiquette" among the Wisconsin Oneidas today. She then describes the rampant factionalism that plagued Oneida society after the American Revolution, weakening the nation and making it more susceptible to removal pressures promoted by the federal and New York State governments, the Ogden Land Company, and the ambitious missionary Eleazer Williams.

Judy Cornelius, the former Oneida Nation librarian, then scrutinizes Eleazer Williams, adding information about his bizarre life. Although Eleazer Williams converted the Oneidas to the Episcopal faith, Cornelius shows that the development of Oneida Episcopal traditions owes much to others, such as Edward and Ellen Goodnough and Oneida chief Cornelius Hill. Loretta Metoxen, former vice chairman of the Oneida Nation of Indians of Wisconsin and current tribal historian in the Oneida Cultural Heritage Department, describes the process of Oneida settlement in Wisconsin in the early years, the negotiations with the Menominee Indians, the economic modes of Wisconsin Oneida existence, the pulls for allotment of tribal lands that followed the Buffalo Creek Treaty of 1838, and the continued insecurity caused by rapid white settlement surrounding Oneida and by Wisconsin statehood in 1848.

The subsequent three essays in chapter 7 were written by Oneidas representing other Oneida communities. Although none of the three directly focuses on Wisconsin, they have much to say about Oneida existence, what anthropologist Jack Campisi has called the Oneidas' common estate. Eileen Antone, band historian for the Oneida of the Thames, describes the Oneida diaspora to Canada from 1839 to 1845. Today the Oneidas' second largest community exists near London, Ontario, as a result of the same pressures that drove the ancestors of the Wisconsin Oneidas out of New York. Liz Obomsawin, screenwriter, educator, and graduate student in Oneida history, an Oneida representing the traditional government in New York State, then shows the impact of removal on the 210 Oneidas left behind in New York in the 1840s. Obomsawin also clearly brings out that, despite removal, there were continuing connections among the Oneida communities throughout the nineteenth century. Last, the late Richard Chrisjohn, an Oneida born in Canada but raised at Onondaga and the most famous Oneida artist of the twentieth century, describes a major legacy of Oneida removal to Wisconsin and Canada, the continuing Oneida quest for justice through their pursuit of land claims suits against the state of New York, rooted in their dispossession from 1785 to 1846.

Notes

1. Laurence M. Hauptman and Jack Campisi, "Talking Back: The Oneida Language and Folklore Project, 1938–1941," *Proceedings of the American Philosophical Society* 125 (Dec. 1981): 441–448.

Stories of the Oneida Language
and Folklore Project, 1938–1941

This chapter reproduces, exactly as they appear in the original, various stories
from Maria Hinton, *A Collection of Oneida Stories.*

ONEIDA SPELLING

Vowels:

Oneida has six vowel sounds. Unlike English each letter stands for one
and only one sound. Here are the letters used and the sounds they
represent.
  'a' has the sound of the 'a' in ah or father
  'e' has the sound of the 'e' in egg or eight
  'i' has the sound of the 'i' in ski or machine
  'o' has the sound of the 'o' in hope or low
The remaining two vowels are nasalized. That means they are pronounced
more through the nose than the usual English sounds. Roughly, then:
  'u' has the sound of the 'un' in tune
  'ʌ' has the sound of the 'on' in son

Consonants:

Most of the consonants have the same sounds as they usually do in
English. This is true for:
  h, l, n, w, and y
The letters 't', 'k', and 's' each have two pronunciations depending
on the other sounds near them.
  't' normally has the sound of the 't' in city, water or stove.
     Notice in those words 't' sounds more like 'd'. If a 'k',
     'h', or 's' follows then the 't' has the usual English sound
     as in top.
  'k' normally has a g-like sound as in skill but if a 't', 's',
     or 'h' follows, it wounds like the usual English 'k' as in
     kill.
  's' often has a sound halfway between the 's' in sea and the
     z-like sound of the 's' in was. When it comes between two
     vowels it always has the z-like sound and when it comes before
     or after 'h', then it has the sound of the 's' in sea.

Other symbols used in writing Oneida:

'ʔ'   is used to represent a special consonant sound (called a glottal stop) that English doesn't have. The sound is made by quickly stopping the flow of air in the throat, a kind of catch.

/   this symbol is written above a vowel to indicate the stressed syllable in a word.

·   this symbol is used after a vowel to indicate the vowel is lengthened or dragged out a bit. (Vowels marked with both the dot and the stress mark have a slightly falling tone.)

_   underlined sounds are whispered and not said aloud

This, then, is the Oneida alphabet used in this booklet.

   a, e, h, i, k, l, n, o, s, t, u, w, y, ʔ, ʌ

Some special combinations are:
   'tsy' or 'tsi' sound like the 'j' in jam or judge
   'tshy' or 'tshi' sound like the 'ch' in church
   'sy' sounds like the 'sh' in shoe or hush

Tsiʔ nu Nikahya·tú neʔn Lanukwehu·wé Laotiyantlʌhsla·kʌ́
Where it Was Written, The Oneida Laws

Asuhkʌ́ kʌ́·tho thahʌ·néwe neʔn Oʔslu·ni   lotiyantlʌhslayʌtáhkwe neʔn
Not yet there   arrived   the   white people they used to have laws the

Lʌnukwehu·we. Onikó·la   yakʌ?   kahya·tú tho kʌs   kati?   wahawʌnahno·tú
Oneidas.   Wampum they say writes there he used then to read from there

tsiʔ ka·yʌ́·   tyohʌtú nʌ náhte? wahali·wʌhte? tsiʔ nahte? nʌyawʌ́·ne to·kát
the one who heads (chief) what   he decided just   what would happen if

lutliyóhsle?   tat uni úhka?   sholihwateʔwáhtu.   Tho kʌs   yakʌ?
they are going to war or if   someone had committed a crime. That was they say

nú nahawʌnahno·tú   tsiʔ ni·yót tsiʔ ʌhuwahlewáhte̲?.   Tho kʌs
the place he would read just how that he should be punished. There used to be

yakʌ?   laháwe? ostaló·kwa neʔn onikó·la kuwanatúkhwa?. Tho   nu nikahya·tú
they say holding   beads   it was wampum they called it. There was written

neʔn laotiyantlʌ́hsla̲.
their laws.

Where It Was Written, The Oneida Laws

What I have to tell you refers to our laws that we had before the white people came over here. Wampum (oniko·la) is where it was written and only the head person (Chief) would read from the Wampum to them. If a man had committed a crime, he would decide what his punishment would be if there is a war, he will tell them what would happen. In his hand he holds these beads, where he reads from, this is called wampum (oniko·la) where their laws are written.

Told by Miss Melissa Corneluis to Ida Blackhawk (8-23-39)
Transcribed and Taped by Maria Hinton (3-11-81)

The Customs of The Oneida's

Tsi? nihotilihotʌ·hné ne?n Lʌnukwehu·wé Tkana?alóhale? tshithatinákele
The ways   of the Oneidas,   Oneida Castle they still lived,

wahatikhu·ní   kʌs wa?thutʌnuhwelá·tu.   Tsi? nikú kukwité·ne nale? yakáhe·we
they would have a   of Thanksgiving.   Every   spring   when it was time

tsi? nʌ   nihatitsi?khetu·níhe? khale? tsi? nihatiyʌthos   okhale? o·nʌ́
for them to make maple sugar and when they start planting and   now

ʌwatahyu·ní   awʌ́hihte?, khale? tsi? nʌ nikanʌstótha, khale? tsi? nʌ
they will start to ripen the strawberries, and now then corn will ripen and now

nihatiyʌthókwas. Ya?teyoké·tohte?   o·nʌ́ ohsla·sé o?yan   ni twana?túkhwa? tho
harvest time.   Most important one now is the New Year as we call it   about

úhte? nikaha·wín owískla nikaya?tó·tʌ é·lhal wa?kuwaya?tatsa?áte,
that   time,   white in color,   a   dog they burned the dog sacrifice,

thó niyolihotʌ·hné ot nahte?   Tahuwanuhwelá·tu.   Akwe·kú kʌ́s
was the custom to for giving   thanks to our Creator. Everyone was

wahuwatikwáhte? oskánhne ahutekhu·ní. Yah né· tehotináktohte? ahutkáttho
invited   together to the feast. Not allowed were they to see

ne?n ukweho·kú ot   nihatiyélha   tsi? wakuwályo ne?n é·lhal.
the people how it was prepared for the sacrifice this dog.

Oneida Castle

It was the custom of the Oneida's, while they still lived in Oneida Castle, New York. *Tsi? Tkanʌ́?alohale?*, to give thanks in the spring when they finished making Maple Sugar and Syrup. They gave thanks when it was planting time and when the strawberries became ripe, when the corn became ripe and most of all when the harvesting was done.

The biggest ceremony is when the New Year comes in, New Years or Dawn of Light, that is when the people celebrate and give Thanks by sacrificing the burning of the white dog. This was their custom of giving Thanks for whatever they were thankful for, when this Ceremony takes place everyone is invited. Together they would feast, but not everyone knew how this was prepared for the sacrifice. This custom is no longer practiced, now we use the white basket with burning of tobacco for sacrifice.

Told by Jim Antone to Tillie Baird (5-10-39)
Transcribed and Taped by Maria Hinton (6-6-92)

O·nʌste? Kukwite·ne Latiyʌthos
Corn is Planted in the Spring

Wa?akwayʌtho o·nʌste? kukwité·ne thó né· o·nʌ́ wa?akwa·yá·ke? kanʌná·ke
We planted   Corn   In the spring then now we cut it   In the fall

thó né· o·nʌ́ wa?akwa·kéhlụ·   Thó né· o·nʌ́ wa?akwastáthahte? o·nʌ́ste? okhale?
then   now we husked the corn. Then now   we dried it   the corn and

wa?akwatlʌ·nú·ni   kanyó o·nʌ́ wa?akwatlʌ·nú·ni   wa?akwanʌstalú·ko kʌs tát
we made corn soup and when   we make the corn soup   we shelled corn   ust about

kayé nikatsé·take o·nʌ́ste? thó né· o·nʌ́ ʌyena?tsyá·lʌ,   otsistá·ke yutákwʌ ohká·lạ?.
four quarts of   corn   then   now put the kettle on, use ashes taken from fire.

Corn is Planted In the Spring

We planted corn in the spring. Then we cut it in the fall and husked the corn.
Then we dried the corn and made corn soup. To make corn soup we would shell just
about four quarts of corn. Then we put the kettle on. We would use ashes taken
from the fire. Then you mix it with the corn in the kettle. Then, let it boil about
four hours. Take the kettle off the stove and wash the corn. Wash the corn again
and let it boil again. Let it boil again until all the ashes are washed out. Now you
start your soup. You put your meat and salt in. Boil your soup again until it is
done. Put your kettle of beans on until they are done. Put the beans into the soup,
Now eat, my isn't it good?

Told by Jonas Elm to Morris Swadish (1939)
Transcribed by Maria Hinton (1-24-80)

Tehutsi?kwa·eks Tewa?a latụ
Playing Ball Lacrosse

Wahu·níse? tehutsi?kwá·eks kʌ́s ne?n tewa?a·látu   kʌ́h nu ne?n
Long ago   they played ball used to this game of lacrosse   here was

Lʌnukwehú·we. Thó ne· tehati·yʌ́he?,   ne?n tsi? ok nahte?shúha ʌhatiye·ná·
Oneida men.   At that time, they played for all kinds of things they will get,

tsi? ka·yʌ́· ʌhutkwe·ni. Né· kʌ́s kʌ na?tehatiyélha? ne?n, kʌh nukwáti latinákele?
whichever side would win. They used to take turns   those at this end lived

Talu·kowanha·kạ́. okhna? tsi? ka·yʌ́· ʌtyʌnukwá thatinákele? Kanatakuha·ká né·
Episcopalians   and   the ones   west of here lived the Methodist   as

luwatina?túkhwa?, kanyó ná·le tehutshikwa?ékẹ. Lonukwé·tayʌ? kʌ́s
they were called, when again they play ball.   One of their members used to,

yakʌʔ,   shakonukwaʔtsláhohs   kanyó kʌs kaló tsiʔ niyo·lé
they say, would give a rub-down of medicine when it was just shortly before

ʌthutáshsawʌʔ.   Kwah kís,   yakʌʔ,   lotahséhtu isiʔ niyo·lé
they would start.   It used to be, they say, he was hiding a short distance away,

neʔn onuhkwaʔtkó· nʌ lotnaʔkwa·tú   kwah tsiʔ nikú yo·tú·u kwah kís
this medicine man during his false face, try as hard as he could used to be,

yákʌʔ   tsiʔ ok naʔtethayaʔtó·tʌ   tho thatakhéhse
they say, with different images that back there he was running around

oská·waku ot naya·wʌ́ne   ahutkwe·ní   laotyóhkwaʔ okhaleʔ
in the brushes, waiting for the outcome for them to win, his group   and

takʌʔ ahotinú·lahke laotyóhkwa.
not to get hurt   his group.

Shayá·tat thó layá·taleʔ   teyotanú·yanit tsiʔ lakwá· nʌ.   né· katiʔ wí· tsiʔ
One man there was of the group was huge   in size,   so   then while

shakonuhkwaʔtslálhohs   né· nuwa thó sahohké·tohteʔ neʔn
he's rubbing them down with medicine this time again, he appeared the

lakwanʌhkó usahonuhkwaʔtslálho.   Waʔhʌ́·luʔ neʔn onuhkwaʔtkó,
huge man   returned to get a medicine rub-down. Said   the   medicine man,

"ottsye   naʔtehonhuskalá naʔkʌ kwah hanyó tsiʔ ni·yót yaku·kwe." Okhaleʔ
"Oh dear, look at the big hips just, it seems that's like a woman." and

úskah útlatsteʔ kayhuhákta tsiʔ tehoti·yʌ́ thó   wahotyaʔtoyaʔakeʔ
one   time   near the river while they were gaming he gave him a body slam,

shayá·tat,   yakʌʔ, isiʔ naʔkayhuháti yaʔkanaʔkʌtslakwʌ́htalaneʔ neʔn
one of the, they say, across the river he went sprawling   this

tehatshikwaʔekskwekó·
great ball player.

Told by Guy Elm to Oscar Archiquette (2-17-39)
Transcribed and Taped by Maria Hinton (10-19-76)

Tsiʔ Ni·yohtu·ne Tsiʔ Yakonyaks
The Way They Used To Get Married

ʌkuka·látuhse   tsiʔ ni·yót tsiʔ yakonyáku   aknulhkʌ́ tsiʔ ni·yót·tsiʔ
I will tell you a story about how that she got married my mother the way that

yakonyákskwe.   Nʌ thóha tsya·ták niyohsláshʌ ok yá·yahk
they used to get married. It's almost a seventy years   and six

yeswakathlo·lí.   Yeksá   tsaʔakohtʌ́tane   tehnitsyá·lu
ago, that I'm talking about. A small girl became an orphan, both of them

wa?thuíheye kuwayáhạ okhna? ohsótha   wa?kuwayótyakẹ. Wísk ok yawʌ·lé
they died   her parents then her grandmother brought her up.   Only fifteen

teyakaohsliyá·ku tsautatenyákţʌ.
years old she was when arrangements were made for her marriage.

Kwah ok thautye·lʌ́ ohsótha wa?etstotslaye·ná atslunyáhkwạ.   Tho na?utsanu·ní
Such a suprise   her grandma received a package of clothing. She was so happy

aknulhá,   wá·yʌlhe?   onʌ kati? wi ʌyutya?tahslu·nị. Ne?n tho né
my mother, she thought now then she will dress up.   But then

na?akonehla·kó   tsi?   onʌ́ yahu·wé yautatokʌ́htu wa?í·lu? ohsótha "Sosana
was very suprised when that time came, Sunday.   Said her Grandma "Susan,

satahkwaslú·ni   akwe·kú ne   ʌhsátste?   ka?i·kʌ́ kantstotsláhele?
get yourself ready all of what you will wear that   bundle

atslunyáhkwa". Kwah kwí né· tsi? niyosno·lé wa?utslu·ní   okhna?
of clothes".   It was just in a big hurry that she got dressed and

wautahkwahslísa·hnẹ. Tho né· onʌ wa?í·lu?, akokstʌ́ha,   "tyatlʌnayʌ·ná"
she was ready.   Then   now she said, the grandmother "Let's go to church?"

kwi onʌ́ kwi wakyahtʌ·tí yaháknewe? onuhsatokʌ́ti·kẹ. Tho ne tha?utyelʌ́
now then so they left   they arrived at the church. There she had her suprise

tho i·late   lanikʌ́htluha   okhale? luwayʌ́ha   ne   tutye·lʌ́hte? wahuwa·kʌ́
there he stood, the young man and   his parents, that's the first time she saw

lanikʌ́htluha,   onʌ́ uni wa?utathlo·lí tsi? ne onʌ́ ʌhotínyake.
this young man, now too they told her that that now they are to be married.

wa?tyushʌ́tho ka?i·kʌ́ yeyá·tase, wa?í·lu?, "ákhsot   onʌ́ se ʌkeksatiyóhakẹ.
She cried   this   young girl, she said, "Grandmother, now I will be a good girl,

i·kélhe? ni autsíten,   yah se tékelhe?   aukényakẹ". Wa?aí·lu?
I want me to go with you, I really don't want to get married." She said

ohsótha?,   "nʌ kwi yah thya?etni·yele? kwátle?,   tho ne onʌ́
the grandmother, "Now we can't help it   granddaughter, that now

nitese·nú   tsi? niyakónyaks   u·kwe. Luwayʌ́ha okhale? í·
you are of an age they get married people. His parents and I

teyukwalihwayʌtá·se   nʌ uni akwe·kú kakwatákwʌ.   Kʌh
have made the agreement now too all   the arrangements are made. Now

i·twéhse kʌ́·tho kanúhsku onuhsatokʌhtí·ke yetsiyatlʌnayʌní·hne   okhale?
we are all here   inside   of the church they are going to marry you and

ʌwatʌ?nyo·tákẹ,   akwe·ku kakwatakwʌ, wáhs kati? onʌ́ oskánhe?
there will be wedding feastivities, all   is arranged,   go on then now together

tsyahtʌ·tí   anikʌ́htlu·ha."   "ákhsot, yah se nité·kelhe? ayuknínyke
you will walk with the young man." "Grandmother, I really don't want to marry

thi·kʌ́ lanikʌ́htehlu.   I·kélhe? se ni utsítene? ńʌ   ʌsesahtʌ́·tj", okhna?
that handsome man. I want for me go along when you go home." and

ohsótha   kwah nok tayakoswá·tʌ ok uni wa?aí·lu?, "yah, se
her grandmother really became annoyed now too she said, "No, you

thutsíten   onʌ́ se nisé ʌhsányake".   Onʌ kati? wi oskánhe
will not go along with me now you are getting married." Now then together

wahyahtʌ·tí ne?n lanikʌ́htlu wa?etsi?totáti   ne?n aknulhá.   Tho ne
they walked the young man crying along the way, this mother of mine. That's

tyakonyáku   ne?n tho né nu, tho né ni·yót tsi? yakonyákskwe. Ne?n lotikstʌ́ha
when she got married that's the place, that is how they were married When the parents

tʌhotilihwayʌ·tásę.   Nok tsi? lanikʌ́htlelu wahathlo·lí   kʌs úhka?
would make the agreement. But the young man would tell them to who

washakonú·wene. Ne kwi yeyá·tase?   yako·tʌ́t shekú ok onʌ
he took a liking. Well then pity the young girl all of a sudden,

wa?utathnú·wene   onʌ ki? ne lotikwʌná·ta? ʌhatikwata·ko.
someone takes a liking to her, now then they the parents will make the arrangements.

Tho kwi ka?i·kʌ́ ni·yót tsi? yakonya·kú   aknulhakʌ́. Onʌ kati? wa?kalóktʌ.
This then is how that she was married, my mother. Now then I finish my story.

The Way They Used to Get Married

I will tell you a story about how they used to get married. It's about seventy-six years
ago, my mother was married that way. My mother was left an orphan, both of her parents
died at the same time and she was left to live with her grandmother. She was only fifteen
years when there was a bundle of clothes left to her grandmothers. She was happy now
she thought she would get to dress up. She didn't know that the custom was to buy
clothes for the young girl that was about to get married. One Sunday her grandmother told
her to get ready for church and to wear the clothes in the bundle. When they arrived at
the church, she was really surprised to see this young man standing there with his parents.
Now they told her that he was to be her husband and this was the day she will be married
to him. This young girl cried and told her grandmother, "I don't want to get married, I
will be good". The Grandmother said "You will have to go with him, arrangements have
already been made, we can't help it, now go and walk with him." She did, but she cried
all the way. She also told her she was of an age to be getting married. So that is how
my mother was married. But from then on there wasn't too many marriages like that.
Except on a few rare occasions when a young man will tell his folks about which young
girl he took a liking to. Well this is the end of my story.

Told by Mrs. Katie Cornelius to Ida Blackhawk (3-17-39)
Transcribed and Taped by Maria Hinton (11-13-80)

Tehalukwe?nya·ku Okhale? Lo·ne·
Broken Spine and His Wife

Wahu·níse onʌ́ lakhsotkʌ́, Tehalukwe?nyá·ku kahle? lo·ne?kʌ́
Long ago when my grandfather Tehalukwe?nyá·ku and his wife

tshutahyanakla·kó· ne?n tkana?alóhale? kʌh nukwá· nutá·ne Ukwehuwé·ne né·tsi?
when they moved here from Oneida Castle this way they came to Oneida because

yah ne té·nelehe? O?slu·ní ahya·tụ. Yakowi·láyʌ yeksá ne?n lo·nẹ.
they didn't want like white people to become. She had a child, his wife.

Tiksʌ́nne tahyatitáhko?. Onʌ́ kwi wahahle?nu·ní· tashakoya?táhawe? shakoyʌ́·ha,
DePere is where they got off. Now then he bundled·her up and carred her, his child.

ehta?késhu kwah ok tsi? niyo·lé· kalhakúshu nutahnihle?notáti kwah nok
walking all the way through the woods with their bundles they just

washakoti?lhóloke? yeksá só·tsi? kutinákele? okalyahtánẹ kalhakuhkó
covered her up this small child because so plentiful were mosquitoes in the forest

kanawakúshu tsi? tehonatawʌlyeháti khale? onʌ́ tho wá·newe Tehawya?tí·lu
swamps that they were travelling in and finally there they arrived at Daniel Bread

tsi? nú nihonúhsote? Kukwité·ne kwi tshikaha·wị. Onʌ
where his house is. In the spring was the time of year. Now

tshihotiyʌthóslụ tahnú tsyotilyó·u lotiyʌthóhslu? Onʌ kwí
they had already done their planting but the frost had killed their plants. Now then

ka?i·kʌ́ lakhsotha tahatáhsawʌ? kwah ok tha?thalutá·libte? wahatnuhsu·ni·
this grandfather started, he just split the logs hurriedly he built his house.

kwah ok ohósele? waha·kálʌhte? ne· né· wahahwánhaste? tsi? yonoká·lʌhte?
Just only bassswood he stripped it that's what he tied the door with.

Ka?i·kʌ́ lo·né· kwáh kʌs teyushʌ́thos yah te?yakauweskwaní·u. Nya?tekalyó·take
This wife just used to cry she was so unhappy there. All kinds of wild game

ne kaná·kele? khale? ohkwe·sʌ́ sʌ kutináklehkwe? khale? nya?tekʌ́tsyake sʌ́. Khale?
were plentiful and partridges too were plentiful and all kinds of fish too. And

onʌ́ tékni wa?thonaskwayʌ·táne? tyotná·kales onʌ́ kwi wahate?slehtu·ni·
finally two animals he got oxen now then he made himself a sleigh

né· kʌs né· akwe·kú tsa?tehútsta tho latinákele? khale? né onʌ́
they used to all use it together, he shares, with the neighbors and he finally

wahanha?slisákha?. Kanatá·ke wahoyo·tʌ́ khale? né onʌ́ tho nikú
went looking for a job. Green Bay he worked and finally that much

wahohwistayʌtáˑne onʌ́ ne kohsaˑtʌ́s wahatathniˑnúseʔ   onʌ́ tahatáhsawʌʔ wahathʌtuˑniˑ
money he had   now then horse he bought for himself now he started   to clear land

néˑ kʌs néˑ eˑsó shakoyaʔtákeɒhʌ tehanuhsanekháni néˑtsiʔ wahatkwataˑkóˑ   nú néˑ
it was that a lot he helped   his neighbors   because he became well off, that he did

Tehalukweʔnyaˑku Okhaleʔ Onˑneˑ
Broken Spine and His Wife

It's a long time now since my grandfather (now deceased) and his wife came to Oneida, Wisconsin from Oneida New York, Oneida Castle. They came here because they didn't want to change their ways to a white man's way of living and his laws. His wife had a small girl child. They got off at DePere, they had come by boat. They walked when they left the boat. There were still large forests and mostly swamps yet at that time and they had to go through all that to get to Daniel Bread's house to where they were going. They bundled up their baby and covered her face because there were so many mosquitos and wild game was plentiful too. Finally, they came to his house. This was in the spring of the year, people around there had already planted, but they were killed by frost.

Now my grandfather started right in to build them a house, he took logs and split them hurriedly, he used basswood and he stripped the bark and used that for ties to a door. His wife was very unhappy here, she used to cry. There were all kinds of game and partridges and fish were plentiful. Finally, he was able to get two animals, they were oxen. Now he made a sleigh, he shared this with his neighbors. Now he was ready to go job hunting. He went to Green Bay, where he worked on the boats where he was hired. Then he was able to buy a horse, he cleared the land for planting. He helped his neighbors a lot because he became well off, that he did.

Told by Sarah Summers to Tillie Baird (3-21-39)
Transcribed by Maria Hinton (5-4-79)
Taped by Maria Hinton (7-21-80)

Crime Story

Swatyeˑlʌ́ kʌs waʔtwatʌ́ˑnuke   neʔn sóˑtsiʔ yaʔteyakolíˑwahkẹ. Tsyaˑták
Sometimes   accidents happen when too much joking around.   Seventy

niyohsláshʌ   oˑnʌ́ tsiʔ nahe thotlihwateʔwáhtu   neʔn "Yakwekkowan"
years (winters) now it's been he committed a crime this   "Big Jake,"

néˑ win "Tyoslehtákat"   lolyóˑu tsiʔ niyawʌˑu   kaʔiˑkʌ "Yakwek".
that is "Train" (deceased) he killed was how it happened this   "Jacob".

Tho nu tshikaháˑwi, akiˑluʔ,   yah uhteʔ teskanaˑnu   neʔn laonikúhla, néˑtsiʔ
In those days   I would say, that maybe he was short that of his mind because

théˑtʌ tshítkʌ   yutkʌhuˑníheʔ?   yakʌ́ʔ   neʔn loˑné ahtsatuhkwaku
yesterday before she was quilting, they say, his wife, when in the cellar

yahakwenʌ́hteʔ, néˑtsiʔ oˑnʌ́ tatahaláhthʌ   onikwʌ́htalaʔ niˑyót atkahanyáks
he went   when now he came back up, a red   like   handkerchief

saháˑwi, tho nutáˑle   tsiʔ yéˑtlu neʔn loˑnẹ́, kʌh uhteʔ niwatekhwahlaʔsla.
he carried, then he came where she sat,   his wife, I guess just a small table

tsi? yakota?nikhuslahele? tho yakʌ? wahanohkwaˑlʌ ka?iˑkʌ? nʌ
where she had her sewing there, they say, he set a bundle, this   then

wahakaˑtshi ohwista yakʌ? tho kahwenúˑnj. Tho yakʌ?
he unwrapped money, they say, there was wrapped. There, they say,

wahathwistashete kwah akwéˑku akte?, na?thaˑyʌ ne?n skahwistatsu,
he counted the money, it was all separately, he put the dollar bills,

kayeliˑshu silu, teknishu?sílu oyeliˑshú kwénis khale? ne?n okweni?tashúha,
half dollar, twenty-five cents, ten cent pieces and even the pennies,

kwah yakʌ? nok luwatlóˑlu tsi? oˑnʌ waháhsane?, yaˑuahk yakʌ? kwénis,
they say that she just watched, now then he finished, six they say, cents

tho tahaláˑko, wa?hʌ́ˑlu?, koh ahtya?tawit ʌhsatathniˑnuhse. Tho
from there he took, he said, here a dress you will buy for yourself. Then

kati? nu na?weˑnene? tsi? yah se? thyeskayeˑli okhale? tsi? oˑnʌ
at this time, it became clear that not right was he and when now

wahanuhwetha, tho yakʌ? wahaˑyʌ laohule? laya?takta. Néˑ úhte?
he went to bed, there they say, he laid his gun near his side. That I think

oskánhe? latiˑtlu ka?iˑkʌ? "Tyoslehta?katkʌ," tahnu? yakʌ?, né nahte? ne?n
together they lived this man named "Fast Train", also, they say, that kind that

yateholihwa?kéˑhne ne? "Tyoslehtáˑkat" Neˑ kati? tsi?
kind of person always joking around "Train" (fast running vehicle). So then when

oˑnʌ wa?olhʌne?, laulha yakʌ? ka?iˑkʌ "Tyo?lehtáˑkat" ahstéhtsi? okhna?
now that it's morning, he they say, this man "Train" in the morning already,

wahtkétsko wahateka?tányu ne?n yutnuhsataliha?tákhwa Néˑ kati? tsi? oˑnʌ
he was up making fires in the heaters of the house. So then that now

wahoˑtékseˑ okhna? yakʌ yahonáˑtu ne?n Yakwek. Wa?hʌ́ˑlu?,
his fire was going good then they say, he called to this Jake. He said,

"Yakʌ hao satkétsko iˑnuwa? thoyuhsakáˑlat." Tahahulotsyáhte? ne?n Yakwek, tho
"Come on, get up now I there lie down." He pulled out a gun, this Jake, that

kaˑyʌ́ thotehotsaktuhatyéhse? layʌtúthos thó
was lying there, he was bending over putting the wood in the stove

wathohna?tsoya?akke waholuˑtate, kwah kwiˑ neˑ ok tho wa?otstenyoˑtaˑne
he aimed his gun at his rear end he shot him, right then and there, he fell in a heap

ne?n "Tyosléhta?katkʌ" okhna? tahatketskwáhte? ne?n Yaˑkwek wahatéko. Nʌ kwi
man named "Fast Train" then he jumped up fast this Jake escaped. Finally

wahuwaya?tíˑsakc? khale? oˑnʌ́ wahotitókʌhse? kʌh yakʌ nu kanúhsote?
they looked for him and soon they found out where he was, it was there was a house,

tekaluˑtátu kalhaˑku tho yehotahsehtu?. Néˑ kwi oˑnʌ́, úhka kati? nahte? tho
built of logs in the woods where he was hiding. Well now, then who then will to go

nyʌhʌ́·le ʌhatatwʌhtehte?, ne· tsi? yehohulahawi·htu? tsahatketskọ. Khale? o·nʌ
there   volunteer,   because he carried his gun, when he ran. Finally now

utetsʌhli   shaya·tat wa?hʌ·lu?, "I kwi tho yʌhʌ·ke, yukya?tʌlu? thi·kʌ?
they found someone one male said, "I then there will go, we are friends this

Yakwek, yah uhte? I·kelhe? thahakwalu·tatẹ".   Nʌ kwi wahunityoku·ni tho
Jake,   I don't think he would shoot me." Now then they gathered together

wahʌnehte? tsi? tetkalu·tatụ. Ne· kati? o·nʌ ka?i·kʌ "Sakwayak" wahathukalyahke? tho
they went to this log house. So then now this "Aaron Hill" volunteered   there

yʌhʌ·le   ʌthoya?tinikʌ·we tsi? nu thotahséhtu,   wa?hʌ́·lu? yakʌ?,   "Tsi? nʌ
he will go, he will bring him out the place he is hiding, he said they say, "Now when

tho ahnúkwe tsyaha·newe kanyo o·nʌ yakatawyahte?. kʌ́·tho kwi nu naeswatahséhtanyu
these people arrived there, when now I'll enter there. here then is where you will hide,

kanyo o·nʌ yʌkatawyáhte? tho né· o·nʌ yʌswahtʌ·ti, kwah tsi? ni·ku ʌwa·tú
after now I have entered then now you will go ahead, just as much as possible

yʌswatlanʌ·tákte? nok tsi? takʌ ʌhetswa·kʌ.   kanyo ʌwa·tu yʌkye·na ne?n laohule?,
get very close but then don't let him see you, if possible I will grab his gun,

tʌtwakehuhuhti, atste?   ʌtkalu·tate tho ne· o·nʌ ya?tʌswalahtate?
I will open the door outside, I will shoot then now you will all come running

ʌhskwaya?takenha kanyo tʌwatuhwʌtsyohwe." Tho kati? wi na?ya·wʌne?   tsi? nu
to help me   if I need you."   That then is how it happened there.

u·tu yahatawyahte?   yahothalhahase? wahohlo·li tsi? yolhalatste? ne?n tahatukohte
He was able to enter, he talked to him he told him that there was he had a chance

kanyo ʌhathu·tate?   usa·ne   tho yʌhʌ·ne? tsi? nu
if   he would consent to go with him, they will go to the place,

na?tehuwaya?tolehtane, wahathu·tate? kati? ne?n Yakwek nʌ kwi taho·yu ne?n laohule?
where he will be judged, he consented then now Jake   gave   his gun to him

okhna? atste, nukwa yahalu·tate? nʌ ki?ok wi ne· yahatinhoho·kahte?.
and then outside direction he shot at quickly then they entered the place.

yuhsahuwasha·li·ne? Kanata·ke nukwa yahuwanho·tu.   Nok tsi? sheku ne·
They led him   Green Bay was the place he was put in jail. But then still they

tshihati·hawe lonulha laotiyanlʌsla yah kati? te?yotu·u ne?n o?slu·ni,
had their   own   laws   not then were they able, the white people,

utahuwa·wike katsatste? tsi? ʌhathle·wahte? ne· ka?i·kʌ ne· latikwa·nʌse lutna?tukhwa tho
to give him a severe   punishment. It was these. chiefs   they are called at

nu tsutskaha·wi nʌ tehuwaya?tolehta·ne ne· uni yotkwe·ni ne?n wahuwahya?hsanhake tsi?
that time   when he will be judged, also they decided that they would hang him, was

wahuwali.   Kwah wakatkattho nʌ tsutahusʌhte tsiʔ nu natewaskwʌhtu tho
they killed him   I did see them when they dropped   there.

yahuwʌskwaˑlʌ tho neˑ oˑnʌ wahonaktotane neʔn thok nahteʔ ahʌˑluʔ kalo tsiʔ niyoˑle
they set him   now then he had a chance to   something   to say   before

ʌtwasʌˑne, nʌ uni teʔyotshiʔtoˑkwʌ   tekukshʌthos
it drops, now too there were many tears being shed, they were crying,

luwʌtʌlheʔ   wahakweˑni waʔhʌˑluʔ "Takʌʔ tʌtsyashʌˑtho waʔ tkatʌˑnke
I feeling sorry for him, he was able to say   "Don't   cry,   I made the mistake

nok sniʔnikuˑlalak, takʌ sheˑku tho nʌtsyawʌhne tho nikawʌˑnake".   Nʌ kwi
just be careful,   don't again let it happen   this is all I have to say". Now then

tahuˑsʌte tsiʔ Lʌtskahele   waʔtwatkalhatenihu tsiʔ wahoyaʔtʌˑtuneʔ tahnuʔ tsiʔ nʌ
they dropped where he sat, revolving around where his body hung and   then when

tshyaʔtwatotate   tkakeˑtohse nukwa nahatyelahteʔ kwah ok uni ok tho thywayaʔtatʌ.
it stopped rotating to the east the direction it faced, right then and there he was buried.

Crime Story

Sometimes accidents happen when there is too much joking around. Seventy years ago a
crime was committed. Big Jake killed Train because of too much joking. They also say
that Big Jake may have been short of mind, because one time he went to the cellar and
brought out a handkerchief full of money. He counted it all out and then gave his wife
six cents to buy a dress. When he went to bed that night he laid a gun by his side. I
think they lived together this "Fast Train" and Big Jake and his wife. Anyway, they say
that Fast Train was the kind of person that was always joking around. So that morning,
they say, that Fast Train was up early making fires in the heaters around the house.
When the fire was going good he called to Big Jake and told him to get up. Big Jake
sat up and pulled out his gun and as Fast Train bent over to put more wood in the
heater Big Jake aimed his gun and shot him in the rear end. Fast Train fell in a heap.
Big Jake jumped up and ran as fast as he could. Finally, they found him at a log house
in the woods. Because he carried a gun they needed a volunteer to go in and bring him
out. Aaron Hill stepped forward and said "I will go, we are friends, I don't think he
would shoot me." Aaron told the people when they arrived there that he would enter
and they should hide, he would try to talk Big Jake into turning himself in. But, he
wanted the people to get very close just in case he needed them. Aaron was able to
enter and talk to Big Jake. He told him that if he would consent to go with him he
may have a chance with the judge. Big Jake consented and gave Aaron the gun. They
led him to Green Bay and was put into jail. However, Oneida still had their own laws
so the white people weren't able to punish him. It was the Chiefs that judged him and
they decided to hang him. Before he died, I was feeling sorry for him and a lot of tears
were being shed. He said, "Don't cry, I made a mistake, just be careful and don't let it
happen again, this is all I have to say." When his body was dropped it was revolving
around and it stopped rotating to the east, right then and there he was buried.

Told by Elizabeth Huff to John A.Skenandore (5/11/39)
Transcribed and Taped by Maria Hinton, (1978)

Ukwehu·we Okhale? Kayotʌ·sla
Oneidas and Work

Kwah nya?tekú wahotiy·tʌ kʌh nu   tsahʌ·néwe Ukwehu·wé. Otyahke?
Just   all kinds of work did, here when they arrived, the Oneidas.   Some

wahutyʌtahni·nú okhale? ka·lúte? wahutʌhni·nú okhale? kanehushúha
sold wood   and   logs   they sold   and   hides.

ótyahke? uni?   Kanatá·ke yahutsyo?tʌhslo·lí·ne? latinʌstalukó·nehse?
Some of them in Green Bay they found work   where they went to shell corn.

Kahu·wáku ka?i·kʌ́ nitku·néhse? onʌ́ste? tahnú né· laonatkalayá·ksla? onʌ́ste?
In the boats they came in   corn   also that was their pay   corn

yotitshe?nútslayʌ? yakʌ?   kunúkwe. Né· kʌ yakʌ?
they had baskets, they say, the women. It was that they say,

tʌtakuthle·náhkwe tsi?   nahte? atʌná·tsli?
they carried their bundles on their back what groceries and staples

wa?thutʌ·tsá·ne.
they needed and had received for pay.

Oneida's and Work

When the Oneida's first arrived here from Oneida Castle, New York. They were
ambitious people, they did all kinds of work to make a living, such as cutting
wood and selling it, they sold logs, they hunted and sold the hide and some even
found work in Green Bay, they shelled corn which came on the boats and this was
part of their pay. The women had baskets, they filled this with their groceries and
other staples they needed, this they bought with their pay which was part of the
corn they had shelled. They always carried whatever load they had on their backs.

Told by Rachel Swamp to Dennison Hill (12-17-39)
Transcribed by Maria Hinton (1-9-78)
Taped by Maria Hinton (11-6-80)

Lutlutʌ?awitha
Driving Logs

Wahu·níse? ki? úhte? wí· yusakathlo·lí· tsi? ni·yót tsi?   lutlʌ?awítahkwe
Long ago, I guess I'll talk about   the way it was that drive logs, they used to.

kukwi?té·ne   nu   tshikaha·wí· nʌ ale? tahutáhsawʌ? latinha?tsli·sáks ka?i·kʌ́ ne
in the spring, about about that time again they started looking for help these   here

lʌnu·kwé ahotiyo?tʌ́hsa kalute?o·kú kaybuhakúshu? nyashakonatolihátye?hne.
men   to go to work on the logs in the rivers to drive the logs.

TeyotΛnú·yanit kΛs uni né·tsi? ni·yót tsi? lotiyo?táti ne?n kayhuhakúshu. Tho
It was a sight to see usually the way they were working along the river. There

nu tshikahá·wi tsi? nú yeswakathlo·lí· tho ni·yót tsi? tekutwΛlyéhahkwe ka?i·kÁ
at that time is what I'm recalling the say that they used to travel these

kalute?o·kú, tho kati? úni ní· wakataténhane? yotlátsu?. Tahnu? yah akwáh thau·tú
logs, all kinds, there then I hired out too, one time. And not hardly can you

kwah ok thikawΛ·niyó tsi? nu nikaha·wí· ahsatkÁlahte? tsi? satatenhá·u tsi? ki?
just any old time of the season to quit that you have hired out to only

niyo·lé· akwe·kú kalute?o·kú yaku·néwe tsi? tetkahsu?kaloskó· Askas nú·
until all the logs have arrived to this big lumber mill. Oshkosh is

kahwistowa·nÁ tΛhsatÁ·tsane? tát Λwa·tú yatΛhsóktΛ. July kΛs
where the big money you will earn if you are able to finish your agreement. July

kwi nú o·nÁ ale? wahatísane? ne?n lutlutΛ?awítha. Wa?akwatu?wéskwahte? kΛs
then is usually the month they finish the log rolling. We have a good time, used

kanyó o·nÁ ya?ákwawe? ne?n Askas kuwa·yáts kanatayΛ?kó· Tho kati? ka?i·kÁ
to when we arrived to Oshkosh the name of this big town. That then was

ni·yót tsi? watkatu·kóhte? yotlátstu?. April nú niwehnitatáti nΛ wakahtΛ·ti·.
it was what I went through one time. April it was during that month I left.

Kwah yakóktΛ July úskah thsiska·le? wa?akwásane?. Tho wí· nú tkali·wayΛ ne?
Well I finished, July first of the month, we finished. There is the word of

kákhwá kwah tsi? ok nahte?shúba tho yotstenyote·kó. Kwah ok thikawΛni·yó
food just about every kind of food was spread there. Just about anytime

nú nikaha·wí· tsi? niwΛhnísles Λwa·tú ki? Λwa·tú ki? Λhsatekhu·ní. Tho kati? ni·kú
or whenever time of the day you are able to you will be able to eat. Now then is all,

Kwátle? nuwa wakka·láyΛ.
grandchild this time, stories I have.

Driving Logs

I guess I will talk about the way it was long ago, when they used to drive logs in the spring. About that time again, they started looking for help to work on the logs in the river I hired on at this time. It was a sight to see the way the men where working on the river. What I'm recalling is the way the logs traveled until they reached the big lumber mill. When you hired on you had to stay the whole season, usually July is the month all the logs arrived at the lumber mill. Oshkosh is where the big money is if you are able to finish your agreement. We had a good time when we arrived in Oshkosh, this big town. They had a big spread of food there, just about anytime of the day you are able to eat there. Now then, grandchild, that is all the stories I have.

Told by Abrahms Archiquette to Guy Elm (4-11-39)
Transcribed and Taped by Maria Hinton (3-10-80)
Recopied by Maria Hinton (8-3-88)

Nik^tsyanakl^·ne
Fish Story

Yotká·te   wa?kanuhtunyu·kó ka?i·k´ wakukwitehslu·ní tsi? k´s
Quite often, I think about   these   spring days,   it   used

nik^tsyanakl^·ne   wahunihsa?nu tsutakahá·wi tahnú yah kwi
to be fish were so plentiful long ago   in those days and   it was

te?yakway^telí·hne úhka?   ayukhinustátse tsi? yakw^tsyákwas.   Kwah
unheard of   someone to forbid us about our fishing.   They

tehonat^na?keláhtu, lotikst^hoku·k^   tsi? nikahá·wi nale? tk^tsyanákle? tsi?
always have an idea, the old timers, about the time again it is fishing time

thatitsyakwathákwe?   tho nu tsutakahá·wi.   Kwah n^ hutá·ti· tó·tis
at their old fishing place at that time.   Just then, they will start croaking

okhale? tekal´·tut   khale? tshikl^?tányak. Tho·nu nikahá·wi nale? tok´ske
and   spring trout and   frogs.   At that time   again,   really

tk^tsyanákle?   Emesnehk^   wi·nu nihatitsyakwatháhkwe?   tho nu
plentiful fish where Amos's place is, where their old fishing place was at that

tshikahá·wi lotiwy^natsahnitú·ne   ayetsyá?ko   ka?i·k´
time.   They were very ambitious about fishing,   these

yukhisothoku?k´   Kwah ok thiyotká·te? shakotiba·wí·se   laotinalhkwa?shú.
our deceased grandparents. It was quite often they brought along   their spouses.

Kwah k^s kwahsutáti tho tyonanitsyute?   atsyákta   ne?n kunu·kwé.
It was   all night   there they fried fish near the river bank the women.

Kwah uni k^s tsi?ok nu   niyonateka?táni   ne wi·n otyáhke? né·
It   even was here and there they had a fire agoing, you see some of them had

yotihnekakli?tslú·ni   ka?i·k´ tsyon^hali·yó onú·tsi? kató·k^ na?teká·lu nale?
had a pot of soup on these   sucker   heads. Every so often   again

sahutekhú·ni   ale? k^s   yah oksa? thutahatihnaw^nhálane?   k´·tho tsi?
they would eat again, sometimes not right away would they get busy here not

niyóle tayolh^?uhatye? ok yah kwi thahutuhkalyahke? yah u·ni thahatiwistóske?
until towards morning they don't even get hungry   they didn't get hungry

alu?bati kwa?hsutáti? latitsyákwas.   Yotká·te? tho na?k^tsyanakl^ne,
even if all night they have been fishing.   Quite often the fish would get so plentiful,

kwah ok thyehsakotiyé·nas   kwah tsi? nihotitsanítha. Kan^?tkalá·ke
with their hands, they grabbed the fish as fast as they could.   On the river bank

yehonatyéhse.   Astéhtsi?   n^ kwi ^seshakotiya?tanyu·tú otyáhke? se
they tossed the fish. In the morning now then they will hitch up, some of them

wi loti?sléhse? tsi? latitsyakonéhse? ne· ʌshakohá·wé· tsi? ka·yʌ
are riding   as they went fishing, he will bring them those who

yah tehonaskwayʌ́·tu okhna? ne· kwi ne· awʌ́·ke tʌhutawʌ·li katsa?nu nʌhatitsyá·ko.
didn't have animals.   Then they will in the water inspect   just where they would fish.

Ne· tʌhati?kaháhsi· tsi? ni·ku ʌhatitsyá·liḥ.   Kwah ok thiyotka·te?
They will divide   of all the fish they caught. It was quite often

tʌhutsuhti·k   tsi? ni·kú wahotitsya?yʌhtá·ne. Ale? sʌ tho
they will have a wagonfull, is how much fish they got.   And too again,

sahonata?kló·ko   tsi? latitsyakwas   ok yah ki? ne· thakalihú·ni
they would have snow as they are fishing, but that wasn't the reason

usahutʌhtyú·ku   tsi? niyó·le kwah ʌ́·te   ʌwá·tu.   nʌ nuwa? ne·ok
for them to go home, not until   it's daylight becomes. Now again then

ʌyukwʌtsyaslú·ni   ne?n ʌtwʌtnʌskwáhte? tsi? ʌtwʌtysyáhko. Tahnu? u·ni ne· tho
only we'll have fish is by sneaking around to get some fish.   And   even then there

tkanyá·tu   tsi? yukwatehyuhatáti yah te·wé·ne kanhke usakʌtsyanaklʌ́ne?
is a dam built above our own river there's no hope when fish will be plentiful again

tsi? nu kwah niyakwʌtsyakwathákwe?   wahú·nise?nu·.
where just   where we used to fish a long time ago.

Fish Story

Quite often, I think about these spring days when the fish were so plentiful. Long ago, it was unheard of someone to forbid you to fish. Every year at the same time when they hear the frogs croaking the spring trout are here, the old timers head for their old fishing place by Amos's place. These old timers were very ambitious about their fishing and would take their spouses along with them. They would fish all night and the women would fry the fish on the river bank. Here and there, there would be fires going and maybe a pot of sucker head soup cooking. Through the night they could eat if they wanted to. Quite often the fish would be so plentiful that they could grab them with their hands and then toss them on the riverbank. In the morning they would bring a wagon and after inspecting the fish would divide the fish they caught. Now and again, we try to fish by sneaking around, but there is a dam built above our own river so there is little hope when there will be fish again at the spot where we used to fish long time ago.

Told by J. Peters to Dennison Hill (5-9-39)
Transcribed and Taped by Maria Hinton (10-1-93)

7

Contemporary Oneida Perspectives of Oneida History

The Archiquette Genealogy
by Amelia Cornelius with the Assistance of Todd Larkin

While the 1784 Treaty of Fort Stanwix was being negotiated, the marquis de Lafayette, who had helped recruit Oneida soldiers during the American Revolution, made an appearance and scolded the British-allied Six Nations because they had fought against the American colonies as well as France. He made an odd appeal to his allied Oneidas. He asked them to allow him to take back two of their male children to France. The two that he was specifically referring to were said to be the children of Lafayette's former clerk, a man named Otsiquette, and an Oneida woman named Sarah Hanyost. Otsiquette had long before returned to France, leaving the boys and Sarah behind. After much deliberation, the Oneidas decided to allow the boys to go back with Lafayette. One of the boys, Edward, better known as Neddy, ran off into the woods and rebelled by throwing stones at those who pursued him. As a result, Lafayette took only Edward's brother, Peter, with him back to France, where the boy received a classical education and learned French fluently. Later, when Peter heard of his people's troubles, he decided to return to try to help them recover their homeland. Instead, he became mixed up in the elaborate schemes of Peter Penet, a French trader from Nantes who attempted to weasel his way into Oneida affairs and secure a personal empire in the late 1780s. Peter's brother,

Neddy, the boy left behind by Lafayette, much later as a leader of the First Christian Party, brought one of the earliest contingents of Oneidas to their Duck Creek reservation near Green Bay in 1823. Over time, the Otsiquette surname became Archiquette, the family name of one of the leading Oneidas of the twentieth century, Oscar Archiquette.

Tribal Discord and the Road to Green Bay
by Amelia Cornelius

From the 1790s onward, Oneida Indian existence was marred continually by conflict between the so-called Pagan Party and the Christian parties. Though the Oneidas repeatedly maintained that they intended not to sell any more land, New York State officials quickly took advantage of this discord and the increasing economic dependence of the Indians. By 1805, these religious divisions led to the partition of Oneida lands between the two groups, whereby the Christians took reservation lands in the southern half of the Oneida Territory and governed them independently of the "Pagans," who administered the northern part. The two parties even entered into an official agreement with New York State officials, who recognized the Oneida division of their lands. The two Oneida representatives in this state agreement were Cornelius Doxtator, who headed the Pagans and was the son of Hanyere, and Skenandoah, the centenarian leader of the Christian Party. With the coming of the message of the Seneca prophet Handsome Lake in the early years of the nineteenth century, divisions became even more clearly defined. Three Oneidas became Longhouse preachers—Jacob the Blacksmith, Henry Cornelius, and Pagan Peter—who spread the *Gaiwiio* or Code of Handsome Lake, to the Oneidas.

During the War of 1812, Oneidas from central New York fought in defense of the United States. They were led by Captain Adam Skenandoah [Skenando] and Pagan Peter, who by then had assumed the name of Captain Peter Elm. In the last days of May 1814, approximately 120 Oneida riflemen trapped three British gunboats armed with congreve rockets along Sandy Creek just south of Sackett's Harbor. This Oneida-led American victory contributed directly to the lifting of the British blockade of Sackett's Harbor and to a slow end of Great Britain's dominance on Lake Ontario. Oneidas also fought bravely at the Battle of Chippawa in Lower Canada on July 5, 1814. Cornelius Doxtator, the head of the Pagan Party, was killed in the Battle of Chippawa; he had two sons, Daniel and George, who were very young boys at the time. A Chippewa Indian felled Cornelius, the father, with a tomahawk and took off with the two boys. The Chippewa in turn was attacked by other Oneida soldiers when he was climbing a fence, and the two boys were recovered.

Soon after the war, the Episcopal church sent Eleazer Williams to the Oneidas as a missionary. He quickly gained influence among the Oneidas and was even able to convert many within the Pagan Party to Christianity. In 1816, the

aged sachem Skenandoah, head of the Christian Party, died. In 1817, members
of the Pagan Party held one last round of traditional dances and then formally
denounced their traditional ways. They renamed themselves the Second Christian Party. Skenandoah's Christian Party now became known as the First Christian Party. Though both parties were now Christian, the ill feelings between
them continued.

Eleazer Williams soon began promoting the idea of reestablishing the Six
Nations in the West. Much like Peter Penet earlier in the late 1780s, his ideas
were controversial and produced bitter discord among the Oneidas. Most of the
older leaders and those of the Second Christian Party refused to listen and aggressively denounced his ways. But Williams was clever, and he convinced
scores of younger chiefs from the First Christian Party to consider his idea. He
then acquired the backing of Cornelius Baird. Baird was a very respected
young chief of the Oneidas and had quite a following. Cornelius had a brother
named Henry, and they took the surname Bear in honor of their father, Cornelius the Great Bear. When they moved to Green Bay, the name was changed
to Baird. Williams used his influence with Cornelius Baird to convince another
young chief by the name of Daniel Bread to consider the thought of moving
west. Soon Williams had the approval of the younger chiefs of the First Christian Party to begin making inquiries into the possibilities of moving west, but
the older chiefs of the Second Christian Party still refused. During the summer
of 1821, a delegation of New York Indians, made up primarily of the Stockbridge and a few of the younger chiefs of the First Christian Party, went to
Green Bay. When they returned they told of their mission in grand terms, but
they were rebuffed by the Second Christian Party and the older chiefs of the
First Christian Party; however, the Stockbridge [and Brothertown] Indians were
anxious to move.

In 1822, another delegation went to Green Bay and this time a treaty was
signed giving the Six Nations and the other New York Indians joint occupation
of the Menominees' lands. This Oneida delegation remained in Green Bay that
winter while the Stockbridge Indians returned to lead parties from New York to
Green Bay the following summer. When word of this treaty reached the Oneidas in New York, the Second Christian Party again denounced the plan; however, this time some of the older Oneidas of the First Christian Party began to
weaken, since many of the First Christian Party members had intermarried
with the Stockbridge Indians.

One of these was Neddy Archiquette. He was about 50 years old and carried
some influence as a chief of the First Christian Party. His grandson was married to Daniel Bread's sister, and Archiquette led the first contingent of permanent Oneida settlers to Green Bay. He built a cabin together with his friend and
grandson-in-law, Armister Janis Ninham. Their settlement increased slowly
until a total of 179 Oneidas, all members of the First Christian Party, were living at Green Bay by February 1829. One of these was a son, named Daniel,

who was born to Armister Janis and Margaret Ninham on December 27, 1827. He was the first Oneida child born in Wisconsin.

Additional Notes on Eleazer Williams (1787–1858) and the Origins of the Episcopal Tradition among the Oneidas by Judy Cornelius

As early as 1825, the Oneidas built a small, log-constructed, Episcopal church along the banks of Duck Creek, which they named after the bishop of New York, John Henry Hobart. At that time the land where they settled was largely unbroken forest of pine, oak, chestnut, and maple. The establishment of the Episcopal tradition among the Oneidas came with the appearance of Eleazer Williams in 1817, a most controversial figure whom I previously wrote about in *The Oneida Indian Experience: Two Perspectives* (1988). This essay adds to my previous writings, elaborating on Williams and the establishment of the Episcopal religion among the Oneidas.

There are a number of stories that surrounded Williams, including his claim to have been the lost dauphin of France, that is, the son of Louis XVI and Marie Antoinette. He was born among the St. Regis Mohawks. His oratorical ability and knowledge of the Indian languages allowed him to communicate with the Oneidas in their own language. He approached Bishop Hobart and was given the assignment of working with the Oneidas. I believe Williams came to the Oneidas with rather dubious ethics, and there is reason to believe that he was hired to lure them out of their original homeland. The Ogden Land Company was one of the primary levers, its owners using whatever motivating force they could to encourage the Oneidas as well as other Six Nations members to move to a new home in the West and give up their original homeland.

Eleazer Williams was born into the Catholic faith among the Caughnawaga Mohawks in Canada around 1787. His father, Thomas Williams, was a great-grandson of Eunice Williams, whose family had been captured at Deerfield, Massachusetts, in 1704. Eleazer's mother, Mary Ann Rice, was also of mixed blood, her ancestors having been captured and adopted by the Mohawks. Thomas and Mary Ann had at least 11 children.

In 1800, Deacon Nathaniel Ely, whose wife was related to Thomas Williams, invited Thomas to send one of his sons to Longmeadow (Massachusetts) to live with them and to provide him an education in the Congregational faith. Ely's aim was to prepare the boy to become a missionary among the Iroquois. Thomas complied by sending Eleazer and a younger brother, who did not stay.

Eleazer attended school for short periods and became acquainted with a number of influential people. Francis Parkman, the historian, indicated that Eleazer was educated at Dartmouth, but records show he attended only a few months there. He did, however, intermittently spend three years with Enoch Hale at West Hampton. During his stay with Hale, Eleazer came under the influence

of Bishop Hobart. The bishop saw Eleazer, with his Indian ancestry and his educational and religious background, as an ideal candidate to missionize among
his fellow Indians.

As a result of his enlistment with the Americans in the War of 1812, Williams
was banned from returning to the family's homeland. He gave up a fortune—
an estimated estate of several thousand pounds and an annual annuity of £250.
After the war the rest of the Williams family moved across the border from
Caughnawaga to the St. Regis reservation on the United States side. Eleazer
was soon approached by the Jesuits to be a missionary for them at St. Regis. Instead, he rejected the Catholic faith of his birth as well as Enoch Hale's Con-
gregationalism. In 1815, he was confirmed by Bishop Hobart of the Protestant
Episcopal church, a most significant event which was to shape later Oneida
history.

Eleazer was able to provide an 11-letter alphabet in Mohawk, thereby making it easier to learn the language. He had also translated part of the Book of
Common Prayer, which was published in 1816. He was fluent in the Iroquois
languages, a strong and persuasive orator, and knowledgeable in both church
and civic functions. In his travels through the East, he had picked up a number
of sermons written by his ancestor, the Reverend John Williams, sermons that
he would later claim he wrote.

In 1816, with authority from Bishop Hobart, Eleazer traveled to Oneida
Castle to serve as catechist, lay reader, and religious leader to the Oneidas. He
was warmly received by the Oneidas, especially by members of the First Christian Party. Not too long after his arrival, another group, the Second Christian
Party, also acknowledged him as their religious leader. Thus, by 1817, three-
fourths of all the Oneidas saw Eleazer Williams as their spiritual adviser.

In 1819, Eleazer asked Albert G. Ellis to join him in teaching the Indian children at Oneida Castle. In return, Eleazer agreed to teach Ellis French, Greek,
and Latin. Ellis recorded his surprise to find that Williams himself needed tu-
toring, because he did not know the basics of the English language, especially
the written aspects of it. Ellis was also responsible for doing all of Williams'
correspondence and recordings. For the next four years, Ellis worked under
Eleazer's direction but was never allowed to teach, even though a school room
was added to the old Skenandoah homestead, which Eleazer occupied. Ellis
recorded in his journal how the Oneidas would sit through lengthy sessions
while Eleazer talked of his childhood, youth, and ancestors at Caughnawaga.
Eleazer's evangelizing efforts were very well received at first. Shortly after
Ellis joined him, Eleazer began to talk about establishing a grand Iroquois empire somewhere in the vast regions west of Lake Michigan. His plan was for a
government split into civil, ecclesiastic, and military departments.

Ellis states in his records that Eleazer was in almost daily correspondence
with the War Department, the Ogden Land Company, and various missionary
societies. In a letter to the Ogden Land Company (dated September 1833),

Eleazer complained about the insignificant amount of money he received from the land speculating company for his part in the "Great Cause" of removal of the New York Indians. It is clear that Eleazer was directly in the pay of New York landed interests intent on dispossessing the Indians from the Empire State.

In the summer of 1820, Williams and a small delegation traveled west before they found out that the land which they were interested in at Green Bay had been granted to the local Indian agent, John Bowyer. The delegation returned to Oneida Castle but were not completely discouraged. Another delegation traveled to Green Bay in 1821. This time they were successful in securing a small strip four miles in width, crossing the Fox River at a right angle, and extending equidistantly from Little Chute, at the center of the strip. Both the Menominees and the Winnebagos agreed to this, for which they would receive payment and rations the following year. When the delegation returned to Oneida Castle, its members received some very strong criticism from most of the Iroquois, who wrote to Bishop Hobart complaining of Williams' plans and requesting his removal. The following year another delegation was sanctioned by the Episcopal church, the federal government, and the Ogden Land Company, with funds to return to Green Bay.

The Menominees and the Winnebagos met with the New York Indians— Oneidas, Stockbridges, Munsees, Brothertowns—to receive their deferred payment. At this point, both the Menominees and the Winnebagos were asked for an extension of the cession. The Winnebagos absolutely refused and withdrew from the council. Eleazer was very persuasive with the Menominees and made all kinds of promises; after some time, he was able to negotiate a treaty whereby the New York Indians would be joint occupants to nearly half of the present state of Wisconsin. President Monroe, with slight modification, approved the treaty in March 1823. The following year, about a hundred Oneidas and just about as many Stockbridge Indians moved to their new home. Williams and his delegation spent the winter at the vacant Indian agency at Green Bay, which Ellis tried unsuccessfully to convert into a school.

In 1823, Williams, who was about 36 years old, married 14-year-old Madelaine Jourdain, the daughter of the agency blacksmith, Joseph Jourdain, who also owned 4,800 acres. She came from a Franco-Indian (Menominee) background. It was an arranged marriage, and Madelaine, who was said to have had a suitor, had to abide by her parents' wishes. She is described as being a very attractive but "uneducated half-breed." Prior to his marriage to Madelaine, Williams had approached one of the daughters of Louis Grignon, but she politely refused his offer of marriage. Williams took his new bride to New York in 1825 to be baptized and confirmed by Bishop Hobart, who gave her his surname to be used as her middle name. The next year, Williams was ordained a deacon but never received any higher ecclesiastic rank than that.

Madelaine and Eleazer had three children, but two daughters died in infancy. Eleazer largely lived off his wife's inherited wealth. The large tract of land that

Madelaine inherited would gradually be lost to cover his debts. She died in 1886, living alone in a desolate cabin on a small parcel of land near Green Bay in Brown County. The area is now a part of Lost Dauphin State Park.

In 1827 the Menominee tribe at the Treaty of Butte des Morts showed its opposition to the New York Indians by choosing not to recognize these eastern Indians as owners of the territory ceded by the Menominees earlier. Three years later, Colonel Stambaugh advised the Menominees to sell their land to the government and disregard the interests of the New York Indians. In 1830 commissioners appointed by the president appeared at Green Bay to establish boundaries for all the Indians in the area. Chief Oshkosh, a Menominee chief, denied that the New York Indians had any right to their land, but instead insisted that they were merely tenants as long as they demonstrated good behavior. In 1831, the Menominees ceded half of their lands to the federal government and ignored the New York Indians. Finally, in 1838 the United States government would formally confirm a 65,000-acre reservation for the Oneidas, approximately 100 acres per Oneida, in the Treaty of Buffalo Creek.

Williams' dream of an "Iroquois empire" was slowly fading, as was his Iroquois following, because of his lack of attendance at the Duck Creek settlement, his lack of concern for their spiritual and educational needs, his condemnation of other denominations, and the exposure of his financial irregularities. By the 1830s the Oneidas began rejecting Williams' leadership. In 1832 the Oneidas, with Chief Daniel Bread as their leader, asked Colonel Boyd, the Indian agent, to sit in on a council meeting. Boyd complied and brought along a few Green Bay citizens. Boyd was asked to draft a copy of the Oneidas' complaints against Williams to send to the War Department, the governor of New York, and the proper authorities of the Protestant Episcopal church. The communication was witnessed and signed by the chiefs of the First Christian Party. Other complaints against Williams followed. Missionary Solomon Davis, who had been working at Oneida Castle since 1821 and who had led a group of about 250 Oneidas to the Duck Creek settlement in 1830, also sent a letter of complaint. Consequently, Bishop Hobart formally reprimanded Williams, leading to his removal.

In 1841, while at St. Regis, Williams learned that the prince de Joinville (third son of Louis Philippe, then emperor of France) was planning to retrace the expeditions of early French missionaries and go, via the Great Lakes, to Green Bay. Learning that the prince was looking for someone who knew Indian habits and history, Williams traveled to Mackinaw and met the prince's ship. In later years (1851) Williams would tell Mr. Hanson, author of *The Lost Prince,* about this encounter with the prince de Joinville. Eleazer stated that he was asked to abdicate his claim to the throne of France; however, he refused to abide by the prince's request. Thus began the outlandish "story" of the lost dauphin, namely that Williams was the lost heir to the French throne.

Williams faced repeated failures in the last two decades of his life. In 1846 the Society for the Propagation of the Gospel among the Indians and others in North America appropriated money for Williams' support as a missionary, but after two years the stipend was withdrawn. In 1850 he went east to offer his services for the removal of the Senecas from Indian Territory to the upper waters of the Mississippi; his offer was declined. He did not return to his family after this but took various missionary positions for short periods of time. He spent the remainder of his life at St. Regis. On August 28, 1858, rejected by all his followers, Eleazer died in great poverty, in a cottage at Hogansburg.

In 1947, at the impetus of Oneida leader Oscar Archiquette, Eleazer Williams' remains were exhumed from St. James Cemetery at Hogansburg, New York. He was reinterred at the cemetery of Holy Apostles Church in Oneida.

Although Eleazer Williams did establish the Episcopal tradition among the Wisconsin Oneidas, other leaders, both Indian and non-Indian, contributed significantly to the promotion of the Episcopal religion among the Oneidas. Especially influential was Reverend Edward A. Goodnough, who came to Oneida with his wife, Ellen, in 1853 and ministered to the needs of the community in the second half of the nineteenth century. Ellen Goodnough's published diary is a major source on Oneida history during those years. Besides serving the spiritual needs of the Oneida people, the Goodnoughs also served as their postmasters, justices of the peace, bankers, teachers, doctors, and political advisers.

One of the more prominent leaders of the Holy Apostles Church who stands out in my mind is Chief Cornelius Hill. A leading political leader of the Oneida Nation during his lifetime (1834–1906), Chief Hill became an ordained Episcopal priest in 1895, serving in that capacity for almost a decade before dying of tuberculosis. Thus, the strong roots of the Episcopal tradition at Oneida go far beyond the controversial Eleazer Williams.

The Oneidas in Wisconsin: The Early Years, 1822–1848
by Loretta Metoxen

The Oneida Indians did not leave all their problems behind when they migrated to the Wisconsin frontier from the early 1820s onward. They were now face-to-face with two Native American cultures—the Menominees (Algonquian) and the Winnebagos (Siouan)—that were quite distinct both from each other and from the Oneidas themselves. Moreover, almost from the time of the Oneida arrival in Wisconsin, these Indians, as well as their New York Indian allies—Stockbridge-Munsees and Brothertowns—were faced with rapid white settlement that put increased pressures on their world. These unrelenting pressures ultimately led to the disastrous policies of the Dawes General Allotment Act of 1887, which resulted in the Oneidas' loss of nearly 65,000 acres of land before the Indian New Deal.

After signing "treaties" with New York from 1785 onward under pressures exerted by that state, the War Department, and the Ogden Land Company, the

Oneida Indians, under the influence of Eleazer Williams, the Episcopal missionary of Mohawk descent, migrated to Wisconsin beginning in 1822. Wisconsin was not a state at that time and would not become a state until 1848. It
was then part of Michigan Territory, headed by Governor Lewis Cass from his
offices at Detroit.

In the summer of 1822, a council of Menominees, Winnebagos, and Oneidas convened at La Baye (Green Bay). This remarkable intertribal negotiation
led to an agreement whereby the Oneidas and other so-called New York Indians were allowed by the other two Indian nations attending to settle in the vast
Menominee Territory and undertake subsistence enterprises such as farming,
hunting, and fishing. In return for their right to settle and make use of these resources, the New York Indian emigres compensated the Menominees in goods
and cash payments.

This Menominee–New York Indian Treaty of 1822 was bothersome to the
French fur traders at Green Bay, many of whom were married to Menominee
women. Pressure was brought to bear on the Menominee chiefs to negate or
change the terms of this accord. The restlessness resounded all the way to the
War Department in Washington. Colonel John Stambaugh was appointed
United States Indian agent at Green Bay. His particular assignment was to settle the unrest within the Menominee community caused by the discontent with
the Treaty of 1822. Stambaugh's concerted efforts led to a federal treaty with
the Menominees in 1831, one that defined the Menominee lands to be used and
occupied by the New York Indians. These lands encompassed 500,000 acres
north and west of the Fox River, including several miles along the riverbed itself. Despite this provision, the Oneidas were not a direct party or signatories
to the Stambaugh Treaty.

In January 1838, the federal government and the Iroquois signed the Treaty
of Buffalo Creek. This treaty provided that the Oneidas settled in Wisconsin
and other Iroquois nations still in New York would move to lands provided for
them in Kansas, just north of the Cherokee Strip. Some Senecas and Cayugas
were removed; their descendants, the Seneca-Cayugas, are in the northeast corner of Oklahoma today. A few Oneidas went to the Indian Territory, and some
later returned. One month later, this Buffalo Creek Treaty was amended in a
separate 1838 federal agreement with the Oneidas which defined the boundaries of the Oneida Nation in Wisconsin. The original reservation was established as 8.5 miles wide and 12 miles long, encompassing 65,428 acres. The ar-
bitrary formula used to determine the size of the reservation was to allow
100 acres per person. In 1838, there were 654 Oneidas resettled in what had by
now become Wisconsin Territory. The reservation as established was not situated on a north-south longitudinal or an east-west latitudinal axis, but lay on its
side parallel to the Fox River. It never included the several miles of river
frontage defined in the 1831 Stambaugh Treaty. This omission limited the economic prosperity of the Oneidas, since they did not have access to the key

waterways up the Fox River to Lake Winnebago and also north through the Straits of Mackinac to the eastern seaboard. Such access was reserved for the descendants of French fur trappers and Franco-Menominee middlemen.

The Oneidas attempted to make the most of their lands on the ridges along Duck Creek and its tributaries. Log homes were situated where cool, clear springs provided adequate water supplies year-round. The Oneidas also had access to bountiful fishing places. Most of the Indians, nevertheless, depended on their fertile fields to farm white corn, raise livestock, or grow orchards. Yet, in and around Oneida Country were sources of concern—mighty pine forests for lumber, hardwoods that could be ideal for furniture. To the north and west of Oneida Country were valuable fur-bearing animals and minerals for smelting, which attracted both eastern capital and non-Indian immigrants in great numbers to Wisconsin Territory. The completion of the Erie Canal in 1825 unleashed a great westward movement of colonizers to the Old Northwest.

These colonizers wanted new lands and new opportunities. They pushed for Wisconsin statehood by inducing even greater immigration to and settlement in the state. In many respects they re-created the same pressures that had forced the Oneidas out of New York in the first place. Yet, these non-Indian settlers were legally prohibited from moving and establishing homes within the boundaries of any federally recognized Indian nation. As a result, these non-Indians clamored in the territorial legislature and lobbied Congress for Indian land cessions. Thus, it is not surprising to realize that Wisconsin Indians as a whole faced allotment pressures to divide their lands in fee simple title from the 1840s onward, four decades before the Dawes General Allotment Act became national policy, and even faced concerted efforts at removal from the state.

The Oneida Move to Canada
by Eileen Antone

After the Treaty of Buffalo Creek of 1838, 241 Indians led by Chief Moses Schuyler decided to relocate to lands along the banks of the Thames River in Delaware Township in the London District of Upper Canada. Previous to this move, Schuyler and August Cornelius had been part of an exploring party which went out and looked for a new abode and attempted to purchase lands from the Ojibwes in the same region. The Ojibwes sent them across the Thames River, where fertile land was available and selling for three dollars an acre. With the encouragement of the local British Indian agent, the Oneida exploring party returned to central New York and reported the potential for relocating to these lands. These Indians then "sold" their central New York lands in an accord with New York State on June 1, 1840. With permission from the British government, the Oneidas then used the proceeds from this land sale to purchase 5,000 acres. On October 10, 1840, 200 Oneidas emigrated. A second wave numbering 160 Oneidas occurred in May 1841. A third contingent of 28 Oneidas arrived in November 1845. Because the Oneidas had to purchase the land they were going to occupy, every man, woman, and child who wanted to move was required to make a payment of $42, which in later years became the single criterion for determining band membership.

According to Oneidas of the Thames oral tradition, Albany officials had given them an ultimatum before the accord of June 1, 1840, to sell their land and leave the Empire State or suffer untold consequences. Apparently when the Oneidas were trying to negotiate with state officials, the money for their New York lands was thrown at their Indian leaders, and they were told to pick it up and leave as soon as possible or suffer untold consequences.

The Oneida removal and initial settlement in Ontario were not unlike the Oneida removal to Wisconsin. They packed up their bags and traveled along the Erie Canal to its terminus at Buffalo. There they had to hire a steamer to bring them across Lake Erie to Port Stanley on the British Canadian side. After much difficulty, they secured passage on a rickety ship that was barely seaworthy. According to Oneida tradition, the Indians eventually reached Port Stanley, where they disembarked and traveled by foot overland. The ship that brought them to their new land sank on its way back to Buffalo in October 1840.

In the early years, the community evolved into three general areas based on religious practices. The River Settlement was the first land to be claimed, and it consisted mainly of Methodist followers. The second area became known as the Upper Settlement, and these residents were of the Anglican, or Episcopal faith. The third general area was called the Bush Settlement, which was composed of the people who were in need of land whether they were Methodists, Anglicans, or not practicing any particular religion.

As soon as the Oneidas settled, they invited the chiefs of the Six Nations at Grand River to come and assist in instituting the Hereditary Chiefs Council, similar to the Six Nations Council. The Hereditary Chiefs Council was recognized by the Canadian government until 1934 when it was replaced by the elective system of chief and councillors, which has since been the official council of the Oneidas of the Thames. The Oneida people lived in relative harmony for approximately 70 years with the Hereditary Chiefs Council as the governing body. In the early 1900s, John Jones from the Six Nations Reserve, along with a few other people, decided to organize the Longhouse religion, based on the Code of Handsome Lake. This religion appealed to the segment of the Oneida society who believed that cultural traditions and beliefs were being forsaken in favor of white practices. The Longhouse was formally established in 1904. After this time the Longhouse followers, including some of the former chiefs of the Hereditary Chiefs Council, set up their own council. It was a duplicate structure of the Chiefs Council, but it was never recognized by the Department of Indian Affairs as a legal governing body of the community. Although it was not considered the legal representative body of government, it continued to operate in a section of the settlement and still exists today.

The Oneidas arrived in Ontario in the midfall of 1840, at a time when the Canadian winter was fast approaching. An early winter snowfall hit long before they had begun building their homes. Thus, the first order of business was building some kind of protection from the elements, so the men got together and worked hard to build houses to shelter the people for the remainder of the winter. The first buildings were large log houses with a fire in the center and beds all along the side walls. Once they had their initial shelters erected and were settled for a while, they decided among themselves that, whatever land a person was willing to clear, he could have. This decision was possible because the title of purchased land was made by the Crown in trust to and for the use, benefit, and behalf of the Oneida Nation of Indians and their posterity forever.

The land was soon cleared of heavy virgin forest. Any land that these first settlers cleared they had the right to sell or will but only to other band members or their descendants. Since these people had been good farmers in New York State, it wasn't long before the land was cleared and small farmsteads were established. These farms usually consisted of a log cabin and outbuildings for the farm animals. An 1844 report made by the Indian agent stated that there were 6 frame and 48 log houses with wigwams and a total of 335 acres under cultivation. The first brick buildings were owned by the Methodist minister, Reverend Abraham Sickles, and William Taylor Doxtater, a leader of the Episcopalians.

When the Oneida people first arrived in Ontario, they had very little contact with the surrounding community. There was one nearby white farmer who lived directly across the river from their first camp and from whom the Indians bought some of their supplies. If he couldn't fill their orders, they would go to the general store in Delaware to make their purchases. In the early years, they grew corn, beans, squash, pumpkins, potatoes, turnips, and grain and stored them as food supplies during the winter months. Pigs and cattle were also slaughtered and stored in brine until used. The money that was needed came from the sale of baskets and cornhusk mats, which were carefully crafted during the cold winter months. In the spring, when it was time to start preparing for the next crop, the men got together and moved from farm to farm, helping each other through the seasonal work until the crops were harvested and stored for the winter. Community togetherness was also the method that was used to erect new buildings, repair old ones, clear land, and keep the roads in repair.

As the years passed, there were some major changes in the settlement. By 1860, a few families were producing commercial crops on their large holdings of 90–200 acres, but the majority of farmers, averaging 10–15 acres, could no longer provide subsistence. For this reason, many of the people turned to the white society for employment, usually by someone making contact with whites who were in need of workers. The main occupation available at this time was cutting wood. Upon confirmation of a job, a group of families would move into the bush, where they spent the fall and winter living in shanties and cutting wood. Come spring, the families would move back to the settlement. By 1880, the forest on neighboring white-owned land also became a source of income, with more and more of the Indian men starting work as day lumbermen to provide for their families. Other seasonal labor jobs that the Oneidas participated in were cutting ice in winter, picking berries, and working in canneries. Following World War I, farming continued to decline, until there were only five men in 1956 who were involved in farming as an occupation.

Differences of opinion led to the dispersal of the Oneida people from their lands in New York. The Indians who went to the Thames could have gone to the Indian Territory, left for Green Bay, settled with the Six Nations of the Grand River, Ontario, or even remained in New York State. Yet, they chose to seek their destiny along the banks of the Thames River, where they have survived for nearly 160 years.

Those Who Remained: The New York Oneidas
by Liz Obomsawin

With the great moves of the Oneidas to Wisconsin and Canada in the early 1840s came a time of great sadness among all Oneida people. The Oneidas experienced a tremendous cultural and social upheaval. Many families were torn from each other by these moves. There was much confusion and bitterness toward state officials, toward the federal government, and toward Oneida religious and political leaders. The Oneida people who stayed in New York were filled with an indefinable emptiness. There was almost nothing left of their homelands or their once strong, proud nation. With sad hearts they looked toward their seemingly bleak future.

The loss of family, friends, and land was compounded by the ever-growing loss of cultural identity and unity. Although all the remaining Oneidas spoke their own language and some could even read and write it, the assimilationist nature of the white man's school system went far in fostering white values.

By 1840, Oneidas remaining in New York still held one united landbase consisting of approximately 1,110 acres—a far cry from the original 6 million acres once possessed by the Oneidas. In 1842, the commissioners of the Land Office of the State of New York arranged for the state to purchase "such portion of the reservation as represented the equitable share in the proportion to the number of Indians" who had moved to Wisconsin. This was realized through one of the last treaties with New York State, in which the remaining and intact Oneida "reservation" was divided into lots and another 371.34 acres were ceded. The cohesiveness of the New York Oneidas suffered even more as their lands became fragmented into a checkerboard pattern of landholdings.

In 1845, the New York State government took it upon itself to initiate a census, the so-called Schoolcraft Census, of all Iroquois people remaining in the state. According to this census, there were 157 Oneidas in the Oneida Creek valley. Additionally, there were 30 Oneidas living with the Senecas, 2 with the Tuscaroras, and 21 with the Onondagas. This census also recorded that the Oneidas were using 421 acres of land in the Oneida Creek valley and leasing out another 89 acres, presumably to non-Indians.

Isaac Honyoust was one of the last Oneidas who held onto Oneida land. In 1888, he gave Philander Spalding a mortgage on his 32 acres to secure the payment of $1,250. This mortgage was then assigned to Patrick Boylan. When Boylan died in 1897, he left the mortgage to his wife, Julia. In March of 1905, the executor of Boylan's will commenced a statutory foreclosure of the mortgage. Julia Boylan then filed action in the New York Supreme Court. After much maneuvering, Julia Boylan won the case, and the interest of the Oneida Indians in this property was alleged to have been extinguished. The Oneida occupants were forcibly removed. Although the other 22 Oneidas on the remaining Oneida lands experienced similar situations, only the Boylan case was taken to the United States Court of Appeals for the Second Circuit. In a United States Supreme Court decision in 1920 [*United States* v. *Boylan*], the court affirmed that the land had been taken illegally from the Oneidas and it was returned to the Honyoust [Honyost] family. It was this 32 acres that later became known as the Oneida Indian Territory.

Over the years, many families missed their relatives in both Wisconsin and Canada and simply moved to these Oneida communities to be with them. In fact, the elders tell us that the rolls that were kept by the Oneidas in all three communities were surprisingly fluid. Some Oneidas from Canada moved back to New York and were added to the enrollment list there, while some Oneidas from New York moved to Wisconsin and were put on their rolls. Indeed, two of the Oneidas who fought with the Wisconsin Oneidas in the Civil War were New York Oneidas. These connections continued through the nineteenth century. The obituary for Daniel Scanandoah, grandson of Chief Skenandoah, presented in the *Utica Democratic Union* on August 12, 1908, demonstrates the close ties among the three Oneida communities: "Surviving are his widow; son Nelson of Vernon; daughter, Mrs. Daniel Honyoust; brothers John of Green Bay, Wisc., and Abram of Canada; and sisters, Mrs. Catherine Burning and Mrs. John Johns of Oneida."

Some of my favorite stories are those that show the continued relationships among our different Oneida communities. Just before the turn of the century, my great-grandfather, Wilson Cornelius, who was a member of the Oneidas of the Thames, fell in love with Julia Christine Carpenter, who was an Oneida Indian in New York State, over 300 miles away. While courting her, he would regularly walk back and forth between Canada and New York with nothing but the clothes on his back and a knapsack slung over his shoulder. Fortunately, he was a medicine man of the Bear Clan and knew how to "live off the land." He would eat berries, boil the leaves, roots, and bark of edible plants, and snare small animals along the way. Needless to say, his efforts were rewarded, and he and Julia were married around 1895. Wilson then moved to New York, where he lived the rest of his life.

Most of the Oneidas who stayed in New York were farmers and could support themselves quite well by selling their barley, oats, wheat, corn, and potatoes. Many of them owned horses or cows and even pigs. Making butter was a favorite pastime. A great many of them made a living by making and selling beadwork and baskets. Both men and women engaged in basket-making. The men prepared the black ash splints, and the women gathered the sweet grass, which grew extensively in the area. The men also made many wooden objects such as canes, cradles, and carvings, and the women excelled in crafting bead-work—needle cases, watch holders, purses, pin cushions, and picture frames. Another way many Oneida women made their living was to work as house-keepers. Chief Skenandoah's granddaughter Catherine Burning worked as a housekeeper to the Higgenbotham family, a leading family in the city of Oneida. Around the year 1890, the old horse-drawn streetcar in Oneida killed her husband. A number of Oneida Indian women were employed by John Humphrey Noyes, the founder of the famous Oneida Limited Silversmiths Company in Sherrill, New York. Although there was a great deal of economic interaction with non-Indians outside their close-knit communities, the Oneida people kept to themselves. There were rare cases where one would marry a non-Indian, but more often, if they married outside the Oneida Nation, it was with another Iroquois person.

The original arrangement with the federal government at the time of and just following the American Revolution (in which the Oneidas were referred to as the faithful allies) was that the government would deal with the Oneida Nation as a separate nation and protect their interests. All Oneidas had been intensely disappointed when the federal government turned a deaf ear to their pleas to intervene in their dealings with land speculators and New York State. Feeling betrayed, this situation left a crimp in their relationship with the federal gov-ernment thereafter; however, this did not stop them from enlisting in the Civil War. A large council of Oneidas met to decide whether they should enter the Civil War in spite of their betrayal by the federal government. Although they made a decision as a nation not to get involved, some of the Oneida men de-cided to join anyway. At least three Oneida men from New York joined the army during the war.

Ray Elm, who was one of our oldest elders in New York, shared with me some wonderful stories of his two grandfathers, who had joined the Civil War. The first was Nicholas Honyoust, who was quite a colorful character. He was well liked by whites and Indians in and around the city of Oneida. He decided that he would like to join the Civil War. He walked up the long hill to Peterborough, where he heard the government was enlisting men, stayed for three days, then decided to desert because he felt that the army was starving him to death! He turned around and went back home. Nobody bothered him, and that was the end of that.

Ray Elm's other grandfather, Abraham Elm, was quite a different story. He and several other Oneida Indians decided they would enlist in Vermont rather than in New York because Vermont paid bigger bounties. They hired a horse and buggy, with a white driver, and rode off to Vermont. Abraham Elm fought hard and well during the war. In one battle, the cannon that he was manning backfired and rolled over on him and one of his fellow soldiers. The Union army then retreated, leaving Abraham and his friend at the mercy of the Confederate soldiers. The enemy freed him from the wheels and then most humanely nursed them both back to some degree of health. As a result of this accident, Abraham was crippled for the rest of his life. Yet, he was an inspiring individual, full of strength and integrity. Later, because of his political activism, Abraham Elm was one of the founders of the Society of American Indians. Founded in 1911, this was the first American Indian civil rights organization in the United States. Elm was an exceptional person. Unlike most Oneidas, who made no attempt to become involved in American politics and did not push for United States citizenship and suffrage, he attempted to vote. In 1876, he was arrested and indicted for voting illegally in an early test case involving American Indians and United States citizenship [*United States* v. *Abraham Elm*].

Many other elders have shared fascinating stories about the Oneidas who remained in New York. Oral tradition remains a powerful means whereby our histories are preserved and handed down. One fact remains clear and irrefutable: The Oneidas in New York have survived, as individuals and as a people. We have come a long way since those early days. Many Oneidas have moved from areas around the United States to return to the original homeland. Many are relearning the Oneida language, and a good many of us have still held on to much of our culture. A traditional government is now in place and various Oneida Nation businesses in New York ensure the Oneidas a secure future. May we all hold hands as we face the future together.

Legacy of Removal: The Oneida Indian Land Claims
by Richard Chrisjohn

The Oneidas were forced west. One group went along Lake Erie and settled between the towns of London and St. Thomas, Ontario. The other went across the Great Lakes, settling in Wisconsin, being allowed to settle there by the Menominees. The hunting was so plentiful near Green Bay that the Oneidas decided to stay, buying land from the Menominees. Yet, they did not forget what had happened to them in New York, and they continued to remember the injustices they faced there. [Between 1785 and 1846] we lost about 5 million acres in New York.

I was born in Canada at Oneida on the Thames. As a young man of 13, I went to live at the Onondaga Reservation near Syracuse in 1934, where I came in contact with some Oneida families. At the time there were few families at Oneida, New York, on the 32 acres. In New York, the Oneidas were always talking about their land claims. My mother-in-law, Mary Winder, had me go around all over looking for Oneida deeds. She collected information about the claim and found out that every town on the north shore of Oneida Lake had land reserved for Indian camps. Moreover, she found that the shoreline up to 10 feet was reserved for the Oneidas when they wanted to travel. Mrs. Winder would also send letters to Washington about the claim, but nothing happened. In the 1940s we formed an elective system of government so that we could present the claim. Two decades later, after the death of William Rockwell, the 600–700 Oneidas began in earnest to pursue the claim. More Oneidas moved back to the 32 acres with the hope of building good homes and improving the life of the people.

PART III

DOING ONEIDA INDIAN HISTORY: NEEDS, APPROACHES, AND RESOURCES

Introduction

One major aim of this collection is to promote future research in Oneida history. The following chapters focus on this objective in very specific ways. Francis Jennings, director emeritus of the D'Arcy McNickle Center for the History of the American Indian at the Newberry Library in Chicago, attempts to demystify the nature of historical research and encourage the Oneidas themselves to become professional historians. Jennings readily admits the lack of objectivity and bias in some past historical treatments on the Oneidas and other American Indians, but he urges Oneidas to overcome their resentment over these accounts and begin to write down their own histories. Jennings calls for "honest scholarship and fair play in opposition to the assumptions of conquest" in the writings of Indian history. He warns against filiopiety, namely, the tendency of all cultures to promote the idea that they are the greatest on earth.

Jennings' chapter is followed by two chapters focusing on two distinct forms of historical materials: governmental documents and maps. James Folts, senior archivist of the New York State Archives in Albany, describes the rich resources on New York's official relations with the Oneidas. He shows clearly that the record groups of the New York State Archives and the document collections of the New York State Library offer a wide variety of opportunities for researchers in Oneida history. They include the records of Indian councils, treaty negotiations, annuity records, expense accounts, and special censuses. In his carefully documented study, Folts gives the reader a road map to undertake his or her own research in Oneida history from the colonial period through Indian removal to Wisconsin and Canada.

In chapter 10, Jo Margaret Mano, associate professor of geography at the State University of New York at New Paltz and an expert on the cartographic records of New York State, describes how the Indians were removed from the mapped landscape in New York from 1792 to 1845. She clearly shows the importance of the master cartographer Simeon De Witt, as well as of Joseph Ellicott, in shaping New York State's cartography and surveying. To Mano, maps are social constructs, and often their "visual impact is more immediate and intuitive than a written description." The cartographic records show the increasing pressures that the Oneidas and other Indians in New York State faced after the American Revolution and are another form of documentation of the process of dispossession. She concludes: "In the case of the Oneida and the Six Nations, the juxtaposition of map ingredients and the *missing* information speak volumes."

To encourage future research, Debra Anderson, the archivist at the University of Wisconsin–Green Bay Area Center of the State Historical Society of Wisconsin, then provides the reader with an index of pre-1887 manuscript collections and governmental records available at the State Historical Society of Wisconsin in Madison and Green Bay. Anderson's index, which has a cutoff date of 1887 (pre–Dawes General Allotment Act), is followed by a select bibliography of works on Wisconsin Oneida history, 1820–1870.

8 *Francis Jennings*

Doing Oneida Indian History

Anyone with average intelligence can dig up information after learning a few skills and tricks of working with collections of documents. The hardest part of historical research is opening one's mind to evidence after carefully testing its authenticity. I do not mean that in some mysterious fashion the professional historian has freed himself from preconceptions. No one can arrive at adulthood without having picked up all sorts of preconceptions and biases. It is nonsense to speak of approaching research with an empty head. So the most difficult and painful part of research comes when the evidence contradicts those preconceptions. When that happens the historian has to change his mind and conceive new ideas that fit the evidence. That's tough, but it is also absolutely fundamental.

On the surface, the life of a historian seems ideal; one deals with interesting subjects and has the glow of satisfaction that comes from making a contribution to knowledge. Life in libraries is calm except for the excitement of discovery. Working conditions are clean, reasonably comfortable, and there are bright, informed people to talk to. I almost said that this is an occupation without hazards, but I've learned better. As in every other vocation, as soon as one tells the truth about a situation or a person, he acquires the wrath of parties interested in keeping the truth unknown. It will be hard for a pioneering tribal historian to resist the pressures, which are bound to come, for him to espouse some sort of propaganda. And it must be confessed that after centuries of growth and improvement of the historical profession, we still have in the profession itself altogether too much racism, nationalism, jingoism, and bigotry to contend with. But we've made some progress or there would be no non-Indian contributors to this book. I look forward to the great day when a significant number of Indian historians contribute to the annual conferences of the major professional associations. They can tell us much that the professionals and the general public need to learn.

A historian is worthless unless he writes honestly according to his evidence. To look for bits and pieces of fact just to support a preconceived program is the antithesis of history, a false substitute that would simply be propaganda. It would be a great mistake for new American Indian historians to huff and puff and blow hard about how their people are the greatest people in the world, and they're always right when everyone else is wrong. I remember on an occasion in Ottawa when an Ojibwe, a very sophisticated government official, claimed that Ojibwes are the greatest people in the world. He excited me. I asked a Cree chief on the same platform if he agreed that the Ojibwes are the greatest people in the world. He was a polite gentleman, so he did not fire up, but we all agreed that maybe the Crees are pretty good too. What Oneida historians will have to accept if they are to be taken seriously, as I expect them to be, is that Oneidas are human beings, much like other people. All sorts of characters will be found on the family tree; maybe some of them were hanging there, although undoubtedly there are heroes and heroines also. But most of those ancestors, without any doubt at all, were just people trying to make a decent living for themselves and their families and willing to get along with anyone who would leave them at peace.

I am reminded of what happened one day when I was pushing a pencil in the library of the Historical Society of Pennsylvania. An elderly woman who had seen my name on the sign-in register rushed up to inquire if I was one of the Jennings of New Jersey. Even though I did live in Glassboro, New Jersey, at the time, this was a surprise; one might almost say that nobody was paying any attention at all to me. Then, light dawned as she told me that a very early governor of colonial New Jersey had been named Jennings. The woman who was so breathlessly interrogating me had high hopes of finding glamour in the connection. I disappointed her. I told her that the furthest back I have traced my ancestry was to one Solomon Jennings, who had been a thug in the pay of Thomas Penn. She never bothered me again.

The history of American Indians is special in its events and people. But it is very much like histories of other peoples and what historians do with them. In one sense all the happenings of those thousands of years present an opportunity for the writer to show what he's capable of thinking. A remark has often been made that each new generation rewrites history to reflect its new interests. I've often thought that every historian does the same. Basically we now have general consensus that American Indians belong to the same human species as

Europeans, Asians, Africans, and so forth. As progress goes, this improvement is not a slight matter. It has greatly restricted the writings of the "conquest map" about Indians having nothing human but their shape. In consequence it compels writers to conceive Indians within the bounds of the same moral obligations due persons like themselves. Nothing less is at stake than the conceptual foundations of the caste system that masquerades under the name of race. Yet there's a way of evading recognition of Indian humanity, namely, the long-established way of blind semantics. This approach is not limited to past historians such as Frederick Jackson Turner or anthropologists such as Lewis Henry Morgan, who thought in evolutionary terms about the transformation of so-called savages roaming in wild license through the wilderness into persons living in human communities governed by law.

Even recent historians are guilty of blind semantics. For example, Professor Bernard Bailyn, of Harvard University, began publishing a project, *The Peopling of British North America,* which is interesting on several accounts. His work on that peopling starts after 1770. His word *British* uses a legal fiction to ignore the existence of even the French Canadians, and he fails to notice there were Irishmen among his immigrants coming to join other Irishmen already scattered through the colonies. Professor Bailyn reveals his attitudes by qualifying the word *peopling.* The project he writes does not involve to any significant extent the movements of either of the two non-caucasian peoples—the Native Americans and the Africans. The language is straightforward. What should we think of the history it describes?

So long as Amerindians and African Americans are marginalized or conceived as inherently inferior by nature, no obligation exists in the upper caste to give equality of opportunity to lower-caste creatures. Indeed the uppers feel an obligation to rule over the lowers for their own good. The common excuse has it that those inferior creatures would not know what to do with equality. It used to be said that they could not be trusted with the right to vote. Such excuses could not be sustained intellectually or morally after the full humanity of blacks and Indians became fixed in common consciousness. The traditions of honest scholarship and fair play stand in opposition to the assumptions that conquest and rule are a homogeneous and exclusive tradition of United States history. Abolitionists are as much a part of history as slavery and a more inspiring one. Ethnohistory and its predecessors, especially among anthropologists, are every bit as indigenous to our history and have as long a pedigree as the ramshackle conceptual contrivance called Western civilization. Now, this is not the place to explore all the faults and contradictions in Western civilization. It may be dismissed here as another variant of the cant of conquest.

Present concerns require examination of the idea of tradition as it has manifested itself among Indians. Once more we must make distinctions. It is obvious enough, I think, that there's no such thing as generic Indian tradition. What ordinarily passes under that name is the mass of specifically tribal traditions which, insofar as they have historical relevance, often contradict each other. I remember the distress of a midwestern Indian at the idea that his tribe might be confused with its neighbor tribe. No way. We dance in opposite directions, said he. And for him that settled their separate identities. Ways of doing things as in rituals and crafts are one form of tradition. This must be distinguished from spoken accounts, the oral tradition passed from elders to children. Like some historians of European descent, reciters of oral tradition may have purposes other than simple preservation of truth. I've explored various tribal traditions concerning Iroquois domination over the Delaware Indians, and I found them full of discrepancies.

As traditions are plural, so are traditionalists. Some are concerned with preventing knowledge of ancient ways from falling into oblivion. They seek to keep the tribal language alive and to preserve rituals that maintain the people's unity and pride. This kind of traditionalist does not necessarily set himself or herself against cultural accommodation to change in other respects. Historians and Iroquois people have every reason to feel grateful to the ceremonial chiefs of the Six Nations Council in Canada for their preservation of the tradition narrative of the formation of the confederation of the Five Nations and to the Iroquoian, an institute on the Six Nations Reserve, for its educational activities. Here at Oneida, Wisconsin, much effort is given to preserving the tribal language. Yet neither at Six Nations Reserve nor at Oneida, Wisconsin, do Indian people oppose new technology.

For those Oneidas who want to take up my invitation to go looking around in dusty archives, I can't always offer you the dust. The Newberry Library in Chicago is a clean place, but you will be welcomed there. These Oneida conferences and the proceedings produced are a long step in the right direction. It is now time for the Oneidas to join in the ranks of professional historians in order to elucidate their remarkable past.

9 *James D. Folts*

Before the Dispersal
Records of New York's Official Relations with the Oneidas
and Other Indian Nations

Documents of the relations between the government of New York and the native peoples who lived (and live still) from Montauk to Niagara are preserved in colonial, imperial, state, and national archives—in Albany, Washington, D.C., Ottawa, and London. Much of the information is also available in libraries; many of New York's Indian treaties and related documents have been published, and some official documents of New York Indian relations have passed into other hands. In the late twentieth century new publications of these historical source materials are appearing for the benefit of scholars and students. However, these editions (paper or microfilm) are by their nature a selection, a compromise in one way or another. The original documents retain their intrinsic and symbolic values, as well as their usefulness to researchers.[1]

In light of the tortuous history of New York's archival records and the late start of its institutional state archives, it is a small wonder that so many documents of New York's official Indian relations have survived (many have not).[2] The extant records of Indian affairs in New York from the seventeenth through the early nineteenth century are found in scattered bodies of documentation, large and small, in the New York State Archives and in several other institutions. This chapter will provide an overview of that documentation, particularly as it relates to the Oneidas before and during their dispersal west from New York; and will assess the various efforts, some of them still under way, to preserve and disseminate that documentation.

European notions of diplomacy, sovereignty, legality, and property have shaped the archival record of Indian relations in New York, other states, and the United States as a whole. However, the ponderous phraseology of the common law, as found in Indian deeds and treaties, is ill-suited for describing the complexities and the peculiarities of Indian-white relations in early New York. Diplomatic proceedings between the Five Nations and the colonial representatives of European powers incorporated the formalities of the traditional Iroquoian Condolence Ceremony. The Indians and whites described their mutual alliances using the metaphors of familial relationships and the "covenant chain."[3] After the Revolutionary War, the triumphant Americans considered the Six Nations to be dependent nations, or simply wards of the government. Both state and federal treaties soon dispensed with traditional protocol, though the fiction of a friendly alliance was maintained; treaties were typically land cessions and took the form of a "bargain and sale" or "quitclaim" deed.[4] Treaty documents have limitations as sources of information about the diplomacy of native peoples because of the difficulties of translation and the bias or ignorance of the European-American negotiators and clerks.[5] However, Indian treaties, deeds, and associated documents provide abundant data on treaty protocol and discourse, on native leaders and spokesmen, on Indian personal and place names, and on the use of diplomacy to gain political advantage and to acquire or defend lands. Most important for the history of the Oneidas, the official records of New York's Indian relations over a period of two centuries contain indirect but important evidence of the intimate, intense world of native villages, often riven by competing factions and interests.[6]

Evidence of treaty proceedings and agreements took various forms. Europeans considered a signed and sealed document, engrossed on parchment or paper, to be enduring evidence of the treaty or deed. As extra insurance against loss, Indian treaties and deeds were copied ("recorded") into books. Both the original treaties and deeds and the recorded copies were maintained by the secretary of the colony of New York, and by his successor after 1777, the New York State secretary of state. However, the original treaties retained their importance as visible, tangible evidence of continuing commitments. The original parchment treaties between the Oneidas and other nations and the state of New York after the Revolutionary War bore receipts by chiefs and warriors for payment of annuities by the state into the 1820s. (Thereafter the receipts were filed separately.)[7]

The Native Americans considered wampum strings or belts as symbols of messages exchanged at the treaty, and also as mnemonic devices to help them remember the treaty proceedings.[8] The Six Nations Council at Onondaga had custody of a "whole pile" of wampum belts, which were temporarily housed in the cabin of two Moravian brethren who resided at Onondaga in 1754–1755 in order to learn the language.[9] On at least some occasions, Indian chiefs who were parties to a treaty or a deed received duplicate originals of the paper or parchment document.[10] At the Treaty of Fort Stanwix, negotiated by Sir William Johnson with the Six Nations and other Indian peoples in 1768, the signing of the deed of cession on November 5 was the final act of the Indian chiefs after agreement was reached. Signing was done on the parade ground of the fort, prior to the distribution of presents, which were set out for public display.[11] The Indians were well aware of the uses of documents. During the proceedings at Fort Stanwix, the Iroquois chiefs borrowed from Johnson a map to help develop a counterproposal on the contentious issue of where to run the Indian boundary line through the Oneida Country.[12]

Most wampum belts have been lost over the centuries. Likewise, many of the early records of New York Colony and State relating to Indians are no longer extant or have been alienated from state custody. In fact, there never has been a unitary, complete "archive" of documents on Indian affairs in New York. An inventory of records in the New York secretary of state's office, made by or for Secretary John Van Ness Yates in 1818, found dozens of manuscript volumes and innumerable filed, bundled papers relating, in whole or in part, to Indian affairs in the colonial and early national periods.[13] The inventory lists original, signed and sealed Indian treaties and deeds; copies of the same, recorded into various books of treaties, deeds, and patents; books of warrants of survey and licenses to purchase Indian lands; numerous large packets of "papers relating to Indian affairs" dating from the 1670s to the 1760s; and receipts for annuities paid to the Oneidas and other Indian tribes pursuant to treaties made after the Revolutionary War. The inventory remarked that the papers relating to Indian affairs "in fact form a very small portion of the negociations between the natives and the Colonists." It was noted that the books of Dutch and English records "abound with transactions" relating to Indians, and that "it would be utterly impossible to present in this place a suscinct or satisfactory account of this subject."[14] Unfortunately, there was no attempt to make an inventory of records on Indian affairs kept by other state officers, such as the governor, the comptroller, the surveyor general, and the Indian commissioners and agents.

The 1818 inventory stated that few original Indian treaties from the colonial period were to be found in the secretary of state's office. The maker of the inventory noted that one or more of the treaties may have been retained by the family of Sir William Johnson, the superintendent of Indian affairs for northern North America from 1755 to 1774. He also noted that during the Revolutionary War a book of recorded Indian treaties or land cessions was stored with some other records of New York Province in a locked chest which was kept in various British warships anchored in New York harbor. Unfortunately the book of treaties was not among the records, now damaged by bilge water, which the British government transferred to the New York secretary of state in 1783.[15]

Conscious of the losses of or damage to important records, Secretary of State John Van Ness Yates obtained a legislative appropriation to rebind and to some extent reorder the old record books in his office.[16]

The midnineteenth century saw a reorganization of New York's colonial records, which accommodated the needs of the school of imperial-colonial, Eurocentric history best represented by the works of Francis Parkman. The documentary evidence of the conduct of New York's Indian affairs was integrated into new chronological series. In the early 1850s, Edmund B. O'Callaghan, M.D., an accomplished amateur historian, arranged most of the various series of documents in the office of the secretary of state in chronological order and prepared a calendar to those documents. The result was one large series entitled "Colonial Manuscripts," comprising over 25,000 documents, incorporating the formerly separate series "Council Papers," "Indian Papers," one group of William Johnson documents, and so on.[17] This simplified organization of archival documents tended to obscure both the administrative and the native perspectives.

The New York State Library was established by the legislature in 1818, received its own building in 1854, and moved into the new state capitol in 1883. The growing library seemed an appropriate repository for the historical records of New York State government that were no longer in regular use.[18] In 1881 the secretary of state transferred several hundred volumes of records and mounted documents to the state library.[19] Particularly important for the study of Indian relations were the Dutch and English "Colonial Manuscripts" (103 volumes); the English council minutes (28 volumes); licenses to purchase Indian lands, warrants of survey, and so on (7 volumes); Indian traders' bonds required to be filed pursuant to the Royal Proclamation of 1763 (2 volumes); New York Assembly documents relating to Indian affairs after the Revolutionary War (2 volumes); and the first volume of recorded Indian treaties (commencing 1692).[20] (The second and third volumes of recorded treaties remained in the secretary's office.) Despite the crowded condition of the state library, the precious records received better care there than in the secretary of state's office. In 1864 a report on historical records in the secretary's office had noted that the original parchment Indian treaties and annuity receipts were stuffed into drawers, "without index, order or arrangement."[21] An inventory of the library's manuscript collections published in 1900 carefully listed the contents of seven file cases of these treaties with the Mohawks, Oneidas, Onondagas, Cayugas, Senecas, Tuscaroras, and the Stockbridge Indians.[22]

On March 29, 1911, a catastrophic fire swept through the state library, then located in the state capitol. The book collection was almost totally destroyed, but many of the bound manuscripts were salvaged because they were buried under wet debris. Among the records that were lost were the original and recorded Indian treaties and the Indian traders' bonds. However, the other series of records of New York Colony and State relating to Indian affairs survived to a greater or lesser extent, and were repaired by library staff during the 1920s.[23] The archival records in the custody of the state library were transferred to the newly opened New York State Archives in 1978.

Despite the losses in the 1911 fire, the New York State Archives today holds many records containing information on the native peoples of New York, past and present.[24] One significant category of records is Indian treaties and deeds.[25] The secretary of state's office transferred two volumes of original (signed and sealed) treaties and associated documents, dating from 1781 to 1847, to the state library in 1924.[26] The second and third volumes of recorded Indian treaties and deeds of cession, dating from 1748 to 1847, were transferred to the state archives in 1979.[27] These two record series contain dozens of documents relating to Oneida land cessions between 1785 and 1842. Other Indian deeds, mostly for lands in the Hudson and Mohawk valleys and on Long Island, are scattered through various record series. The Duke of York's Laws of 1665 required that a purchaser of lands from the Indians first obtain a license from the governor and council and that Indian deeds be recorded by the provincial secretary.[28] For that reason, books 2 and 3 of the secretary of state's "Record of Deeds," originally and more appropriately titled "Miscellaneous Records," contain numerous seventeenth-century Indian deeds, as well as a few treaties.[29] The applications for land grants by letters patent contain scores of original Indian deeds dating as early as the 1670s.[30] Two other series in the archives contain scattered Indian deeds from the decades of the 1680s and 1720s.[31]

The officials of New York Colony and State preserved Indian treaties and deeds because they documented title to real property. It was a different story in regard to the diplomatic record of proceedings with Indian nations. For over a century New York conducted its official proceedings with the Indians through appointed commissioners, and almost all the records of those commissioners have left the custody of New York's government. Some of those alienated records were subsequently lost or destroyed. The magistrates of Albany were keenly interested in Indian relations because of the community's dependence on the trade in furs and skins. After 1675 the Albany magistrates were formally designated as provincial commissioners of Indian affairs and were guided by instructions from the governor. One of Robert Livingston's duties as the Albany city clerk was to record proceedings of meetings with the Indians. His position as secretary of Indian affairs was formalized in 1696, and he served in that post almost continuously until 1721. His son Philip Livingston served as secretary of Indian affairs until 1749.[32] Meanwhile, in 1746, Governor George Clinton dismissed the Indian commissioners and entrusted Indian affairs to a single individual—William Johnson, an Anglo-Irish immigrant who first managed a relative's Mohawk Valley estate and then turned Indian trader.[33] The proceedings of the Indian commissioners were recorded on folded sheets and maintained in that format until 1751, when they were bound into four folio volumes at the order of William Johnson.

Johnson resigned as "colonel of the Six Nations" later on in 1751, angered that he had not been reimbursed fully for his expenses. The Albany magistrates were reappointed as Indian commissioners in 1752. However, in 1755 the Crown appointed Johnson sole superintendent of Indian affairs for northern North America. Johnson again got custody of the records of the Albany Indian commissioners.[34] The secretaries of Indian affairs recorded detailed minutes of the numerous treaties and conferences held by Sir William Johnson with the Six Nations during the French and Indian War (1755–1760), the subsequent Indian war led by Pontiac, an Ottawa chief (1763–1764), and the periods of uneasy peace that followed those conflicts. After Sir William's death in 1774, the new superintendent, Guy Johnson, assumed custody of the records of the Albany Indian commissioners and the Indian superintendency and took them with him on his flight to Canada after the outbreak of the war in the spring of 1775.[35] The manuscript proceedings of Indian conferences held by Sir William Johnson and Guy Johnson during the period 1755–1775, and the third and fourth of the four volumes of the records of the Albany Indian commissioners covering the period 1723–1748, are now in the Public Archives of Canada.[36] The first and second volumes, covering the period 1677–1723, disappeared sometime in the nineteenth century.[37]

Most of Sir William Johnson's official and personal papers were acquired by the state of New York, in four different groups (1801, 1850, 1863, and 1866).[38] These documents were deposited in the state library and were grievously damaged in the 1911 fire. The 14-volume edition of the *Papers of Sir William Johnson* published the charred remnants along with numerous letters to and from Johnson held by other repositories.[39] However, the editors did not reprint documents that had already been printed elsewhere.[40] The index volume, a monument of thoroughness, lists several hundred page references to the Oneida Indians. Other Johnson documents relating to New York Indian affairs have only recently been made public.[41]

The proceedings of the New York commissioners of Indian affairs are important because they contain minutes of numerous informal meetings with the Six Nations that did not result in formal treaties that were recorded elsewhere. References to the Oneidas and other tribes of the Six Nations are innumerable. Fortunately, there are summary or substitute sources of information for many of the lost proceedings. Peter Wraxall, whom the Crown appointed in 1750 as clerk of Albany City and County and secretary of Indian affairs, prepared in 1754 an abridgment of the commissioners' proceedings through the year 1751. Wraxall's abridgment was purchased by the New York State Library in 1854 and was destroyed in the 1911 capitol fire. However, a well-edited transcript made in 1904 was published in 1915.[42] Wraxall's abridgment must be used with caution; he supported William Johnson's political interests, as well as his own, and berated the Albany merchants and traders for dishonest dealings with the Indians and for smuggling goods to Canada.[43]

The personal papers of Robert Livingston, the long-time secretary of Indian affairs, contain numerous drafts or transcripts of proceedings of the Indian commissioners between the years 1666 and 1723. These documents were edited and published in 1956.[44] The papers of Cadwallader Colden at the New-York Historical Society include other copies of proceedings of Indian conferences for various dates, 1677–1690.[45] Colden was the New York surveyor general for 40 years, acting governor for some periods, and a scientist and historian. Colden's *History of the Five Indian Nations of Canada, Which Are Dependent on the Province of New-York in America, and Are the Barrier between the English and French in That Part of the World,* first published in 1727, drew liberally on the proceedings of the Albany Indian commissioners.[46] Extracts from the lost proceedings of the New York Indian commissioners, evidently prepared in the 1720s for New York governor William Burnet, are now in the American Antiquarian Society in Worcester, Massachusetts. This document was published in 1982.[47] Other unpublished transcripts of the commissioners' proceedings survive for various dates in the 1740s and 1750s.[48] Finally, the filed papers of the governor's council contain occasional reports from the Indian commissioners, particularly in wartime.[49]

During the Revolutionary War the Continental Congress appointed Indian commissioners in the "Northern Department," chief of whom was General Philip Schuyler, a New Yorker.[50] However, New York also designated its own Indian commissioners in 1779, 1783, 1784, and 1788. New York asserted its exclusive right to negotiate with the Indians living within its boundaries, under a provision of the Articles of Confederation. After the war the New York Indian commissioners in effect expropriated the millions of acres of lands occupied by the Six Nations (including the Oneidas and Tuscaroras, allies of the United States). The Indians were confined to reservations, which in turn were reduced or eliminated within a few decades. This sordid story has been told often, generally from the same array of printed sources.[51] The manuscript proceedings of the New York State Indian commissioners during the period 1784–1790 were later donated to what is now the Albany Institute of History and Art. They were published, with extensive annotations by Franklin B. Hough, in 1861.[52] The commissioners concluded their services in 1790, when the federal government assumed its constitutional responsibility for Indian relations. Thereafter, appointed state agents were responsible for paying the annuities required by New York's treaties, most of them not ratified by the United States Congress, as required by the federal Trade and Intercourse Acts of 1790 and 1793. They and the commissioners of the Land Office carried on other state business relating to the Indians residing in New York and, in the cases of the Oneidas and Cayugas, those residing in other states.[53]

The archives of the state of New York contain numerous fiscal documents of the post–Revolutionary War Indian commissioners and agents. This routine evidence of fiscal transactions yields new data on the Oneida people and their relations with the New York government during the period 1780–1840. Again, use of these documents is facilitated by a knowledge of their history and of the losses that have occurred. The state comptroller, an officer established in 1797, was required to audit and approve all vouchers for payments out of the state treasury. In the 1890s historically minded individuals began mining the huge mass of comptroller's records for significant documents. Thousands of accounts and claims of Revolutionary War officers and soldiers, audited after the war, were mounted into volumes and transferred to the state library. Some of these documents referred to Oneidas who had served in the American forces. Regrettably these documents on the Oneidas were destroyed in the capitol fire.[54] However, there survive numerous claims by warriors of the Six Nations, including 11 Oneidas, for reimbursement for the expense of arms, equipment, clothing, and travel during the War of 1812. These claims are evidence of the continuing warrior tradition among the Six Nations in the nineteenth century.[55]

In 1910 many additional comptroller's documents were selected for preservation because they related to the activities of the Indian commissioners and agents and other state officers in the decades after the Revolutionary War. A bit smudged from the capitol fire but otherwise intact, they provide graphic details about the postwar conferences and treaties between New York and the Six Nations.[56] There are accounts for the making of wampum belts, for the trade goods presented to the Indians, for the substantial travel expenses of the Indian commissioners and agents, and for the purchase of the vast amounts of food and drink consumed at the conferences. While the Indians' liking for liquor cannot be gainsaid, the Americans were also heavy drinkers.[57] When Governor George Clinton and the other Indian commissioners met on August 27, 1784, to discuss the forthcoming treaty with the Six Nations at Fort Stanwix, their bill for "Supper" was £3 11s., for "Wine, porter, punch, Grogg &c.," £8 15s. Other vouchers reveal the plight and the pride of the Oneidas. In 1791 the sheriff of Herkimer County submitted an expense account for himself and his posse for the costs of evicting white settlers from the Oneida and Cayuga reservations and arresting the squatter Honyost Schuyler. The next year 22 Oneida warriors were awarded blankets as had been promised to them by Colonel Marinus Willett for special services during the Revolutionary War.[58]

Unfortunately, many of the comptroller's documents relating to the expenses of Indian commissioners and agents and the Indian annuity payments were destroyed through an inexcusable accident. In 1951–1952 employees of the old Division of Archives and History in the State Education Department examined over 10,000 cubic feet of filed papers of the comptroller's office. From the approximately 200 tons of documents, 1 ton (88 cartons) was considered "historical" and designated for preservation. Among the documents were four cartons of "Receipts for Indian annuities & Indian enumeration[s]," among them documents for the Oneidas, 1795–1850.[59] In October 1955 the 88 cartons of historical documents were mistakenly hauled away to a paper mill in Québec to be pulped. Near the Canadian border some Onondaga Indian annuity receipts flew off the truck. They came into the hands of the president of the Onondaga Historical Association in Syracuse, who went to Montréal and purchased 262 pounds of records as waste paper for the sum of $8. These documents remain at the Onondaga Historical Association to the present.[60] The newspapers reported the affair in embarrassing detail, and in early December 1955, the state historian sent four staff members to Québec to purchase the remaining documents, amounting to 265 pounds.[61] These records are now in the state archives.

The salvaged documents include additional accounts, claims, and receipts for expenses of Indian commissioners and agents, and related documents. For example, a visit of some Oneida chiefs to Albany in the winter of 1814 cost the state $1,000.05 for their "entertainment," mostly board and lodging in local inns. (The "Chiefs & warriors of the Christian party" declared they "Received good treatment in any way and maner from the Land Lord of the house and of his wife.") Documents from 1819 concern the $4,500 cost of a new church at Oneida, intended to serve the two Christian parties of the Oneidas. John W. Quinney, a chief of the Stockbridge Indians, petitioned Governor De Witt Clinton in 1825 for $42 to cover additional expenses "for the transportation of the Poor of our Nation & for provisions from New Stockbridge [New York] to Green Bay [Wisconsin]." In 1826 Thomas Dean, schoolteacher to the Brothertown Indians, claimed $26.16 for school books and slates he purchased for his pupils at a stationery store in Utica, New York.[62] The records saved from the paper mill also document the state's regular payments of annuities, as required by the post–Revolutionary War treaties. For several decades Oneida "sachems and chiefs" marked or signed the receipts.[63] Annuities to the Oneidas were discontinued in 1841, when the state unilaterally paid a lump sum of $92,489.72 to the New York and Wisconsin Oneidas.[64]

The New York State Archives holds some lists of individuals belonging to the Oneidas and the associated Brothertown Indians. A list of the Brothertowns in central New York was made in 1795, for the distribution of proceeds from sale of their reservation by state-appointed commissioners.[65] In 1840–1842 the New York commissioners of the Land Office obtained cessions of the lands of New York Oneidas planning to emigrate to the township of Delaware, London District, Upper Canada, or elsewhere (some may have gone to Wisconsin). Accompanying the "treaties" are lists of the men, women, and children of the First and Second Christian parties and the Orchard Party. There is also a list of Brothertown Indians then residing in Oneida County, New York.[66] The New York State census of 1845 listed heads of households on the Indian reservations. Supervised by the ethnologist Henry R. Schoolcraft, the census of the reservations provides personal names, both in their native language and in English translation, for the Oneidas, Onondagas, and Tuscaroras.[67] The New York Indian agents also maintained copies of federal annuity rolls or censuses for the Oneidas living in New York (either at Oneida or on the Onondaga reservation) for scattered years between 1891 and 1924. The lists include names of all individuals in a household, and in some cases they state ages and relationships.[68]

Generally the "solutions" to preserving and disseminating the texts of Indian treaties and deeds have suited the needs of academic historians and records custodians, while the needs of other users have been slighted. The earliest form of preservation was the recording of the deeds and treaties into books. The covers of the books provide some protection for the pages inside, and the recorded copy was deemed to be legally equivalent to the original. However, this method of preservation is inadequate, as both the original and the recorded Indian treaties in the New York State Archives reveal. The pages or leaves are weakening overall and are beginning to tear on the edges and in the folds. Some tears were mended with sticky transparent plastic tape, compounding the damage.

A favored method of preserving and disseminating the information in Indian treaty documents has been publication. Starting in the 1690s some New York Indian treaties were printed in pamphlet or broadside form.[69] During the nineteenth and early twentieth centuries, many proceedings of colonial Indian treaties and conferences were published by the state of New York: in the *Documents Relative to the Colonial History of the State of New-York,* 15 volumes (1856–1887); and in the *Papers of Sir William Johnson,* 14 volumes (1921–1965). The former series printed thousands of documents transcribed from English, French, and Dutch archives.[70] Despite their continuing value for historians, both of these editions were selective, not comprehensive. For example, they do not include documents relating to the many eighteenth-century contacts between the proprietary government of Pennsylvania and the Six Nations.[71] The most complete printed collections of post–Revolutionary War treaties involving New York Indians are practically unobtainable in their original editions, because they were published as legislative documents, in small printings on high-acid paper. New York State treaties were printed in New York Assembly document no. 51, the so-called Whipple Report, in 1889.[72] In 1903–1904 federal treaties were edited by Charles J. Kappler and published by the United States Government Printing Office.[73]

In recent decades there have been two major efforts to publish Indian treaties. Both projects are praiseworthy and essential for research, but their products have limitations. In the late 1970s, as a result of the leadership of Francis Jennings, the D'Arcy McNickle Center for the History of the American Indian at the Newberry Library in Chicago sponsored a project to copy, microfilm, and index every available Iroquois treaty document through the year 1842. The project staff obtained the cooperation of dozens of repositories in the United States, Canada, and Britain. Indian groups in the United States and Canada provided information and counsel. Over 9,000 documents were microfilmed (mainly from photocopies). The copies were arranged in chronological order and identified by source, date, and content. Accompanying the 50 rolls of microfilm is a one-volume published calendar of the treaty documents, with a name and subject index.[74] This *Iroquois Indians: Documentary History of the Diplomacy of the Six Nations* is a tremendous resource for scholars, but the editors candidly acknowledged some major deficiencies: many of the documents are nearly illegible on microfilm, many of the documents are printed versions rather than manuscript originals, and the index refers to only about 15 percent of the microfilmed documents.[75]

More recently, a series of volumes called *Early American Indian Documents: Treaties and Laws* has begun to be published. Planned to cover the period 1607–1789, four volumes containing New York documents have appeared so far.[76] The types of documents included are far more varied than the series title implies. These volumes include treaties, deeds, letters, reports, statutes, travel accounts, and other documents that illustrate both formal negotiations and general relations between the colonial, state, and federal governments and the various Indian nations and groups. The aim of the editors and publishers is to put "reliable texts of key documents into the hands of scholars and the general public as quickly and economically as possible."[77] Printed versions of documents are preferred whenever available; manuscript sources are used only if they "differed significantly from the best printed copy. . . . In the majority of cases, of course, no manuscript survives" (this is, even for New York, a questionable statement).[78] Almost all the New York documents reproduced are taken from widely available published sources.

The most valuable intellectual contribution of these two large publication projects is the scholarly commentary on Indian-white relations. The commentary is provided either through chapter introductions and endnotes in the *Early American Indian Documents* series, or through the book of essays on Iroquois diplomacy which accompanies the microfilm *Iroquois Indians: Documentary History of the Diplomacy of the Six Nations.*[79] However, both projects emphasize formal contacts between Indian nations and European-American governments, and both give the most attention to the colonial period. Thus they are far from complete and do not altogether replace the need to go to the original sources themselves to examine fully the history of the Oneidas or other tribes. The document collections of archives and libraries will continue to be valuable, irreplaceable resources for the history of native communities.[80]

Notes

1. The emotive power of archives is well explored by James M. O'Toole, "The Symbolic Significance of Archives," *American Archivist* 56 (Spring 1993): 234–255.

2. The New York State Archives was established by statute in 1971 and became operational in 1978. See Bruce W. Dearstyne, "Archival Politics in New York State, 1892–1915," *New York History* 66 (Apr. 1985): 164–184; "Development of the New York State Archives Program," New York State Library *Bookmark* 39 (Winter 1981): 67–71.

3. Francis Jennings, William N. Fenton, Mary A. Druke, and David R. Miller, eds., *The History and Culture of Iroquois Diplomacy: An Interdisciplinary Guide to the*

Treaties of the Six Nations and Their League (Syracuse: Syracuse University Press, 1985), particularly the essays by Fenton, "Structure, Continuity, and Change in the Process of Iroquois Treaty Making"; Jennings, "Iroquois Alliances in American History"; and Druke, "Iroquois Treaties: Common Forms, Varying Interpretations." See also Mary A. Druke, "Linking Arms: The Structure of Iroquois Intertribal Diplomacy," in *Beyond the Covenant Chain: The Iroquois and Their Neighbors in Indian North America, 1600–1800,* ed. Daniel K. Richter and James H. Merrell (Syracuse: Syracuse University Press, 1987), pp. 29–39. A general survey of Six Nations diplomacy is William N. Fenton, *The Great Law and the Longhouse: A Political History of the Iroquois Confederacy* (Norman: University of Oklahoma Press, 1998).

4. The transformation of the Indian treaty in the decades around 1800 is described by Francis Paul Prucha, *American Indian Treaties: The History of a Political Anomaly* (Berkeley: University of California Press, 1994), pp. 1–22; and Dorothy V. Jones, *License for Empire: Colonialism by Treaty in Early America* (Chicago: University of Chicago Press, 1982).

5. Druke, "Iroquois Treaties," pp. 86–90.

6. On the interrelationship of village factionalism and Six Nations diplomacy, see Daniel K. Richter, "Cultural Brokers and Inter-Colonial Politics: New York–Iroquois Relations, 1664–1701," *Journal of American History* 75 (June 1988): 48–67; and Jack Campisi, "Fur Trade and Factionalism of the Eighteenth Century Oneida Indians," in *Studies on Iroquoian Culture,* ed. Nancy Bonvillain, Franklin Pierce College, Department of Anthropology, Occasional Publications on Northeastern Anthropology no. 6 (Rindge, N.H.: Department of Anthropology, Franklin Pierce College, 1980), pp. 37–46.

7. On the practices of recording receipt of annuity payments, see letter of Albert Ottinger, deputy attorney general, to Charles H. Mullens, deputy comptroller, July 20, 1925, in Comptroller's Indian Annuity Claims and Receipts, box 4, folder 1, NYSA series A0832. For an earlier example of the intrinsic importance of original treaties, see Kenneth Scott and Charles E. Baker, "Renewals of Governor Nicolls' Treaty of 1665 with the Esopus Indians at Kingston, N.Y.," *New-York Historical Society Quarterly* 37 (July 1953): 251–272.

8. The varying forms and meanings of "treaty documents" are discussed by Druke, "Iroquois Treaties," pp. 85–98. Remarkably, in recent years Canadian courts have accepted "aboriginal evidence," oral and ceremonial traditions that would normally be excluded as hearsay. Mary Ann Pylypchuk, "The Value of Aboriginal Records as Legal Evidence in Canada: An Examination of Sources," *Archivaria* 32 (Summer 1991): 51–77. In the early centuries of the common law "the spoken word was the legally valid record and was superior to any document." Michael T. Clanchy, *From Memory to Written Record: England, 1066–1307* (Cambridge, Mass.: Harvard University Press, 1979), p. 56.

9. "Diary of a Journey to Onondaga, Residence There, and Return from Thence, by the Moravian Brethren, Charles Frederick and David Zeisberger, from June 9, 1754 to June 4, 1755," in William M. Beauchamp, ed., *Moravian Journals Relating to Central New York 1745–66* (Syracuse: Dehler Press, 1916; reprint, New York: AMS Press, 1976), p. 215.

10. James A. Sullivan, Alexander C. Flick, and Milton W. Hamilton, eds., *The Papers of Sir William Johnson,* 14 vols. (Albany: University of the State of New

York, 1921–1965), 11: 748. This is a reference to a peace treaty with the anti-British Senecas.

11. E. B. O'Callaghan, ed., *Documents Relative to the Colonial History of the State of New-York,* Vol. 8, London Documents, 1768–1782 (Albany: Weed, Parsons and Co., 1857), pp. 132–133.

12. O'Callaghan, ed., *Documents Relative to the Colonial History of the State of New-York,* 8: 104–128. The map was either the much-used map by Lewis Evans, *A General Map of the Middle British Colonies, in America* (Philadelphia, 1755), or a manuscript copy thereof drafted by Guy Johnson and reproduced in O'Callaghan, facing p. 136 in Vol. 8.

13. New York Secretary of State, *Annalium Thesaurus,* 1818. This 395-page manuscript inventory is the earliest complete surviving list of records in the state's oldest office of record. Ironically, the *Annalium Thesaurus* (Treasury of the Annals) itself disappeared sometime after being microfilmed by the Genealogical Society of Utah in 1973. A copy of the microfilm is in the state archives. The *Annalium Thesaurus* formed the basis for a condensed inventory published in a special report of the secretary of state dated Jan. 4, 1820, *Journal of the Senate of the State of New York . . . Forty-third Session . . . 1820* (Albany: J. Buel, 1820), pp. 13–51.

14. *Annalium Thesaurus,* p. 149.

15. *Annalium Thesaurus,* p. 145; Secretary of State's Report, 1819, Notes D and G, pp. 43–47; Berthold Fernow, "The Archives of the State of New York," *New York Genealogical and Biographical Record* 20 (July 1889): 108–109.

16. Secretary of State's Report, 1819, pp. 13–15. Yates's project is discussed by Victor H. Paltsits, "Tragedies in New York's Public Records," *Annual Report of the American Historical Association for the Year 1909* (Washington, D.C.: 1910), 2: 370–371; repr. in the *Magazine of History* 13 (July 1910): 40–42.

17. E. B. O'Callaghan, comp., *Calendar of Historical Manuscripts in the Office of the Secretary of State, Albany, N.Y.,* 2 vols. (Albany, 1866). On the arranging and binding of the "Colonial Manuscripts," see New York, Senate, Document no. 24, 1853 (Albany, 1854), pp. 1–14.

18. Cecil R. Roseberry, *For the Government and People of This State: A History of the New York State Library* (Albany: New York State Education Department, 1970).

19. New York Laws of Session, 1881, chap. 120.

20. George R. Howell and Charles A. Flagg, comps., "Annotated List of the Principal Manuscripts in the New York State Library," University of the State of New York *State Library Bulletin,* History 3 (1899): 215–225. See also Berthold Fernow, "General Statement of Material Contained in Manuscripts Transferred to the State Library from the Office of the Secretary of State, Pursuant to Laws of 1881, Ch. 120," *Sixty-fourth Annual Report of the Trustees of the New York State Library, for the Year 1881* (Albany: Weed, Parsons and Co., 1882), pp. 11–15. Another description of historical records in the state library is found in Herbert L. Osgood, "Report on the Public Archives of New York," *Annual Report of the American Historical Association for the Year 1900* (Washington, D.C.: Government Printing Office, 1901), 2: 67–112.

21. "Communication from the Secretary of State, Relative to Historical Manuscripts and Records in His Office," New York, Senate, Document no. 46 (1864), p. 3.

22. Osgood, "Report on the Public Archives of New York," 2: 89. The treaties, including many with the Oneidas, dated from the 1790s to the 1820s, with the exception

of one from 1726 and three from the 1760s. In 1877 it was reported that over 300 documents had been stolen from the "Colonial Manuscripts" since O'Callaghan's calendar was published in 1866. Fernow, "Archives of the State of New York," p. 109.

23. *Annual Report of the Trustees of the New York State Library for the Year 1911* (Albany, 1912), pp. 18–32.

24. For a listing of recent records of New York State government useful for understanding Indian relations, see Laurence M. Hauptman, *Formulating American Indian Policy in New York State, 1970–1986* (Albany: State University of New York Press, 1988), pp. 171–172.

25. New York State Archives, *Guide to Records Relating to Native Americans* (Albany: New York State Education Department, 1988). This guide contains information on records of the colonial and early state governments, population censuses taken by New York State, administrative and case records of the Thomas Indian School on the Cattaraugus Reservation in western New York, and records of legislation and public policy relating to Indians.

26. Original Indian Treaties and Deeds, NYSA series A4609 (former series #448A).

27. Record of Indian Deeds and Treaties, 1748–1847, NYSA series A0448. The treaties are indexed by name of tribe or nation, in a card file maintained by the New York State Office of General Services. A microfilm copy of the index is available at the state archives. The archives also hold a burned, fragmentary transcription of Indian treaties, originally spanning the period 1766–1811 (series A0232). The transcription appears to date from the early nineteenth century; it is cited in Osgood, "Report on the Public Archives of New York," 2: 89.

28. *The Colonial Laws of the State of New York* (Albany, 1894), 1: 40–42. The official procedure for land grants is described in a report by Governor William Tryon to the Board of Trade, 1773, printed in O'Callaghan, ed., *Documents Relative to the Colonial History of the State of New-York,* 8: 374–375. Indian deeds recorded by the Dutch government are available in Charles Gehring, trans. and ed., *New York Historical Manuscripts: Dutch,* Vols. GG, HH, and II, "Land Papers" (Baltimore: Genealogical Publishing Co., 1980). On New York colonial land policies, see Armand La Potin, "The Minisink Grant: Partnerships, Patents, and Processing Fees in Eighteenth-Century New York," *New York History* 56 (1975): 28–50; Georgiana C. Nammack, *Fraud, Politics, and the Dispossession of the Indians: The Iroquois Land Frontier in the Colonial Period* (Norman: University of Oklahoma Press, 1969); Thomas C. Cochran, *New York in the Confederation; An Economic Study* (Philadelphia: University of Pennsylvania Press, 1932; reprint, Augustus M. Kelly, Publishers, 1972), pp. 105–108; and William Smith, Jr., *The History of the Province of New-York,* ed. Michael Kammen (Cambridge, Mass.: Harvard University Press, 1972; first published in 1757), 1: 260.

29. Record of Deeds, 1640–1884, NYSA series A0453. The archives hold a microfilm copy of a card index (in the New York State Office of General Services) listing the Indian deeds in this series.

30. Applications for Land Grants (Land Papers, series I), 1643–1803, NYSA series A0272. The Indian deeds are indexed by name of grantee (i.e., European purchaser) in *Calendar of N.Y. Colonial Manuscripts Indorsed Land Papers; in the Office of the Secretary of State of New York 1643–1803* (Albany: Weed, Parsons and Co., 1864; reprint, Harrison, N.Y.: Harbor Hill Books, 1987), p. 1053.

31. Book 5 of Letters Patent (NYSA series 12943) contains about 10 Indian deeds from the 1680s. Warrants of Survey, Powers of Attorney, Indian Deeds, and Other Miscellaneous Records, 1721–1776 (series A1885) includes some deeds from the 1720s. This series was damaged in the capitol fire of 1911; what remains is available on microfilm. The *Catalogue of Records of the Office of the Secretary of State* (Albany, 1898) states (p. 31) that the colonial secretary's book of general entries contained a few Indian deeds. This is now General Entries, 1665–1682 (series A3169), but the portion of the series that survived the fire includes no Indian deeds. See the published version, *Books of General Entries of the Colony of New York, 1664–1688,* 2 vols., ed. Peter R. Christoph and Florence A. Christoph (Baltimore: Genealogical Publishing Co., 1982).

32. On the history of the commissioners of Indian affairs see Allen W. Trelease, *Indian Affairs in Colonial New York: The Seventeenth Century* (Ithaca: Cornell University Press, 1960; reprint, Lincoln: University of Nebraska Press, 1997), pp. 207–227; Lawrence H. Leder, ed., *The Livingston Indian Records 1666–1723* (Gettysburg, Pa.: Pennsylvania Historical Association, 1956; reprint, Stanfordville, N.Y.: E. M. Coleman, 1979), pp. 8–11; and Edgar A. Werner, *Civil List and Constitutional History of the Colony and State of New York* (Albany, 1889), pp. 220–221. Secretaries of Indian affairs in New York after 1750 were Peter Wraxall (1750–1759), Witham Marsh (1759–1765), Richard Shuckburgh (1766–1773), and Joseph Chew (1774–1775).

33. Milton W. Hamilton, *Sir William Johnson: Colonial American, 1715–1763* (Port Washington, N.Y.: Kennikat Press, 1976), pp. 52–55; Stanley N. Katz, *Newcastle's New York: Anglo-American Politics, 1732–1753* (Cambridge, Mass.: Harvard University Press, 1968), pp. 179–181.

34. Werner, *Civil List,* p. 221; Hamilton, *Sir William Johnson,* p. 316.

35. Peter Wraxall, *An Abridgment of the Indian Affairs Contained in Four Folio Volumes, Transacted in the Colony of New York, from the Year 1678 to the Year 1751,* ed. Charles H. McIlwain (Cambridge, Mass., 1915), p. lxxxviii; Jonathan G. Rossie, "Guy Johnson," *Dictionary of Canadian Biography,* 4: 393–394.

36. Peter Gillis et al., comps., *Public Records Division, General Inventory Series, No. 1 Records Relating to Indian Affairs (RG 10)* (Ottawa: Public Archives of Canada, 1975), p. 9. The records are available on microfilm: Reels C-1220 and C-1221 (Albany Indian Commissioners) and C-1222 and C-1223 (Indian Superintendents Sir William Johnson and Guy Johnson).

37. On the records of the Albany Indian commissioners, see Wraxall, *Abridgment of the Indian Affairs,* pp. lxxxvi–xcii; and Leder, ed., *Livingston Indian Records,* pp. 11, 13. Though the minutes prior to 1722 are lost, a rough summary of the contents for the period 1677–1719 survives.

38. On the history of the Johnson papers, see "Annotated List of the Principal Manuscripts in the New York State Library" (1899), p. 210; and Sullivan et al., eds., *Papers of Sir William Johnson,* 1: xiii–xvi.

39. Vols. 1–8 comprise one chronological series of documents; Vols. 9–12, another; and Vol. 13 contains still more documents, plus a chronological listing of all documents in Vols. 1–13. The prefire contents and arrangement of the Johnson papers are discernable through Richard E. Day, comp., *Calendar of the Sir William Johnson Manuscripts in the New York State Library* (Albany, 1909).

40. Most of the Johnson letters acquired by New York State in 1801 were incorporated into the "Colonial Manuscripts" assembled by E. B. O'Callaghan, and published

in O'Callaghan, ed., *The Documentary History of the State of New-York,* Vol. 2 (Albany, 1849–1850), pp. 543–1009 (octavo ed.), pp. 315–584 (quarto ed.). At the end of Vol. 2 is a list of several dozen documents lost since the state acquired the collection in 1801. Many other Johnson documents transmitted to the authorities in London were printed in O'Callaghan, ed., *Documents Relative to the Colonial History of the State of New-York,* Vol. 6, London Documents, 1734–1755 (Albany, 1855); Vol. 7, London Documents, 1756–1767 (1856); Vol. 8, London Documents, 1768–1782.

41.   In June and July 1997 the Montréal auction firm Hotel des Encans sold, by lot, a collection of about 300 documents relating to Indian affairs in New York, Pennsylvania, the Ohio country, and Canada, dating from the 1750s to the 1820s. Though the provenance of the documents is not stated in the auction catalogs, these documents were preserved by descendants of Sir John Johnson and his father, Sir William Johnson. Some of the documents relate to treaties or conferences with the Oneidas and the other tribes of the Six Nations during the 1750s, 1760s, and 1770s (sale of June 16–19, 1997, lots 608, 615, 680, 681; sale of July 16, 1997, lot 612). Archival-quality photocopies of the entire collection were made by the Public Archives of Canada prior to the sales. The documents will be reproduced on microfilm in 1998. The collection is described at the item level in Patricia Kennedy, comp., *Finding Aid no. 2122, MG 19, F 35, Superintendent of Indian Affairs* (Ottawa: National Archives of Canada, Manuscript Division, forthcoming). Patricia Kennedy, pers. comm., May 12, 1998.

42.   Wraxall, *Abridgment of the Indian Affairs,* pp. xciv–cii.

43.   Wraxall denounces the Albany Indian commissioners in a letter to William Johnson, Jan. 9, 1756, in O'Callaghan, ed., *Documents Relative to the Colonial History of the State of New-York,* 7: 14–29. Wraxall's bias has long been recognized; see Wraxall, *Abridgment of the Indian Affairs,* p. xcii; and Thomas E. Norton, *The Fur Trade in Colonial New York 1686–1776* (Madison, Wis.: University of Wisconsin Press, 1974), pp. 63–64, 229–230.

44.   Leder, ed., *Livingston Indian Records 1666–1723.* The Livingston-Redmond Papers were successively deposited at the New York Public Library, the New-York Historical Society, and the Franklin D. Roosevelt Library before being sold to the J. Pierpont Morgan Library. The Livingston Papers are available on microfilm produced by the National Archives.

45.   *The Letters and Papers of Cadwallader Colden,* Vol. 8 of the *Collections of the New-York Historical Society for the Year 1934* (New York, 1937), p. ix.

46.   Colden's history, whose title reflects his imperialist bias, was reprinted in England in 1747, 1750, and 1755; and in the United States in 1866, 1902, 1922, and 1958. The work concludes in 1701, but a continuation for the period 1707–1720 is published in *Letters and Papers of Cadwallader Colden,* Vol. 9 of the *Collection of the New-York Historical Society for the Year 1935* (New York, 1937), pp. 357–434. On Colden's career, see *Dictionary of American Biography,* 4: 286f.

47.   Daniel K. Richter, "Rediscovered Links in the Covenant Chain: Previously Unpublished Transcripts of New York Indian Treaty Minutes, 1677–1691," *Proceedings of the American Antiquarian Society Proceedings* 92, part 1 (1982): 45–85. Governor Burnet's use of the proceedings of the Indian commissioners is noted in Wraxall, *Abridgment of the Indian Affairs,* p. xciii.

48.   Transcripts of the New York Indian commissioners' proceedings Jan. 6, 1746–1747 [*sic*] through Apr. 1746 are held by the Albany Institute of History and Art.

The New York State Library holds a contemporary copy of the commissioners' proceedings for Aug. 2, 1746, as well as documents of Jacobus Bleecker, an Indian commissioner and Dutch interpreter during the 1740s. A manuscript notebook of 112 pages containing proceedings of the Albany Indian commissioners for the period June 29, 1753 through May 4, 1755, was offered for sale by the Montréal auction firm Hotel des Encans in June 1997 (lot 680). See n. 41.

49.   These documents are listed in O'Callaghan, ed., *Calendar of Historical Manuscripts,* Vol. 2, English Manuscripts, 1664–1776. Communications from the Indian commissioners are also referenced in the *New York State Library Bulletin* 58, History 6 (1902), "Calendar of Council Minutes"; reprinted as *New York (Colony) Council: Calendar of Council Minutes,* comp. Berthold Fernow (Harrison, N.Y.: Harbor Hill Books, 1987).

50.   Philip Schuyler's papers as Indian commissioner for the United States and subsequently for New York are in the Manuscripts Division of the New York Public Library. See especially MR 7 and 7a.

51.   David Lehman, "The End of the Iroquois Mystique: The Oneida Land Cession Treaties in the 1780s," *William and Mary Quarterly* 47 (Oct. 1990): 523–547; Jack Campisi, "The Oneida Treaty Period, 1783–1838," in *The Oneida Indian Experience: Two Perspectives,* ed. Jack Campisi and Laurence Hauptman (Syracuse: Syracuse University Press, 1988), pp. 48–64; Helen M. Upton, *The Everett Report in Historical Perspective: The Indians of New York* (Albany: New York State American Revolution Bicentennial Commission, 1980), pp. 17–49; Barbara Graymont, "New York State Indian Policy after the American Revolution," *New York History* 57 (1976): 438–474. On the Oneidas' recent efforts to rectify the injustices done to them, see George C. Shattuck, *The Oneida Land Claims: A Legal History* (Syracuse: Syracuse University Press, 1991).

52.   Hough, ed., *Proceedings of the Commissioners of Indian Affairs Appointed by Law for the Extinguishment of Indian Titles in the State of New York* (Albany: Munsell, 1861). The papers of Israel Chapin, the agent of the United States to the Six Nations from 1792 to 1802, include transcripts of these proceedings and many related documents. Chapin's papers are part of the Henry O'Reilly Collection at the New-York Historical Society. The papers of Governor George Clinton contained many letters and documents relating to Indian affairs during the 1780s and 1790s, but most of them were destroyed in the capitol fire. Many documents relating to the Treaty of Fort Stanwix (Fort Schuyler) in 1784 were printed in *Public Papers of George Clinton,* Vol. 7 (Albany, 1904), pp. 323–398. Much of this material is also found in *DHI.*

53.   The 1818 inventory of records in the office of the New York secretary of state notes that the U.S. Constitution reserves to the federal government the exclusive right to enter into a "treaty, alliance or confederation" with the Indians. In an early instance of bureaucratic rationalization, the inventory then remarks: "The Treaties between this State and the Indians since the adoption of the Constitution almost exclusively relate to Territory or purchases of their lands and may therefore more properly be called grants, conveyances, or cessions." *Annalium Thesaurus,* p. 145.

54.   See published summary of Indian documents in Frederic C. Mather, ed., *New York in the Revolution as Colony and State,* 2d ed., 2 vols. (Albany, 1904), 2: 45–46. The remnants of this series are now in the New York State Archives (series A0200).

55.   See lists of Indian claimants at end of *Index of Awards on Claims of the Soldiers of the War of 1812, as Audited and Allowed by the Adjutant and Inspector Gener-*

als, Pursuant to Chapter 176, of the Laws of 1859 (Albany, 1860; repr. 1969, 1994). The claims themselves are in the New York State Archives (series A0020 and A3352).

56.   Selected Audited Accounts of State Officers, NYSA series A0802.

57.   William J. Rorabaugh, *The Alcoholic Republic, an American Tradition* (New York: Oxford University Press, 1979); Peter C. Mancall, *Deadly Medicine: Indians and Alcohol in Early America* (Ithaca: Cornell University Press, 1995).

58.   NYSA series A0802, Vol. 15, folios 8, 63, 70.

59.   See "List of Comptroller's Records Packed for Transfer from Stratton Building, March 1952," and letter from Albert B. Corey, state historian, to Daniel P. Moynihan, assistant to the secretary to the governor, June 3, 1955. Both documents are in the Charles E. Gosnell (state librarian) Papers, box 4, NYSL, Manuscripts and Special Collections.

60.   Although there is some Oneida material, the comptroller's documents held by the Onondaga Historical Association that relate to Indians concern mostly the Stockbridge and Brothertown Indians. Jack T. Ericson, Reed Library, SUNY College at Fredonia, pers. comm., Mar. 29, 1995; Laurence M. Hauptman, pers. comm., Aug. 7, 1997.

61.   See Gosnell Papers, box 4, NYSL. *New York Times,* Dec. 8, 9, 19, 1954; Syracuse *Post-Standard,* Dec. 11, 19, 22, 1954; Albert B. Corey, "Rescue of Fugitive New York State Records," *Manuscripts* 7, no. 3 (Spring 1955): 183.

62.   These documents are found in boxes 2, 3, and 4, NYSA series A0832.

63.   A memorandum "relative to Indian Annuities," dating from the 1830s, lists treaty and statutory authorities and the annuities payable to the various parties of the Oneidas, the Brothertown Indians, and several individuals, as well as to other Indian nations (NYSA series A0832, box 1, folder 1). Annuity receipts for the Oneida, Brothertown, and Stockbridge Indians are found in boxes 3–4.

64.   New York Laws of Session, 1839, chap. 58. See Campisi, "The Oneida Treaty Period," pp. 61, 64.

65.   N.Y. Secretary of State Field Book no. 27, pp. 195–204, NYSA series A0452. New York Laws of Session, 1795, chap. 41.

66.   Original Indian Treaties and Deeds of Cession, Vol. 1: 5–19, 153–204; Vol. 2: 65–88, 129–156, NYSA series A4609. There are separate lists for those planning to emigrate and those planning to stay.

67.   Population Census of Indian Reservations, 1845, NYSA series A1832. The census volume, available on microfilm, gives for each household data on number of persons, value of farm produce, number of livestock, literacy, and so on.

68.   Lists for the Oneidas are dated 1891, 1900, 1901, 1903, 1904, 1907, 1908, 1909, 1919, 1920, 1923, 1924, 1944, 1946. Indian Census and Annuity Rolls, 1881–1950, NYSA series A0742. These rolls were microfilmed by the Department of Social Services, and the state archives hold a portion of the microfilm. Access to rolls dating after 1925 is restricted to protect personal privacy. The older census lists compiled by federal Indian agents are now in the National Archives (Record Group 75); the lists have been microfilmed (National Archives Microfilm Publication M595). An unpublished microfilm reel list for the New York rolls (1885–1924), including Oneidas residing in New York, compiled by Jack T. Ericson, is available at Reed Library, SUNY College at Fredonia, and at the New York State Library, in Albany.

69.   Henry F. De Puy, comp., *A Bibliography of the English Colonial Treaties with the American Indians Including a Synopsis of Each Treaty* (New York, 1917). Proceedings of several important treaties between Pennsylvania and the Six Nations and their

dependents were published by Benjamin Franklin. See Julian P. Boyd, ed., *Indian Treaties Printed by Benjamin Franklin, 1736–1762* (Philadelphia, 1938).

70. Nicholas Falco, "The Empire State's Search in European Archives," *American Archivist* 32 (Apr. 1969): 109–123; Milton W. Hamilton, *The Historical Publication Program of the State of New York* (Albany: New York State Education Department, 1965).

71. Pennsylvania's proceedings and treaties with the Six Nations are published in *Minutes of the Provincial Council of Pennsylvania*, Vols. 1–10 (Harrisburg, 1838–1852). Related documents are found in Samuel Hazard, ed., *Pennsylvania Archives; Selected and Arranged from Original Documents in the Office of the Secretary of the Commonwealth*, 1st ser., Vols. 1–4 (Philadelphia, 1853). On the Oneida chief Shickellamy, a Six Nations supervisor of the Susquehanna Indians, see James H. Merrell, "Shickellamy, a Person of Consequence," in *Northeastern Indian Lives, 1632–1816*, ed. Robert S. Grumet (Amherst, Mass.: University of Massachusetts Press, 1996), pp. 227–257.

72. *Report of the Special Committee to Investigate the Indian Problem of the State of New York.*

73. Charles J. Kappler, ed., *Indian Affairs: Laws and Treaties*, Vol. 2, *Treaties*, U.S. Senate, 57th Congress, 1st Session, Senate Document no. 452 (Washington, D.C., 1903); enlarged ed., U.S. Senate, 58th Congress, 2nd Session, Senate Document no. 319 (Washington, D.C., 1904; repr. 1930). See Prucha, *American Indian Treaties*, pp. 521–524, on sources for federal Indian treaties. Several important New York State and federal treaties are printed in Upton, *Everett Report in Historical Perspective*, Appendix. Federal treaties with the Oneidas are printed in George R. Fay, comp., "Treaties between the Oneida Indians and the United States of America, 1784–1838," University of Northern Colorado, Museum of Anthropology *Miscellaneous Series*, no. 40 (1978).

74. Francis Jennings and William N. Fenton, eds., *Iroquois Indians: A Documentary History of the Diplomacy of the Six Nations and Their League* (Woodbridge, Conn.: 1985).

75. The reproductions of treaties in the New York State Archives are legible, probably because that institution declined to photocopy the fragile documents and required the project to microfilm them. The project staff obtained from the archives relevant documents in the Colonial Council Minutes (series A1895); the Colonial Council Papers ("Colonial Manuscripts," series A1894); Assembly Petitions, Correspondence, and Reports Relating to Indians ("Assembly Papers," Vol. 41, series A1823), and Indian Deeds and Treaties (series A0448). The project did not film the original Indian treaties (new series A4609, old series 448A).

76. *Early American Indian Documents: Treaties and Laws, 1607–1789*, ed. Alden T. Vaughan, Vol. 7: *New York and New Jersey Treaties, 1609–1682*, ed. Barbara Graymont (Frederick, Md.: University Publications of America, 1985); Vol. 8: *New York and New Jersey Treaties, 1683–1713*, ed. Barbara Graymont (Bethesda, Md.: University Publications of America, 1995); Vol. 9: *New York and New Jersey Treaties, 1714–1753*, ed. Barbara Graymont (Bethesda, Md.: University Publications of America, 1996); Vol. 18: *Revolution and Confederation*, ed. Colin G. Calloway (Bethesda, Md.: University Publications of America, 1994).

77. The hyperbole becomes clear when one learns that the price of the complete collection, by subscription only, is $2,210, and that the 20-volume set began to appear in 1979 and is now (in 1997) just half complete.

78. *Early American Indian Documents*, 7: xxii.

79.   Jennings, Fenton, Druke, and Miller, eds., *History and Culture of Iroquois Diplomacy.*

80.   Native groups wishing to establish their own archives may consult a manual published by the Society of American Archivists, John A. Fleckner, *Native American Archives: An Introduction* (Chicago: Society of American Archives, 1984).

10 *Jo Margaret Mano*

Unmapping the Iroquois
New York State Cartography, 1792–1845

Maps of New York State from the end of the Revolutionary War to the midnineteenth century provide an example of an era of rapid cartographic change. During this period the swift disappearance of the Oneidas and the rest of the Six Nations of the Iroquois from the landscape of official New York State cartography can be interpreted as supporting the political agenda. This perception can be illustrated by contrasting state-sponsored maps with other maps produced within the state, as well as with those published elsewhere. The maps also document the conflict between two different visions of the land, illustrating the Euro-American belief that it is a possession or commodity rather than a shared resource. This chapter will examine the view of maps as social constructs, postrevolutionary New York State policy toward the Iroquois to 1800, the influence of Simeon De Witt and Joseph Ellicott in shaping New York State's cartography and surveying from 1784–1804, and the removal of Indians from the mapped landscape in the years 1792–1845.[1]

Maps are products of their cultural, social, and particularly their political context. As such, they cannot be read as neutral testimony for illustrating history. As primary documents, maps provide a perspective on the contemporary perception of the landscape. Maps also shape the knowledge and understanding of the area they portray. The creation of a map involves a complex filtering of available information, as well as the use of symbols, which may have ambiguous meanings. Thus "a map is a consequence of choices among choices."[2]

Mapmakers depend on a variety of sources to compile a map, using older maps and new information, some collected through surveying. Because accurate surveying and land measurement are costly enterprises, they are often performed for either political and/or economic gain. Surveys and land division impose order and, by extension, civilize the landscape. Accurate mapping is often a prerequisite to the sale and transfer of land. Precise surveying thus facilitates land speculation, which sees land as a commodity rather than a resource. The expense of integrating new geographic data and producing, publishing, and distributing maps makes cartography inherently conservative. Through history, the information on published maps usually has lagged behind updated information or new discoveries. Exceptions to this situation occur only when rapid map publication supports a specific, often political, agenda. A brief time span between territorial change and map documentation can be viewed as a cartographic power play. Maps that continue to preserve past artifacts show the acceptance of slow editorial revision.

The clues to unraveling the motivations of maps are provided by the affiliations of the mapmakers and their sponsors, or even the publishers. Biases are often revealed by the items that are included or excluded. Although larger scale, more detailed maps have the potential to include more data, omissions are not always a function of the map scale. As Blakemore and Harley have observed: "Blank spaces can acquire meaning by cognitive translation. . . . Blank spaces thus make statements or pose questions. The recognition of the cognitive nature of mapping . . . enables cartography to be seen as a memory bank of past perceptions or mental images rather than a record solely of 'hard' topographical reality."[3] The concept of "blank spaces" includes missing information. Maps can also be analyzed as a piece of art can be studied, by viewing the juxtaposition of elements and the overall meaning of the whole.[4] This perspective recognizes that the intuitive grasp of a map's visual message can speak to more visceral understandings than the written word.

A new American style of cartography was developed after the Revolutionary War, using a minimal palette of symbols and enforced by the need for rapid and accurate maps of the new states. Simeon De Witt, who had many contacts with the Oneidas and other members of the Six Nations, was a primary figure in its development. De Witt was appointed surveyor general to the Continental army in 1780, and headed the small mapmaking corps attached to Washington's headquarters that made surveys and road traverses for strategic locations. At the end of the war, De Witt proposed to Congress that he create a map based on the military surveys. Congress did not provide the funds for this proposal, and in 1784 De Witt resigned his commission and became surveyor general of New York State.[5] De Witt served in this office for over 50 years until his death in 1834. During that time he was intimately involved in not only supervising the state's cartography and land acquisition and sale, but also with many of the transportation improvements in the rapidly developing network of roads and canals.

By the end of the Revolutionary War, New York State was critically short of funds and title to lands promised as bounties for veterans for military service. Appropriating and selling land answered both needs. During the war, New York had difficulty recruiting and supporting the troops required by the Continental army. The situation was clearly revealed by the laws passed by the New York State legislature related to raising and paying the militia. In 1778, the state promised a $50 reenlistment bonus. In 1780, a wheat bounty was offered to recruits, and the state, short of funds, floated bonds to be redeemed later if the treasury had funds generated from the sale of lands forfeited by British sympathizers. By 1781, New York began to offer "unappropriated lands" for military service, followed in 1782 by a more generous basic grant of 600 acres for three years' service. A 1783 law guaranteed land to almost every New Yorker with military service, tied to rank.[6]

The 1781 act granted land within New York State in areas that were not already settled or claimed, or part of the Indian lands of the allied Oneidas or Tuscaroras, or part of the lands west of the 1768 Line of Property. The surveyor general had to approve land claims within any of these areas.[7] By 1782, New York realized the quantity of land promised for military service required reserving, at least on paper, a section of the state in Tryon County to satisfy future claims. The parcel designated—the New Military Tract—stretched, on its east side, from the western boundary of the Oneida and Tuscarora lands north and west to Lake Ontario, the Oswego River, and Oneida Lake, south and west to an east-west line from the southern tip of Seneca Lake, and then north from there to the mouth of Sodus Creek.[8] However, the surveyor general was not allowed to receive or accept locations in the tract, except for a small piece between Seneca Lake and Cayuga Lake.

New York's claim to the land was weak, and the area was also claimed by Massachusetts from its western border between latitudes 41.02° and 44.15° under a 1629 sea-to-sea grant from the British king.[9] Moreover, it was situated in the middle of Iroquois Territory. The boundary, or Line of Property, between white settlement and Iroquois lands had been negotiated in 1768 between Sir William Johnson and the Six Nations at the Treaty of Fort Stanwix. This line ran south from Wood Creek, to the head of the Unadilla River, to the Great Bend of the Susquehanna, west to Tioga, and then southwest through Pennsylvania and Virginia to Alabama. The 1768 treaty boundary is shown as the "Line of Property" on the "Country of the VI. Nations," drawn in 1771 by Guy Johnson and dedicated to William Tryon, then governor of the province of New York (see Map 10.1). The map sites the Indian villages with miniature tepees and their chief towns with tepees topped by a flying flag; it also locates Indian paths.[10] The map shows the tribal locations of the Oneidas, Onondagas, Cayugas, and Senecas by their names. It includes a notation north of the Mohawk River stating, "The Boundary of New York not being closed, this part of the Country still belongs to the Mohocks" (*sic*); a notation in the lower left corner

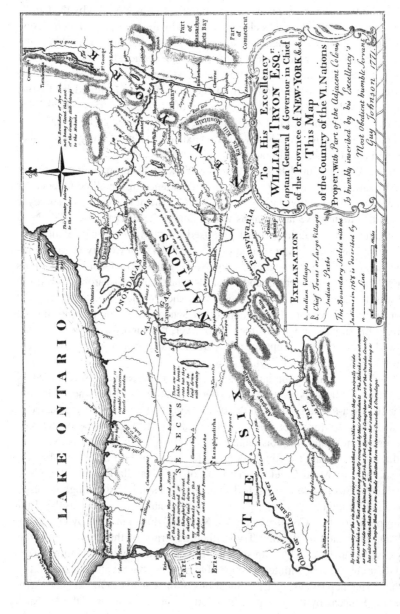

Map 10.1. Guy Johnson's map of the country of the Six Nations, 1771

174

reads, ". . . the Tuscaroras who form the sixth Nation are omitted being a southern People that live on lands allotted them between Oneida & Onondaga."[11]

The Iroquois held territory west of this treaty boundary, which included most of central New York, all of western New York except Forts Niagara and Oswego, and most of northern and western Pennsylvania, as well as large land areas in Ohio and beyond. Members of the Six Nations Confederacy regarded themselves as sovereign nations, the diplomatic equal of the European nations with whom they had negotiated such treaties. During the Revolutionary War, the members of the confederacy had supported different sides. Most Oneidas and Tuscaroras supported the United States, while most Senecas, Cayugas, Onondagas, and Mohawks supported the British; others maintained neutrality.

At the end of the Revolutionary War, the Continental Congress claimed title to the lands, ceded by Britain in the preliminary treaty of peace. The lands were occupied by the tribes, many of which were still in a state of war with the United States. The Articles of Confederation, adopted in 1781, established that only the Congress had the "sole and exclusive right" and power of determining peace and war and "entering into treaties and alliances." Even more important in understanding the complex issues surrounding negotiations, treaties, and land possession was Article IX, section 4, which stated, "The United States in Congress assembled shall also have the sole and exclusive right and power of . . . regulating the trade and managing all affairs with the Indians, not members of the States, provided that the legislative right of any State within its own limits be not infringed or violated."

The two phrases "not members of the States" and "the legislative right of any State within its own limits" complicate the interpretation of this clause. Ethnohistorian Jack Campisi explains the situation by quoting a letter from Madison to Monroe, and commenting:

. . . A tribe could be within the boundaries of a state, yet not part of it. In this instance, while the state possessed the legislative right (the right of preemption), it could not exercise that right without permission from Congress. In the context of the established complimentary principles of the right of discovery, which belonged to the sovereign, and the right of undisturbed use, which belonged to the tribe, the clause would seem to preserve the states' right of preemption without bestowing the power to extinguish. This power resided with the sovereign, in this case the Continental Congress. Preemption was (and is) only a proprietary right.[12]

In 1784 New York State's governor George Clinton moved quickly to embrace the Iroquois as "Members of the State," in order to strengthen his claim that New York was sovereign over Indian affairs within its borders and to circumvent the 1781 Articles of Confederation. Clinton ignored Congress' warning that land transactions with the Iroquois were void, convinced tribal leaders that New York's commissioners were valid negotiators, and began aggressively to coerce the tribes into selling their lands. Postwar state policy was aptly described by historian Barbara Graymont as having three ends:

1. Extinguish any claims of the United States Congress to sovereignty over Indian affairs in the State of New York,
2. Extinguish the title of the Indians to the soil,
3. Extinguish the sovereignty of the Six Nations.[13]

Clinton began this policy by calling together the Six Nations at Fort Stanwix before the United States commissioners convened them for treaty negotiations. At the conference, held from August 31 to September 10, 1784, Clinton hoped to purchase land. He cloaked his intentions in assurances to the Oneidas and Tuscaroras that New York was determined to protect Indian lands, saying, "We have been informed that some designing Persons have endeavored to persuade You that We mean to take away your lands. This is not true; You must not believe it. We have no claim on Your lands; its just extent will ever remain secured to You."[14] Instead, Clinton stated he was only interested in the location of the Oneidas' lands. The Oneidas described their territory as extending from Lake Ontario and the St. Lawrence River south to Pennsylvania's northern border, west to the Oswego River, and east to within about 50 miles from the Unadilla River.[15]

Clinton then met with the nations who had supported the British and offered them peace, but suggested that the Mohawks, Onondagas, Senecas, and Cayugas should offer land as compensation for the damage that they had caused during the war. The Mohawk war chief Joseph Brant accepted the offer of peace, but denied any possibility of granting land, except for the British forts of Niagara and Oswego, which now belonged to the Americans. The conference ended with no land changing hands.

In October the United States commissioners convened the Six Nations, warned them that New York did not have the right to buy land, and promised in the Treaty of Fort Stanwix that the "Oneida and Tuscarora nations shall be secured in the possession of the lands on which they are settled."[16] The peace treaty signed with the Mohawks, Senecas, Onondagas, and Cayugas required the surrender of land claims west of a Niagara-Pennsylvania line, south of Pennsylvania's northern border, and Fort Oswego. The treaty thus extinguished Indian title to Seneca lands in the Ohio Valley and west of the line south of Fort Niagara, while trying to ensure peace between the Indians and whites by protecting the remaining tribal lands. After this federal treaty was ratified, Congress did not intervene to prevent New York from extracting more and more land from the Indians, reducing the territories of the Oneidas, Onondagas, and Tuscaroras to small reservations around their villages within the next four years.

New York's aggressive land acquisition policy included acts in 1784 and 1785 to "Facilitate the Settlement of Waste and Unappropriated Lands." The second act repealed the first, adding a provision to hasten settlement by advertising land sales, including sales of ceded Indian land. Under this act, Clinton and the New York commissioners met with the Oneidas and Tuscaroras in 1785 at Fort Herkimer to ask for a large tract in the southern part of their territory on the Pennsylvania border. A divided Oneida Nation sold the area for $11,500, to be paid in goods and money.[17] The state of Massachusetts protested this purchase to the Continental Congress, claiming that this land was the state's under royal charter. In 1786, Massachusetts and New York finally signed an agreement over the disputed western part of New York State, with New York retaining governmental jurisdiction and Massachusetts having preemption rights to the territory.[18]

In 1787, a group of land speculators called the New York Genesee Company of Adventurers signed a 999 year lease with the Six Nations for a huge tract of land, followed by another similar lease early in 1788, which included most of the remaining Oneida lands. The lease scheme was created to skirt the state regulation that prohibited private purchases of Indian land. In September 1788, Governor Clinton and the New York State commissioners signed treaties at Fort Schuyler with the Oneidas and Onondagas. Clinton assured the Oneidas that he was not interested in buying land, but only wished to protect their interests from the wily and cunning Genesee Company. The Oneidas were tricked into ceding some 5 million acres to the state for money, goods, and an annual payment. They retained a reservation and a tract where 21-year leases might be made, as well as retaining reservations for their Stockbridge and Brothertown dependents.[19] The Onondagas surrendered almost all their lands from Lake Ontario to the northern Pennsylvania line, except for a small area around their main village, for money, clothing, and an annuity.[20] In 1789, the Cayugas ceded their lands from the northern Pennsylvania border to Lake Ontario, save a small reservation, for a monetary down payment and an annuity.[21]

In 1790 Congress passed the first federal Trade and Intercourse Act, which prohibited land sales and trade with the Indians without special federal permission. Despite this law, in 1793 the New York State legislature passed "An Act relative to the Lands Appropriated by this state to the Use of the Oneida, Onondaga and Cayuga Indians," which obtained more land and controlled leases and transfers of Indian land. In November 1793, Simeon De Witt and John Cantine as state agents bought more land from the Onondagas.[22] The Oneidas refused to part with land in their 1793 conference with De Witt and Cantine, stating that the 1788 agreements had been a mistake, based on false advice from the state. A projected meeting with the Cayugas was postponed until the following year because sickness prevented some of their chiefs from coming to the treaty negotiations.[23]

Late in 1794 at Canandaigua, New York, the federal government made two treaties through United States commissioner Timothy Pickering aimed at strengthening federal control over Indian lands within New York. The first, with the Oneidas, Onondagas, Cayugas, and Senecas, confirmed their reservations and promised that no one would claim their lands until they chose to sell them, specifying that such transactions were to occur only under federal auspices. The second paid reparations to the Oneidas, Tuscaroras, and Stockbridge Indians for their losses as allies of the Americans in the Revolutionary War.[24] New York passed another act for separating the Indians from their lands in 1795, called "An Act for the better Support of the Oneida, Onondaga, and Cayuga Indians, and for other purposes herein mentioned." The act purported to make the Indian land "more productive" for the tribes, but this was to be accomplished by non-Indians buying the land.[25] The low prices and annuities paid for the lands meant that greater profit could be made by white land speculators and the state. As the Indians' reservations shrank, they were less and less able to maintain their traditional economy. This law also required that reservation land be subdivided, with individual parcels allotted for each family. Plotting of individual lots for families undermined the traditional concept of land held in common and the solidarity of tribal control. The treaties between New York and the Cayugas in July of 1795 left them with only a small reservation and an annuity payment of $1,800. The Onondagas also signed a treaty in July, relinquishing Onondaga Lake and its rich salt deposits for a $700 annual payment.

These two state accords of 1795 were followed in September by the Oneidas finally selling 100,000 acres. None of these 1795 state-Indian agreements was ever ratified by the United States Senate, and none had a federal commissioner present as required under the Trade and Intercourse Acts of 1790 and 1793.[26]

The mid-1790s map included in Franklin B. Hough's 1866 work, *Notices of Peter Penet,* and called "A Map of the Oneida Reservation, Including the Lands leased to Peter Smith," documents the shrinkage of the Oneidas' lands (see Map 10.2).[27] The 1768 Line of Property from Wood Creek extends off the map beyond the Brothertown reservation. A subsequent boundary negotiated in 1788 is shown in the tinted original with a green shaded line, which darkens to a smudge in black-and-white reproduction. The lands given by the Oneidas to Kirkland are plotted east of this boundary. The 1795 cession can be seen as the division between the plotted lots and the undivided central reservation. Oneida is surrounded by tent symbols. A note on the map explains that the lots south of a line from A to B were those leased to Peter Smith. The numbered square parcels of subdivided land tame and organize the mapped landscape. The visual message of this map is a metaphor for the constricting net of settlement at the expense of Oneidas' landholdings.

During the years 1796–1798 under the governorship of John Jay, federal representatives were present at the three Indian treaties held by New York State. In 1796, the Seven Nations of Canada relinquished all claims to land in New York, except the six mile by six mile St. Regis reservation. In 1797 the Mohawks, now living on the Canadian Grand River and the Bay of Quinte, were paid a final settlement for the lands they lost in New York. The Oneidas

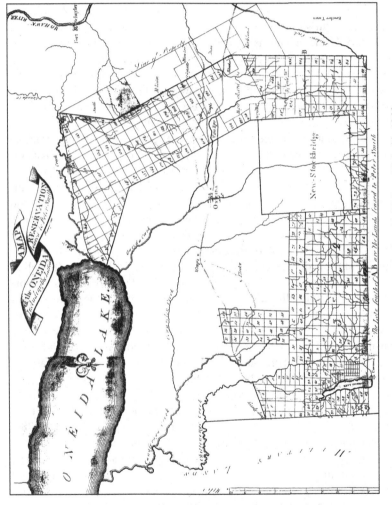

Map 10.2. Franklin B. Hough map of Oneida Country in the mid-1790s, published in 1866

179

sold more land to the state in 1798, over 1,280 acres with several strategic parcels, for $500 (of which $300 was paid prior to the treaty) and an annual payment of $700.[28] Unlike previous or later treaties, this state-Oneida accord of 1798 was formally approved by the United States Senate.

Both Simeon De Witt and Joseph Ellicott had extensive and different impacts on New York State's cartographic landscape. While Ellicott surveyed and subdivided Seneca lands west of the Preemption Line for the Holland Land Company, De Witt's influence was greatest on the Oneidas' lands and in the New Military Tract, which was located on the Onondagas' and Cayugas' lands. In 1789, as New York's surveyor general, De Witt was responsible for overseeing the survey of the New Military Tract, designated to satisfy the land claims of Revolutionary War veterans.[29] The survey was directed by chief surveyors Major Abraham Hardenberg and Moses De Witt (Simeon's cousin). The orthogonal platting used to divide the land employed the newly passed 1785 Land Ordinance township and range system instead of the traditional, irregular metes and bounds and was one of the few areas east of the Ohio River where that system was used.[30] This approach to specifying parcels simplified the identification and location of land, and thus encouraged and facilitated speculation. Ellicott's surveying extended the rectilinear grid of the New Military Tract into western New York, leaving an enduring pattern in the land's cultural landscape. In 1800, Ellicott submitted a map to the Holland Land Company, titled "Map of Morris's Preserve or West Geneseo in the State of New York," which showed the boundaries of the Indian reservations and townships he had laid out, as well as the boundaries of the land purchases and hydrology.[31] De Witt was responsible for collecting and compiling all the survey maps submitted to the surveyor general's office, as well as carrying out acts passed by the legislature, such as the advertising and selling of newly acquired Indian land. De Witt was personally responsible for setting up the arrangements and locations for state land sales. He was also one of New York State's representatives in several of the treaty negotiations with the Oneidas and handled the money for the 1785 treaty.[32]

The township surveys of the New Military Tract were used by De Witt to produce the map titled "1st sheet of De Witt's State Map of New-York" in 1792 (see Map 10.3). This map fulfilled the requirements of the February 28, 1789, act requiring him to make a map of the 25 (later 27) designated New Military Tract townships, each subdivided into tracts of approximately 600 acres. The map extends from Otsego and Herkimer counties in the east to the western edge of the New Military Tract and south to the Susquehanna River. The boundaries of the Oneida, Onondaga, and Cayuga reservations stand out in separating blank, undivided areas from the platted townships. The map shows vividly the vulnerable location of the Oneida reservation, squeezed between existing settlement to the east and the rectangular, subdivided townships of the New Military Tract. The empty spaces of the reservations appear to map readers as "waste and unappropriated lands" requiring "improvement."

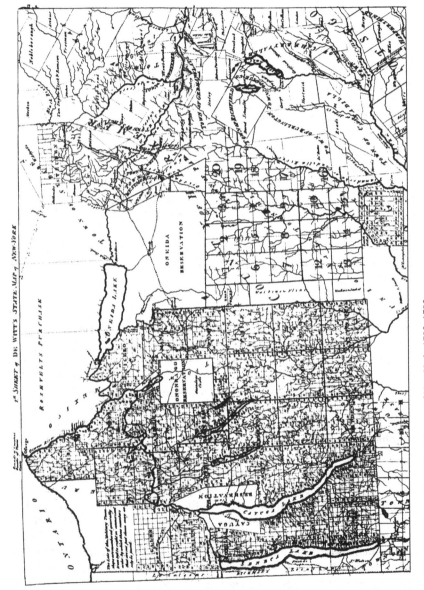

Map 10.3. Simeon De Witt's state map of New York, 1792–1793

The map reproduced here is the Library of Congress copyright deposit, received on January 17, 1793, but the map was deposited on October 26 of the preceding year.[33] A copy of the map, housed in the New York State Archives, has the notation "State Engineer's Office Map" on the side, and obviously served as an updated, "working" map (see Map 10.4).[34] The empty space of the original Oneida 1785 reservation has been filled in with land purchases and "improvements." The land purchases of 1795 from the Oneidas are shown as the "one mile strip" and "2 mile strip" with the new Stockbridge reservation laid out. The lands leased to Peter Smith are named "New Petersb———urgh" on either side of the Stockbridge reservation. A strip of the east side of the tract, representing lands bought in 1795, curiously reads "Oneida Reservation." A new east-west road crosses the reservation south of Oneida Castle. Another notable addition is a line labeled "Canal," running from Fort Schuyler across the reservation to the New Military Tract township of Manlius, then to the southern tip of the "Salt Lake" (Syracuse) and continuing west. This canal is the Western Inland Lock Navigation Canal, a precursor of the Erie Canal. The additions in the Oneida reservation reflect the state's land acquisitions made in 1788 and 1795, shown also on Hough's map of "Peter Penet's Operations," discussed previously (Map 10.2). In the Onondaga reservation, a dotted line reflects the state's purchase of the lands around Salina. To the west of this section of the map, in the Cayuga reservation, the loss of Indian lands is revealed by the extension of neighboring township's names over the reservation.

The loss of Indian land is vividly portrayed by comparing the 1771 map "Country of the VI. Nations" (Map 10.1) with a couple of maps included in the writings of Franklin B. Hough. Map 10.2, included in Hough's *Notices of Peter Penet* and described above, reveals the sequential reduction and subdivision of lands sold to the state. Another map (Map 10.5), originally included in the *Proceedings of the Commissioners of Indian Affairs,* has been preserved in the Library of Congress Division of Maps.[35] The map title explains it is a "Map of Part of the State of New York with Parts of the Adjacent States made in 1793–4 by John Aldam & John Wallis, Coppied from the Original 1/3 off." The map was lithographed by C. Van Benthuysen in Albany and drawn by David Vaughan. John Aldam is a misspelling of John Adlum, who wrote to Moses De Witt in 1792 asking him to sketch the New Military Tract to use in preparing a map of eastern communication with the Great Lakes.[36] The map extends the area covered by Guy Johnson's map (Map 10.1) south to include parts of New Jersey north of Sandy Hook. It is a compilation of data from the Johnson map including the 1768 treaty line, with updated and improved topography, and the New Military Tract townships from De Witt's 1792 map (Map 10.3) are superimposed. The names of the Oneidas, Onondagas, Cayugas, and Senecas are blazoned with large letters over their respective tribal lands. But the addition of the information from De Witt's 1792 New Military Tract map on these lands reveals the true story, and the only mapped reservation is the Oneida

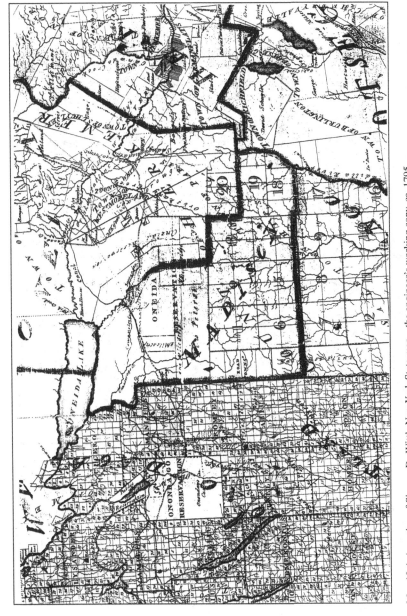

Map 10.4. A section of Simeon De Witt's New York State map—the engineer's working copy. ca. 1795

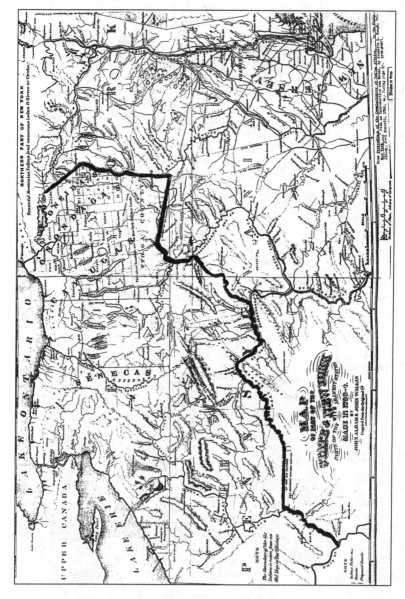

Map 10.5. John Adlum and John Wallis' map of part of New York State, 1793–1794

reservation. This map portrays dramatically the conflict over the possession and control of the New York landscape.

In 1797, New York State passed a law directing the surveyor general to survey "the bounds of any of the counties in the State as have not heretofore been surveyed and marked" and requiring the supervisors of townships in the southern part of the state to submit maps and descriptions by February 1798. De Witt integrated these disparate responses with Ellicott's western surveys, the 1792 map, his own surveys during the Revolutionary War, and earlier maps to produce the large scale, six-sheet, 1802 map of New York State. This map, one of the first state-sponsored maps, was later distributed to the governors of all other states. Not only did De Witt's 1802 map set the standard for the new American school of cartography, but its broad distribution also provided valuable cartographic information which would be used by subsequent mapmakers. In De Witt's 1802 map the Oneida, Onondaga, and Cayuga reservations have been removed, and the western reservations in the Holland Purchase have been added in an insert at smaller scale than the main body of the map.[37]

In 1804, De Witt's smaller scale "contraction" of the 1802 map was published (see Map 10.6). It minimizes the presence of the remaining Indian reservations, including those west of the Preemption Line. Only "Gardeau R" is named, but it is obscured by the map folds in this reproduction. Although the outlines of the Buffalo Creek, Tonawanda, and Cattaraugus reservations are included (east and northeast of Lake Erie), no names appear, just discreet *R*'s, which are made more ambiguous by the fact that the ranges along the southern border with Pennsylvania are numbered as *"R1, R2, R3. . . ." R* is not defined in the map key, so only a keen observer who knew the existence of reservations would find those few. The remainder of the reservations are omitted entirely. De Witt's 1804 map was his last direct cartographic contribution. However, he later supervised the production of David Burr's state map and county atlas.

Burr's *Atlas* was issued after some delay in 1830 with a copyright date of 1829. Burr compiled preliminary draft maps of each township, which were sent to each town supervisor with requests for corrections. From 1827 the surveyor general's office provided official support for Burr's venture and acted as a clearinghouse for the returned and corrected drafts. Burr's introduction acknowledges De Witt's supervision, but it is not known what form this supervision took, other than receiving the corrected maps. In 1829 De Witt reported to the legislature on the proposed format of the state atlas.[38] The *Atlas* includes maps of each county at a large (1" = 2.5 miles) scale. The state *Atlas* was revised in 1839, using a team of "competent agents" to gather material in each county. This method was more reliable than depending on the supervisors' responses, which were often slow and uncooperative. The most significant change was the addition of all the post offices in the state.

Burr's 1829 *Atlas* indicated in Oneida County the small remaining Oneida reservation. In Cayuga, the area of the former reservation is shown as "Late

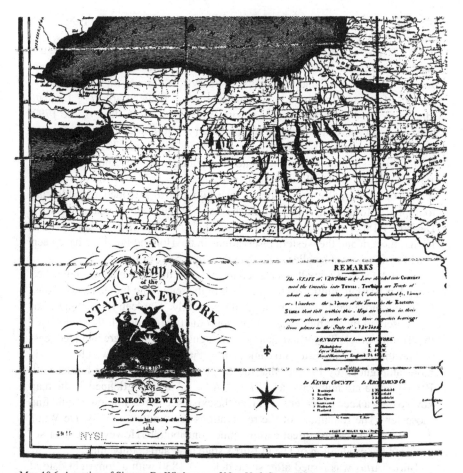

Map 10.6. A section of Simeon De Witt's map of New York State, 1804

Cayuga Reservation." Onondaga County also notes a small Onondaga reservation. The *Atlas* named and mapped the Allegany, Big Tree, Squawky Hill, Canawaugus, Canadea, Cayuga, Cattaraugus, Gardeau, Oil Spring, Onondaga, Oneida, St. Regis, Tonawanda, and Tuscarora reservations in their respective counties. However, Burr's 1830 map of the whole state included with the *Atlas* has only one Indian reference, with the words "Six Nations" and several tents located in Upper Canada. There was indeed a large settlement of Iroquois there, but the map gives the message that all the Indians had left for Canada.

The changes between the 1829 and 1839 *Atlas* editions are also notable. The Oneida, Onondaga, Tuscarora, and Cayuga mappings remain the same as in the 1829 edition. The reservations at Gardeau, Squawky Hill, Canadea, and Big

Tree are plotted over, the outline of the reservations faintly visible. The Cana-waugus reservation remains. The Tonnewanta (*sic*), Buffalo Creek, and Catta-raugus reservations are much reduced by subdivision. However, in the Alle-gany reservation more tent symbols have been added. The state map, imprinted with the words "Stone and Clark, Republishers 1840," is essentially the same as the 1830 map in terms of Indian reservations, showing only "Six Nations" in Canada.

The influence of this state-sponsored cartography can be assessed by com-paring it with later maps. It is not known how widely the 1792 map informa-tion diffused, but that can be deduced by comparing the information it con-tained with later maps. The 1802 map and the Burr *Atlas* must have had wide exposure, since a copy was sent to each state governor and all the New York State offices in Albany.

New York State maps were also produced by independent mapmakers and publishers at various scales and were also published in atlases and pocket trav-eler's guides. During this time period the majority of maps in the United States were produced by small independent mapmakers. Amos Lay and John Stans-bury published in New York City a *Map of the Northern Part of the State of New York* in 1801, which used the New Military Tract information in De Witt's 1792 map and shows the Oneida, Onondaga, and Cayuga reservations. Lay con-tinued to publish large scale maps of the whole of New York State from 1812 to 1826, which showed not only the Oneida, Onondaga, and Cayuga reserva-tions, but also all reservations west of the Preemption Line. Another indepen-dent New York mapmaker, John Eddy, published in 1811 and 1818 *The State of New York, with parts of the adjacent states,* which depicted the "Oneida Cas-tle" surrounded by tent symbols and a similar approach to the Onondaga Cas-tle, although all reference to the Cayugas is missing. This large scale map also depicts most of the reservations west of the Genesee River, as well as the "Shintock" (Shinnecock) and "Montaug" (Montauk) presence on Long Island.

An important European map of New York of this period is included in the *Atlas von Nordamerika,* published in Hamburg, Germany, by Christoph Ebel-ing, with maps drafted by Daniel F. Solzmann.[39] The 1799 map of New York obviously used information from the 1792 De Witt map, substantiated by the map data, and an Ebeling letter complaining that the creation of new counties required reengraving the map.[40] Solzmann's map of New York includes the pre-1788 boundaries of the Oneida reservation, with the prominent words "Oneida Reservation" and "Oneida Castle." Castle appears with large lettering, as does "Cayuga Reservation." The Preemption Line is retermed the "Indian Line" and a "Buffalo Indian Town (Indian Dorf)" stands out in the western end of the state. In contrast with De Witt's 1792 map, where the reservations are hemmed in by platted lots, this map's message reflects a strong Iroquois pres-ence, emphasized by prominent Indian features against a blank background.

Apart from these examples, the Iroquois began to fade swiftly from the cartographic landscape after 1800. The situation can be analyzed by charting mapped reservations on the extant maps of New York State from 1792 to 1845 (Table 10.1). This time span begins with the publication of De Witt's first printed map, that of the New Military Tract, and ends with only the vestiges of Indian notations. The table is divided into three cartographic streams: official state-sponsored maps (De Witt and Burr), maps published in New York State, and maps published elsewhere. Philadelphia was the center of map publishing in the United States at the turn of the nineteenth century, and mapmakers such as Carey, Lucas, Finley, Williams, and Mitchell published series of atlases and pocket editions, borrowing freely from existing sources. Different editions of Burr's New York State maps were reproduced by New York publisher J. H. Colton in a variety of formats and scales.

Table 10.1 shows that the Indian presence on the landscape was not just a matter of scale, for even small scale atlases and traveler's pocket atlases include some reservations. An interesting example of the cartographic and actual marginalization of the Iroquois is seen in the 1813 edition of *Spafford's Gazetteer,* where the term *Six Nations* has been pushed over the edge of the map into the left border. With the exception of Vance's 1823 map and Tanner's 1819 atlas pages, which depict six reservations in western New York, the majority of maps at all scales show only the Tonawanda and/or Tuscarora reservations and the location of the Six Nations in Canada, particularly after 1830. The reason for this can probably be related to Burr's influence, for the various editions of his independently published maps of New York include only those notations, despite the more detailed and accurate portrayals in county maps in his state atlas. The persistence of the Tonawanda on even small scale maps may be traced to their strategic location on the feeder to the Erie Canal. After 1845, the Tonawanda persist only on later editions of earlier maps which have not been revised, and the only other notation is "Indian Village" on the Allegany reservation found on maps by Burr, Colton, and Young.

"Reading" a map involves a mental process different from the sequential reading of a book. Map information is seen as a whole, and the message of the map is shaped by the balance of its visual elements. A map's visual impact is more immediate and intuitive than a written description. Extracting information from the map requires the assembly of piecemeal data, fitting together the jigsaw of sources which result in a cartographic depiction of the "real" landscape. The overall map appearance emphasizes some features and conceals others. In the case of the Oneidas and the Six Nations, the juxtaposition of map ingredients and the *missing* information speak volumes. An absent feature does not exist for the map reader, unless its existence is known. Erasing the Iroquois from the landscape through illegal treaties was the policy New York State pursued in the years after the Revolutionary War. This policy was supported by the state-sponsored cartography, which rapidly eliminated the Indians from contemporary maps.

Table 10.1. Map depictions of Indian presence in New York State, 1792–1845

NYS "Official" maps	NYS-published maps	Maps published elsewhere
1792, S. De Witt Ca, Oneid, Onon 1" = 6 miles		
		1794, Morse (atlas) None 1" = 45 miles
		1795, Carey (atlas), Phila. Ca, Oneid, Onon, tents[a] at A1[b] 1" = 22 miles

	1796, Winterbottom (atlas)
	Ca, Oneid, Onon, tents[a] at
	   Al,[b] BT[b] & Canawaug[b]
	1" = 20 miles
		1796, Morse (atlas)
		tents at Ca,[b] Oneid,[b]
		   Onon[b] & Al[a, b]
		1" = 45 miles

		1796, Carey (atlas), Phila. None 1" = 68 miles

		1799, Ebeling & Solzmann,
		   Hamburg
		B, Tus (in Canada),
		   tent at Al,[b] Ca, Oneid,
		   "Onondago castle"[b]
		1" = 18 miles

	1800, Ellicott
	   (unpublished map)
	B, Ton, Tus, Cat, Al,
	   G, Can, OS, BT, SH
	1" = 11 miles	

	1801, Lay & Stansbury NE New York map Ca, Oneid, Onon, SR 1" = 7 miles	
1802, S. De Witt B, Ton, Tus, Cat, Al, G, Can, OS 1" = 5 miles		
1804, S. De Witt G, "R"[a] at B[b] & Cat[b] & Ton[b] 1" = 15 miles		

NYS "Official" maps	NYS-published maps	Maps published elsewhere
		1805, Arrowsmith & Lewis (atlas) Al, B, BT, Can, Ca, G, Cat, SH 1" = 43 miles
		1808, McCalpin, Oxford None 1" = 20 miles
	1811, Eddy (engr. Phila.) (LC) Al, B, BT, Can, Cat, G, OS, "Oneida Castle,"[b] "Onondaga Castle,"[b] SH, Ton, Tus 1" = 12 miles	1811, Lucas (atlas), Phila. dotted outlines[a] at B, Al & Cat 1" = 42 miles
	1812, Lay Al, B,[a] Ca, Can,[a] Canawaug, Cat G, Oneid, Onon, OS, SR, Ton, Tus, Canawaug, "Six Nations" in Canada[b] 1" = 7 miles	
	1813, Spafford Gazetteer tent at Al,[b] "Six Nations" in Canada[b] 1" = 33 miles	1813, Carey (p.atlas), Phila. tents[a] at Ca[b] & Oneid[b] 1" = 65 miles
		1814, Carey (atlas), Phila. OS, G, "Canadea or Seneca"[b] 1" = 22 miles
		1816, Carey (p.atlas), Phila. (same as 1813 ed.)
		1816, Lucas (atlas), Phila. (same as 1811 ed.)
	1817, Lay (same as 1812 ed.)	
	1818, Eddy (same as 1811 ed.)	
		1819, Tanner (atlas), Phila. B, Can, Cat, SR, Ton, Tus, "Six Nations" in Canada[b] 1" = 18 miles

NYS "Official" maps	NYS-published maps	Maps published elsewhere

	1823, Vance
	Al, B, Can, Cat, Ton, Tus,
	  "Six Nations" in Canada[b]
	1" = 5 miles
		1823, Lucas (Carey & Lea)
		  (atlas), Phila.
		"Canadea Inds,"[b]
		  "Inds" south of Buffalo
		  & on Tonawanda Creek[b]
		1" = 30 miles

	1824, Vance & Dey Al, B, Can, Cat, Ton, Tus, "Six Nations" in Canada[b] 1" = 5 miles	1824, Finley (p.atlas), Phila. "Indian Vill." at Tonawanda[b] 1" = 20 miles
	1825, Lay (same as 1812 ed.)	1825, Jocelyn (p.atlas) N. Haven (LC, 1823 ed.) None 1" = 45 miles
		1825, Finley (p.atlas), Phila. (same as 1824 ed.)
		1826, Finley (p.atlas), Phila. (same as 1824 ed.)

	1827–28, Williams
	B, "Tonawanda Indian
	  Village,"[b] village site
	  at Tus[b]
	1" = 18 miles	

	1829, Williams
	Al, B, Ca, "Tonawanda
	  Indian Village,"[b]
	  village site at Tus[b]
	1" = 18 miles	

1829–30, Burr (atlas)
County maps
Al, B, BT, Canawaug,
  Cat, Onon & Oneid
  reduced, OS, SH, SR,
  Ton, Tus
1" = 0.4 mile		

1829–30, Burr (atlas) State map "Six Nations" in Canada[b] 1" = 20 miles		

NYS "Official" maps	NYS-published maps	Maps published elsewhere
	1830, Burr "Tonawanda,"[b] "Tuscarora Indians,"[b] "Six Nations" in Canada[b] 1" = 8 miles	1830, Tanner (p.atlas), Phila. (LC) "Indians" at Tonawanda[b] 1" = 32 miles
	1830, Williams (same as 1829 ed.)	
	1831, Phelps (p.atlas) None 1" = 21 miles	1831, Pierce (p.atlas) N. Haven, CN "Tonawanda"[b] and "Tuscarora Indians"[b] 1" = 19 miles
		1831, Fenner & Sears, London None 1" = 35 miles
		1832, Huntington (p.atlas) Hartford, CN A1, B, "Tonawanda,"[b] "Six Nations" in Canada[b] village site at Tus[b] (LC) 1" = 20 miles
	1833, Burr "Indian Reservation" at B[b] 1" = 20 miles	1833, Mitchell (p.atlas), Phila. "Indian Vill." at Ton,[b] "Six Nations" in Canada[b] 1" = 20 miles
	1833, Burr B, Tus, "Senecas" in Canada[b] 1" = 20 miles	1833, Tanner (atlas), Phila. "Indians" in N. Genessee Co. on Tonawanda Creek[b] 1" = 45 miles
	1834, Burr "Six Nations" in Canada,[b] "Tonnewanta,"[b] and "Tuscarora Indians"[b] 1" = 8 miles	1834, Case & Waters (p.atlas) Hartford, CN "Indian Vill." at Ton[b] 1" = 22 miles
	1834, Chapin & Phelps None 1" = 16 miles	

NYS "Official" maps	NYS-published maps	Maps published elsewhere
		1835, Buchon, Paris "Indiens" at Can,[b] Ton[b] & B[b] 1" = 30 miles
	1836, Burr (same as 1833 ed.)	
1839–40, Burr (atlas) (revision of 1829 ed.) County maps Al, B, Canawaug, Cat, Oneid & Onon reduced, OS, SR, Ton, Tus 1" = 0.4 mile		
1839–40, Burr (atlas) State map (same as 1829–30 ed.) 1" = 20 miles		
	1841–50, Smith "Tonnewanta Indians,"[b] "Tuscarora Indians,"[b] "Indian Village" at Al[b] 1" = 18 miles	
	1844, Burr (same as 1834 ed.)	
		1845, Young, Phila. "Indian Village" at Al[b] 1" = 10 miles
		1846, Mitchell, Phila. (same as 1832 ed.)

Note: Maps included are sheet and roll maps, atlas pages, and pocket atlases that cover all or a large portion of New York State.

Abbreviations used for Indian reservations: Al = Allegany; B = Buffalo Creek; BT = Big Tree; Ca = Cayuga; Can = Canadea; Canawaug = Canawaugus; Cat = Cattaraugus; G = Gardeau; OS = Oil Spring; Onon = Onondaga; Oneid = Oneida; Ton = Tonawanda; Tus = Tuscarora; SH = Squawky Hill; SR = St. Regis. Other abbreviations: p.atlas = pocket atlas; LC = Library of Congress, Map Division.

Scale is stated as 1" = x miles.

Place of publication is listed after the publisher when known.

N.B.: This table lists only New York State Library holdings, with additions from the Library of Congress, Map Division. Not all editions are shown here, and other maps (and editions) may exist.

[a]Unnamed on map.

[b]Reservation boundaries are not shown. The reservation is identified only as a village site or with a label (shown in quotation marks as it appears on the map).

Notes

1. The maps discussed here are extant published and unpublished maps held by the New York State Library and the Map Division of the Library of Congress. There may be other maps and other editions in other collections. My deepest thanks to the staffs at these libraries for their help.

2. Denis Wood and John Fels, "Designs on Signs/Myth and Meaning in Maps," *Cartographica* 23 (1986): 64.

3. Michael J. Blakemore and J. B. Harley, "Concepts in the History of Cartography: A Review and Perspective," Monograph 26, *Cartographica* 17 (1980): 97.

4. See David Woodward, ed., *Art and Cartography: Six Historical Essays* (Chicago: University of Chicago Press, 1987).

5. Walter W. Ristow, *American Maps and Mapmakers* (Detroit: Wayne State University Press, 1985), pp. 73–75.

6. Richard Huot Schein, "A Historical Geography of Central New York: Patterns and Processes of Colonization on the New Military Tract, 1782–1820," Ph.D. dissertation, geography, Syracuse University, 1989, pp. 67–72.

7. New York State Laws of Session, Session 4, chap. 23 (3-10-1781).

8. New York State Laws of Session, Session 6, chap. 11 (7-25-1782).

9. New York based its claim on a treaty made between the British and the Five Nations in 1701. See Edmund B. O'Callaghan, ed., *Documents Relative to the Colonial History of the State of New-York* (Albany: Weed, Parsons and Co., 1853–1887), 4: 908–911.

10. A copy of this map is reproduced and described in *A Book of Old Maps Delineating American History,* ed. and comp. Emerson D. Fite and Archibald Freeman (New York: Dover Publications Inc., 1969), p. 228.

11. The full map footnote explains, "By the Country of the six Nations proper is meant that part within which they principally reside the rest which is of Vast extent being chiefly occupied by their dependants. The Mohocks are not mentioned as they reside within the limits of N. York at Fort Hunter & Conajohare part of the Oneida Country lies also within that Province the Tuscaroras who form the sixth nation are omitted being a southern People that live on lands allotted them between Oneida and Onondaga." Ibid.

12. Jack Campisi, "From Stanwix to Canandaigua," in *Iroquois Land Claims,* ed. Christopher Vecsey and William A. Starna (Syracuse, N.Y.: Syracuse University Press, 1988), pp. 56–57.

13. Barbara Graymont, "New York State Indian Policy after the Revolution," *New York History* 57 (1976): 440.

14. Franklin B. Hough, ed., *Proceedings of the Commissioners of Indian Affairs Appointed by Law for the Extinguishment of Indian Titles in the State of New York* (Albany, N.Y.: Munsell, 1861), 1: 41.

15. Ibid., pp. 45–47.

16. Charles J. Kappler, *Indian Treaties, 1778–1883* (New York: Interland, 1972), p. 5.

17. Hough, ed., *Proceedings,* pp. 66–116.

18. Graymont, "New York State Indian Policy after the Revolution," pp. 452–453.

19. Ibid., pp. 241–247.

20. Hough, ed., *Proceedings,* pp. 197–203.

21. Ibid., pp. 307–308.

22. *Whipple Report,* pp. 195–197.

23. Simeon De Witt's draft report of these November 1793 conferences is found in the Surveyor General's Land Papers, Series 2, Book 21: 120, NYSA.

24. Kappler, *Indian Treaties,* pp. 34–39.

25. Graymont, "New York State Indian Policy after the Revolution," pp. 462–463.

26. *Whipple Report,* pp. 244–248.

27. Franklin B. Hough, *Notices of Peter Penet and His Operations among the Oneida Indians* (Lowville, N.Y.: Albany Institute, 1866.)

28. Ibid., pp. 249–251.

29. The classical township names in the tract were provided by the New York State Board of Land Commissioners, not De Witt. See Charles Maar, "The Origin of the Classical Place Names in Central New York," *New York Historical Association Quarterly Journal* 7 (July 1926): 155–167.

30. See Hildegard Binder Johnson, *Order upon the Land* (New York: Oxford University Press, 1976).

31. 1800 Ellicott map in inside back cover of Robert W. Bingham, ed., *Holland Land Company Papers: Reports of Joseph Ellicott,* Publication #32, Vol. 2 (Buffalo, N.Y.: Buffalo Historical Society, 1937).

32. Hough, ed., *Proceedings,* p. 79.

33. Ristow, *American Maps and Mapmakers,* p. 76.

34. NYSA Series A0273, Map 481.

35. The map annotation indicates it comes from Hough, *Proceedings,* Vol. 1, facing p. 45.

36. Schein, "A Historical Geography of Central New York," p. 125, citing a May 15, 1792, letter from box 2 of the De Witt Family Papers, SU.

37. De Witt took great pains with the engraving of this map, writing on Jan. 9, 1800, to Henry Glen in Philadelphia, asking for lettering samples of "the very best" for his engraver (G. Fairman) and asking if Joseph Ellicott had returned from western New York, since he wanted a sketch of that area to include in the map. De Witt (Tompkins County) Historical Society, Ithaca, De Witt Miscellaneous Manuscripts.

38. New York State, *Legislative Documents,* 53d Session, Vol. 2, No. 189 (Albany, 1830).

39. See Ristow, *American Maps and Mapmakers,* pp. 169–178.

40. Ibid., pp. 171–174.

Afterword

The history of the Oneidas is the story of their unrelenting determination to survive as a people. The intertwining relationship of the OnΛyotéa-ka and the United States during one of the most significant eras of both nations' history, 1784 to 1860, has been the focus of this book. That this book was organized primarily around the historical conferences of Oneida people themselves is nothing less than that deep primal force of a culture asserting itself, its life, and the belief that its people have a uniqueness in their history, since the Creator made them distinct from others. Telling a part of that story, warts and all, makes this small book a tribute to the Oneidas of the past and recognizes its umbilical connection with the present and future of the people.

The history set forth in this book shows a changing balance of political and economic power. During this period we see the tragic effect that United States expansion had on the Oneida people. Although the book was not entirely written by Oneidas, significant representations of Oneida perspectives are found throughout the edited collection. Indeed, it was the Oneidas themselves who made it worthwhile for the non-Indian academicians to focus their energies: the Oneida History Committee drafted the conference programs; the Oneida Tribal Business Committee funded the endeavor; and L. Gordon McLester III, an Oneida, served as co-editor of the project.

The remarkable story of the Oneida cultural continuity and change from New York State to Wisconsin tells of both a painful and tragic process and a heroic experience at the same time. Oneidas had to respond to the loss of their homeland, new environments, distinct Native Americans with far different cultures, new economic realities, shifting governmental policies, and many other pressures. Yet, in the process, they created the Oneida Nation of Indians of Wisconsin. Today more than 14,000 Oneidas are enrolled in Wisconsin. We hope to continue our efforts at preserving our own history and conveying it to both Onʌyotéa-ka and others in the future with more history conferences and publications, focusing on the period from 1850 to the present, namely the years in which the Oneidas "took root" in Wisconsin.

Appendix
Select Bibliography
Index

Appendix
Oneida Indian Records Prior to 1887 Owned by, or
Deposited at, the State Historical Society of Wisconsin
or at Its Area Research Centers

Archiquette, John. Papers, 1868–1874.
University of Wisconsin–Green Bay Area Research Center.* The microfilm
portion of this collection is also available at the State Historical Society of Wisconsin, Madison.
Diary kept by Archiquette, an Oneida Indian, containing information on
tribal council decisions and on farming, road-building, religious services, and
other aspects of life on the Oneida Indian Reservation near Green Bay, Wisconsin. Translated from the Oneida language by Oscar H. Archiquette. The
original diary is on microfilm; a typewritten translation is on paper.

Boyd, George, 1779?–1846. Papers, 1797–1858.
State Historical Society of Wisconsin, Archives Division.**
Papers consisting of letters received and copies of letters sent by Boyd as Indian agent at Mackinac, Michigan, from 1818 to 1832, and at Green Bay, Wisconsin, through the following decade. His Indian papers consist of reports and
correspondence with his superiors and colleagues. The materials discuss
troubles with British traders; the use of whiskey in the fur trade; the Black
Hawk War; Indian treaties, agreements, petitions, and accounts; payments of
annuities, food, and gifts to Wisconsin Indians. Information on the Indian mission schools at Green Bay and Duck Creek and Indian education and religion
in general may be found in correspondence with the Reverend Richard F. Cadle
and his associates.

Boyer, Joshua. Papers, 1832–1833.
State Historical Society of Wisconsin.
Typewritten copy of a report to the Department of State in the form of a jour-

*University of Wisconsin–Green Bay Area Research Center, Cofrin Library, Room 705, 2420
Nicolet Drive, Green Bay, Wis. 54311.
**State Historical Society of Wisconsin, 816 State Street, Madison, Wis. 53706.

nal kept by Boyer while on a trip to Green Bay as secretary to George B. Porter, governor of Michigan Territory and superintendent of Indian affairs. The report and accompanying letter to Lewis Cass, secretary of war, describe the process of getting both the Menominees and the New York Indians to agree to changes in treaty boundaries.

Bridgman, Frank E. Indian Vocabularies, 1875–1879.
State Historical Society of Wisconsin.
Menominee and Oneida Indian vocabularies.

Brown County. Clerk. Plat Maps, ca. 1830–1928.
University of Wisconsin–Green Bay Area Research Center.
Original surveyor's maps for cities, towns, and villages. Includes maps for Williams' Grant (undated) and the Fort Howard Military Reserve (1863).

Brown County. Clerk of Circuit Court. Original Court Documents, 1818–1953.
University of Wisconsin–Green Bay Area Research Center.
Records relating to civil and criminal cases tried before the territorial district court (Michigan and Wisconsin territories) and the circuit court. Case files may include briefs, petitions, arguments, trial transcripts, judgments, and other documents. There are additional volumes that pertain to court proceedings.

Brown County. Treasurer. Tax Rolls, 1841–1975.
University of Wisconsin–Green Bay Area Research Center.
Annual tax rolls showing date, town, owner, legal land description, acreage, valuation of real and personal property, amount of taxes, total taxes, and individual who paid taxes. Alphabetical arrangement by municipality and, thereunder, chronological.

Christ Episcopal Church (Green Bay, Wis.). Records, 1829–1973 Microfilm.
The University of Wisconsin–Green Bay Area Research Center. This collection is also available at the State Historical Society of Wisconsin.
Records of the congregation and related institutions, including correspondence, minutes, governing documents, financial records, and sacramental records. Also includes historical materials concerning the parish, its related institutions, and Green Bay. Includes correspondence, reports, and financial records, 1869–1915, of the Cadle Home and Hospital in Green Bay; programs and clippings of the Oneida Indian Mission School, Oneida, Wisconsin; and materials, 1836–1838, pertaining to the founding of an Indian Episcopal boarding school.
Restriction: Vital records contained in the church registers, 1829–1961, are closed to research except by permission of the rector or wardens of Christ Episcopal Church, Green Bay, Wis.

Colman, Henry Root, 1800–1895. Papers, 1817–1894.
State Historical Society of Wisconsin.
Correspondence of the Reverend Mr. Colman, who took charge of the Oneida Methodist mission near Green Bay, Wisconsin, in 1840, consisting of letters received from members of the Colman and Spier families in western New York; from his daughter Julia, who was active in Women's Christian Temperance Union work in New York City; his son Henry, while attending Lawrence University, teaching at Evansville Seminary, 1863–1867, and serving as pastor in various Methodist churches in the state; his son Elihu, while attending Lawrence University, 1858–1864, and practicing law in Fond du Lac; and his son Charles L., of La Crosse, Wisconsin. There are also some small memorandum books kept by Colman during his first years in Wisconsin; copies of diaries kept by Charles L. Colman, 1854-1857, describing the operation of a shingle machine and the beginnings of the Colman Lumber Company of La Crosse; and genealogical material.

Davis, Calvin. Letter, 1856.
State Historical Society of Wisconsin.
Letter from Calvin [Davis], De Pere, Wisconsin, describing land and crops in the area and making reference to the Oneida and Menominee Indians.

Dean, Thomas, 1783–ca. 1843. Papers, 1796–1844.
State Historical Society of Wisconsin.
Papers of the Indian agent at Brotherton, New York, including an account book and diary with descriptions of a survey expedition on the Fox River, 1824, and of journeys to Green Bay in 1830, to Washington, D.C., in 1831, and along the Lake Huron coastline starting on the St. Clair River in 1834; deeds for Indian lands; copies of petitions to President Andrew Jackson, 1830, and to Enos Throop, governor of New York, 1831; and a number of letters from other Indian agents and federal officials for Indian affairs. Papers primarily concern negotiations on behalf of the Brotherton [Brothertown] Indians for lands held by the Delaware, Miami, and Shawnee Indians in Indiana, and the Fox, Menominee, Ojibwa, Stockbridge, and Winnebago Indians in Michigan and Wisconsin. Papers also include some information on several New England tribes and on the Oneida Indians of New York.
Unprocessed accessions: M94–178: Papers previously microfilmed, plus four additional travel diaries (1824–1827) and other business papers, such as account books, contracts, bonds, and letters. Also included is a copy of the 1796 "Act for the Relief of Indians who are Entitled to Lands in Brothertown."

Draper Manuscripts: Border Forays Manuscript, 1875–1876.
State Historical Society of Wisconsin.

Draft, written in collaboration with Consul Butterfield, of an unpublished work concerning Indian-white conflict on the frontier from 1538 to 1876, but primarily from 1750 to 1782. Includes speech of Skenandoah, Oneida chief.

Draper Manuscripts: Frontier Wars Papers, 1754–1885.
State Historical Society of Wisconsin.
Papers collected and arranged by Lyman Draper in preparation to writing a series of sketches on border warfare. Though the earlier Indian wars are briefly considered, the larger portion of the material deals with wars waged in the Northwest (1788–1795) and with western operations during the War of 1812. The papers include several significant series of original documents and journals of participants in the campaigns. The portion pertaining to the Oneida Indians is composed of correspondence, interviews, and notes on the Oneidas. Most of the material was gathered by Draper from residents of the reservation in Wisconsin. These papers deal primarily with participation in the Revolution in New York, their allegiance to the Americans, and biographical data on New York Indian leaders of that era: Joseph Brant, Johannes Crine, Captain John Deseronto, members of the Doxtator family, Good Peter, Paul Powless, and Skenandoah. Letters of two ministers, Methodist S. W. Ford and Episcopalian E. A. Goodnough, describe the social and economic conditions of the Oneidas and their mission churches and schools in Wisconsin in the late 1870s. A synopsis of a census of the Oneida tribe taken in October 1877 gives statistics on population, livestock, and agricultural production.

Draper Manuscripts: Joseph Brant Papers, 1710–1879.
State Historical Society of Wisconsin.
Papers concerning Brant, the Mohawk war chief who served as a British officer during the American Revolution, including material on that war and Indian-white conflicts, Brant's life, and his relatives and descendants. Includes an 1878 letter by Albert G. Ellis which contains recollections and comments about Eleazer Williams, the Oneida who claimed to be the "lost dauphin."

Draper Manuscripts: Samuel Bradel and Lewis Wetzel Papers.
State Historical Society of Wisconsin.
Papers gathered by Draper on Bradel and Wetzel, who were noted scouts, spies, and Indian fighters in southwestern Pennsylvania and northwestern Virginia during the Revolution and postwar Indian conflicts. Includes a draft of a book on Brady, which contains appendices of sketches of Indian leaders in the upper Ohio Valley. The latter includes a biographical sketch of the Oneida chief Tanacharison (spelled by Draper as Senacharison), known as Half King (ca. 1700–1754).

Foster, Nathaniel Caldwell, 1834–1923. Papers, 1830–1936.*
    University of Wisconsin–Eau Claire Area Research Center.*
    Fragmentary records of Foster, a native of New York State who came to Wisconsin in 1854 and became a prominent lumberman and logging railroad operator headquartered at Fairchild after 1876. The collection contains political correspondence with representative James A. Frear; miscellaneous business papers including land titles, maps, mortgages, and financial records pertaining to his land and timber investments in Eau Claire and Clark counties; a few records relating to the Fairchild and Northwestern Railroad constructed by Foster in 1913; and a journal, 1908–1936, of the N. C. Foster Lumber Company. One folder contains land deeds and other business papers, 1830–1870, concerning Daniel Bread and the first Christian Party of the Oneida Nation of Indians.

Green Bay and Prairie du Chien Papers.
    State Historical Society of Wisconsin.
    Papers relating to the fur trade in Wisconsin and the Northwest collected by the State Historical Society of Wisconsin from a variety of sources and bound together in 1906. Includes nine volumes of papers concerning Indian affairs. Documents were produced or acquired by Morgan L. Martin, Henry S. Baird, George Boyd, George W. Lawe, Albert G. Ellis, and others in their capacities as agents or subagents for the Indian departments or as attorneys in cases involving Indians. These materials consist of statements of accounts with the government, memoranda on lawsuits, petitions, memorials, claims, minutes of council meetings, censuses, records of disbursements, and correspondence concerning the Menominee, Stockbridge, Oneida, and Winnebago Indians.

Hall, Chauncey. Letter, 1834.
    State Historical Society of Wisconsin.
    Typewritten copy of a letter, dated Statesburgh (near Green Bay, Wis.) from Hall to Edmund F. Fly, concerning his missionary labors and thoughts on the Indian tribes in the area.

Holy Apostles Episcopal Church (Oneida, Wis.). Records, 1829–1979 Microform.
    University of Wisconsin–Green Bay Area Research Center. Reel 1 of this collection is also available at the State Historical Society of Wisconsin.
    Records of an Oneida Indian mission church, originally the Hobart Church, which was the first Episcopal church in Wisconsin. Includes records of church finances, 1854–1894; records of baptisms, confirmations, communicants, marriages, and deaths and burials; accounts of missionary E. A. Goodnough,

*University of Wisconsin–Eau Claire Area Research Center, Eau Claire, Wis. 54702.

1862–1870; names of Oneidas who served in the Civil War; names of Oneidas taken away to school by the Indian agent, 1884; an Oneida Indian Mission Cemetery Association plot book, 1902–1953; and articles, clippings, and booklets concerning the mission.

Restriction: Baptismal records after 1954 are closed to research for 30 years after date of entry, except by permission of the pastor of Holy Apostles Episcopal Church.

Horner, John S., 1802–1883. Communications, 1836–1841.
    State Historical Society of Wisconsin.
    Miscellaneous papers of Horner as secretary and acting governor of Michigan and Wisconsin territories and register at the Green Bay Land Office. Included are petitions received from Wisconsin citizens, an 1839 letter to Horner from an Oneida chief, and a transcription of a published statement by Horner addressing rumors about his exchange of offices with William B. Slaughter. The later items are addressed to Horner's successors in territorial office, James D. Doty and A. P. Field.

Martin, M. L. (Morgan Lewis), 1805–1887. Papers, 1645–1931.
    University of Wisconsin–Green Bay Area Research Center. The microfilm portion is also available at the State Historical Society of Wisconsin.
    Papers of a Wisconsin pioneer and land speculator who served on the Wisconsin Territorial Council, as Washington representative for Wisconsin Territory, president of the state constitutional convention, member of the state legislature, United States Army paymaster, Indian agent, and Brown County judge, including correspondence, diaries, accounts, land patents and other legal and business records, reminiscent articles by Martin, and reminiscences and a brief diary by Mrs. Martin. Business and personal correspondence, which forms the bulk of the collection, largely concerns legal problems, land grants and purchases, Indian affairs, the fur trade, governmental activities, and personal news. Letters after the Civil War deal with his problems as Indian agent for the Menominee, Stockbridge, and Oneida Indians and include comments on claims, annuities, and treaties. References to Indian affairs are found in traders' claims, in a letter by George Boyd in 1841, and in some Stockbridge correspondence in the 1870s.

Outagamie County. Clerk of Circuit Court. Original Court Documents, ca. 1820s–1940s.
    University of Wisconsin–Green Bay Area Research Center.
    Records relating to civil and criminal cases tried before the circuit court. Case files may include briefs, petitions, arguments, trial transcripts, judgments, and other documents.

Outagamie County. Treasurer. Tax Rolls, 1855–1975.
 University of Wisconsin–Green Bay Area Research Center.
 Assessment rolls (1855–1867) and tax rolls (1868–1975). The assessment rolls record name of town, village, city; date; name of owners; legal description of property; valuation assessed; and the various state, county, and local district taxes for each piece of property. The tax rolls indicate name of owners; legal land description; acreage; total valuation; amount of tax; date of payment; and payor. Alphabetical arrangement by municipality and, thereunder, chronological.

Powless, Joseph O. Papers, 1817–1880.
 University of Wisconsin–Green Bay Area Research Center.
 Transcribed diary kept by Joseph O. Powless, clerk of the Oneida Nation, and continued by John Archiquette, recording deaths among the Oneidas (1817–1880), births (1868–1875), and occasional other items about life on the Oneida Indian Reservation near Green Bay. Translated by Oscar Archiquette.

United States. Bureau of Census. Population Census Rolls, 1820–1920.
 University of Wisconsin–Green Bay, Cofrin Library, Special Collections Department.
 Name-specific census data gathered by the federal government for each year ending in zero. Beginning in 1900 there are separate listings for Native Americans. In the 1900 census records, Oneidas are listed in the village of Wrightstown, Grand Chute, Freedom, and Kaukauna. The 1910 census contains listings in the cities of De Pere, Hobart, Howard, Suamico, Kaukauna, Seymour, and West Oneida. In the 1920 census there are listings in Oneida Township, Oneida Town, and a listing for the Oneida Indian School. Includes names, ages, relationship to head of household, literacy, and occupation. Chronological arrangement by decade and, thereunder, alphabetical by county and municipality.

United States. Bureau of Indian Affairs. Great Lakes Consolidated Agency. Records, 1869–1950 Microform.
 State Historical Society of Wisconsin.
 Shelf list of records fathered by the Great Lakes Consolidated Agency in Ashland, Wisconsin; including records from the agency and from predecessor agencies, subagencies, and Indian schools in Iowa, Michigan, Minnesota, and Wisconsin. Records listed include general correspondence, reports, and subject files, 1869–1950; general accounting record books, 1875–1950; account supporting papers, 1875–1950; individual allotment and bank account records, 1883–1950; and timber and land accounts and records, 1883–1950.

United States. Bureau of Indian Affairs. Green Bay Agency. Letters Received, 1824–1881.

University of Wisconsin–Green Bay, Cofrin Library, Special Collections Department.

Incoming correspondence from all sources concerning Indian lands, emigration, treaty negotiations, subsistence, annuity payments, conflicts, depredations, claims, traders and licenses, population, education, progress in agriculture, health employees, buildings, supplies, accounts, other administrative matters, and many other subjects relating to Indians. The letters are arranged alphabetically by name of agency or other subject heading, thereunder by year, and thereunder in registry order. These reels are for the Green Bay Agency.

United States. Bureau of Indian Affairs. Indian Census Rolls, 1885–1940.

University of Wisconsin–Green Bay, Cofrin Library, Special Collections Department.

These census rolls were usually submitted each year by agents or superintendents in charge of Indian reservations. The data on the rolls vary to some extent, but, usually given are the English and/or Indian name of the person, roll number, age or date of birth, sex, and relationship to head of family. Beginning in 1930, the rolls also show the degree of Indian blood, marital status, ward status, place of residence, and sometimes other information. For certain years— 1935, 1936, 1938, and 1939—only supplemental rolls of additions and deletions were compiled. Most of the 1940 rolls are not included. There is not a census for every reservation or group of Indians for every year. Only persons who maintained a formal affiliation with a tribe under federal supervision are listed on these census rolls.

United States. Bureau of Indian Affairs. Records of the Wisconsin Superintendency of Indian Affairs, 1836–1848, and the Green Bay Subagency, 1850.

University of Wisconsin–Green Bay, Cofrin Library, Special Collections Department.

Records of field offices. Superintendents of field offices were responsible for intertribal relationships, relationships between tribes and U.S. citizens, and the agents who reported to them. They attempted to preserve or restore peace and often tried to induce Indians to cede lands and to move to areas less threatened by white encroachment. They also distributed money and goods and carried out other provisions of treaties with Indians. Gradually, as the Indians were confined on reservations, the agents became more concerned with educating and "civilizing" them. The records relate to all aspects of Indian administration in the field.

United States. Office of Indian Affairs. Letters Received, 1824–1881.

University of Wisconsin–Green Bay, Cofrin Library, Special Collections Department.

Incoming correspondence from all sources concerning Indian lands, emigration, treaty negotiations, subsistence, annuity payments, conflicts, depredations, claims, traders and licenses, population, education, progress in agriculture, health employees, buildings, supplies, accounts, other administrative matters, and many other subjects relating to Indians. The letters are arranged alphabetically by name of agency or other subject heading, thereunder by year, and thereunder in registry order. These reels are for the Green Bay Agency.

United States. Office of Indian Affairs. Reports of Inspection of the Field Jurisdictions of the Office of Indian Affairs, 1873–1900.

University of Wisconsin–Green Bay, Cofrin Library, Special Collections Department.

Inspectors examined matters pertaining to the conditions of the Indians. They also examined the extent to which the Indians adopted white civilization, reservation boundaries, the use of reservation land, the state of industry, the character and abilities of the agent and other employees, school conditions, the status of agency fiscal records, and enforcement or violation of the law. Other topics included the health of Indians, the receipt of rations, the removal and treatment of Indians by agents and other officials, traders' dealing with Indians, Indian courts, building repairs, conditions of dormitories, water supply, fire protection, and sanitation and drainage. Arranged alphabetically by Indian agent, superintendency, or school, and thereunder chronologically.

United States. Ratified Indian Treaties, 1722–1869.

University of Wisconsin–Green Bay, Cofrin Library, Special Collections Department.

Reproductions of ratified Indian treaties (1722–1869), with related papers; eight unperfected treaties (1854–1855); a chronological list of the treaties; and indices by place and by tribe. The list and indices include few entries dated as late as 1883. Includes the presidential proclamation of the treaty, the resolution of consent to ratification by the Senate, and printed copies of the treaty. Sometimes there are copies of messages from the president to the Senate, copies of messages or letters of instruction to the treaty commissioners, and journals and correspondence concerning the treaty. Arranged chronologically by treaty date.

United States. Territorial Papers of the United States. Wisconsin, 1836–1848.

University of Wisconsin–Green Bay, Cofrin Library, Special Collections Department.

The Territorial Papers of the United States is a multivolume documentary historical compilation containing archival materials selected from many record groups of the National Archives. The objective of the series is to document the administrative history of the U.S. territories with texts that are annotated, exact, representative, and particularly significant. In addition to governmental operations, the records relate to genealogy, economic development, Indian affairs, geographical features, and partisan politics. These reels contain material relating to American Indians.

Williams, Eleazer, 1787–1858. Papers, 1634–1964.

University of Wisconsin–Green Bay Area Research Center. The microfilm portion of this collection is also available at the State Historical Society of Wisconsin. Portions of the collection are on permanent loan to the State Historical Society of Wisconsin by the Neville Public Museum of Brown County.

Papers of an Episcopal missionary to the Oneida Indians in New York and Green Bay, Wisconsin, who was of mixed English, French, and Indian lineage and claimed to be the "lost dauphin" of France. Williams, who lived in or near Green Bay from 1822 until 1850, was instrumental in encouraging some members of the Oneida and Stockbridge Indian tribes to immigrate to Wisconsin during the 1820s. The papers consist of materials by Williams, including correspondence, 1801–1856, which pertains to his efforts to secure land for the New York Indians, his connections with land companies and French fur traders, his relationship with church and government officials, his repudiation by the Oneida Indians in 1832, and the lost dauphin controversy. Other materials written by Williams include autobiographies covering his life to about 1833; notes about Great Lakes geography and early exploration, fur trade, and missionary activities among the Indians, especially the Six Iroquois Nations; journals and journal fragments; sermons and notes; and a few speeches. Materials about Williams include a scrapbook, clippings, pamphlets, a small amount of correspondence to Lyman Draper from acquaintances of Williams, and an article about Williams by Albert G. Ellis. Materials in Williams' collection include journals, narratives, and sermons of several of Williams' ancestors; two diaries of Mrs. Williams, 1834–1839 and 1858–1878; journals of two acquaintances, Albert G. Ellis and John Sargeant; dictionaries and documents in an Indian language, presumably Mohawk or Iroquois; fur trade accounts of Grignon, Lawe, and Porlier, 1818–1832; and almanacs, pamphlets, and books from Williams' library. The processed portion of this series is described above and dates 1634–1964; there are unprocessed additions, 1853 and 1913.

Select Bibliography
The Oneidas in Wisconsin, the First 50 Years

Basehart, Harry S. "Historical Changes in the Kinship System of the Oneida Indians." Unpublished Ph.D. dissertation, Harvard University, 1952.

Bieder, Robert E. *Native American Communities in Wisconsin, 1600–1960.* Madison: University of Wisconsin Press, 1995.

Bloomfield, Julia Keen. *The Oneidas.* New York: Alden Brothers, 1907.

Campisi, Jack. "Ethnic Identity and Boundary Maintenance in Three Oneida Communities." Unpublished Ph.D. dissertation, SUNY Albany, 1974.

Campisi, Jack, and Laurence M. Hauptman, eds., *The Oneida Indian Experience: Two Perspectives.* Syracuse, N.Y.: Syracuse University Press, 1988.

Colman, Henry. "Recollections of Oneida Indians, 1840–1845." In *Proceedings of the State Historical Society of Wisconsin at Its Fifty-ninth Annual Meeting,* pp. 152–159. Madison: SHSW, 1912.

Cope, Alfred. "A Mission to the Menominee: Alfred Cope's Green Bay Diary," part 3. *Wisconsin Magazine of History* 50 (Winter 1967): 135–155. (This article is in four separate issues of the *Wisconsin Magazine of History;* however, part 3 contains the most on the Oneidas.)

Davidson, John Nelson. "The Coming of the New York Indians to Wisconsin." In *Proceedings of the State Historical Society of Wisconsin,* Vol. 47, pp. 153–185. Madison: Democrat Printing Company, 1899.

Draper, Lyman C. "Additional Notes on Eleazer Williams." In *Wisconsin Historical Collections,* Vol. 8, pp. 353–369. Madison: SHSW, 1879.

Ellis, Albert G. "Advent of the New York Indians into Wisconsin." In *Wisconsin Historical Collections,* Vol. 2, pp. 415–449. Madison: SHSW, 1856.

Ellis, Albert G. "Fifty-Four Years' Recollections of Men and Events in Wisconsin." In *Wisconsin Historical Collections,* Vol. 7, pp. 207–208. Madison: SHSW, 1876.

Ellis, Albert G. "Recollections of Rev. Eleazer Williams." In *Wisconsin Historical Collections,* Vol. 8, pp. 322–369. Madison: SHSW, 1879.

Fenton, William N. *The Great Law and the Longhouse: A Political History of the Iroquois Confederacy.* Norman: University of Oklahoma Press, 1998.

Geier, Philip Otto. "A Peculiar Status, a History of the Oneida Indian Treaties and Claims: Jurisdictional Conflict within the American Government, 1775–1920." Unpublished Ph.D. dissertation, Syracuse University, 1980.

Hauptman, Laurence M. *The Iroquois in the Civil War.* Syracuse, N.Y.: Syracuse University Press, 1993.

211

Kemper, Jackson. "Journal of an Episcopalian Missionary's Tour to Green Bay, 1834." In *Wisconsin Historical Collections,* Vol. 14, pp. 431–433. Madison: SHSW, 1898.

The Oneida Nation in 1866: The Constitution and By-Laws of 1866. Stevens Point, Wis.: University of Wisconsin–Stevens Point, Documents Dept., 1973.

Prevost, Toni. *Indians from New York in Wisconsin and Elsewhere: A Genealogy Reference.* New York: Heritage Books, Inc., 1995.

Richards, Cara. *The Oneida People.* Phoenix: Indian Tribal Series, 1974.

Ritzenthaler, Robert E. *The Oneida Indians of Wisconsin.* Milwaukee, Wis.: Milwaukee Public Museum, 1950.

Ta Luh Ya Wa Gu: Holy Apostles Church, Mission to the Oneidas, 1822–1972. Oneida, Wis., 1972.

Index